IT'S ABOUT TIME & TRAVEL

How I Got from Here to There,
Not Always in a Straight Line

RICHARD S. KAHN

ARCHWAY
PUBLISHING

Archway Publishing books may be ordered through booksellers or by contacting:

Archway Publishing
1663 Liberty Drive
Bloomington, IN 47403
www.archwaypublishing.com
844-669-3957

ISBN: 978-1-6657-0399-4 (sc)
ISBN: 978-1-6657-0397-0 (hc)
ISBN: 978-1-6657-0398-7 (e)

Library of Congress Control Number: 2021904578

Print information available on the last page.

Archway Publishing rev. date: 04/08/2021

PREFACE

This is not a story of time travel. It is a story of time and travel. Time is not on our side. Time is a blessing to be cherished and protected. It is often abused, frequently feared, and usually ignored until it is too late.

We have all experienced the slow moving time in our youth; waiting for summer to come so we could get out of school, waiting for Christmas to come so we could get our presents. It never came fast enough. And yet, as we grow older, time flows ever so faster and we notice another season ending before we wanted it to end, another birthday, another moment come and gone.

Time elevates moments to heights of ecstasy as we anticipate the coming of an event. The anticipation enhances the excitement of the event—a vacation, a celebration, a meeting with a loved one. Anticipation is a wonderful feeling leveraged by time.

Time is everything. We live by time until our time runs out. We are then suspended in the memories of time forever.

I dreamed of writing the great American novel, but Life got in the way. This is a book about real life along a timeline filled with travel experiences. I also dreamed of getting awards and accolades on a big stage. I realize now that the real rewards were gained over time as I traveled the path that brought me here today.

Our true success in life is found in the memories that line the corridors of our mind. The walls of my mind have been painted with a colorful kaleidoscope of images from a truly blessed life.

Richard S. Kahn

ACKNOWLEDGEMENTS

Linda Jean Kahn

For her patience and understanding of all my idiosyncrasies and her astute editing of my often rushed prose. She is beside me, behind me, and always inside my mind.

Henry Paul "Ebbie" Woolley

For his inspiration as I read or listened to his words as they flowed from his mind and onto paper and into songs, painting pictures of life as we knew it. His insights on life always astound me.

Richy Goldfarb

For his unconditional friendship, his easygoing ways of seeing all sides which always brought me back to reality and his fierce chess playing that brought us together on our bus rides to and from work for years.

Sue Roach

For her infectious laugh that reminded me to smile and not take myself too seriously.

Neil Skolnick

For his passion for life and his sage advice over 20 years of close friendship that disappeared with the distance of 3,000 miles.

For **Erik** & **Ryan** who became my sons providing me with great love and warmth.

For **Josh**, my sometimes brilliant son, who I will always love.

To all the people who worked at Kahn Travel Communications over the years, especially **Leigh-Mary** and **Theresa**, who worked with me for nearly 25 years. You put up with a lot and I thank you for all that you did. For all my many friends, family, cousins, business associates and others that I met along the way who provided me with the fuel that powered me to move forward.

For **Steve Czarnecki** and **Lou Baim** and others that we lost. Please know that you are missed.

Thank you all for being a part of my life that resulted in this book.

DEDICATION

For **Elora, Emilia,** and **Ronan,**

I dedicate this book.

I wrote this so that my grandchildren will know and understand me, and continue to laugh at my feeble jokes, even long after my time runs out.

CONTENTS

Preface v
Acknowledgements vi
Dedication vii

Chapter 1   Escape from China 1
Chapter 2   It's Now Really About Time, and About Time 20
Chapter 3   On My Way to Paris 26
Chapter 4   Finding the Mythical Gods of Greece 37
Chapter 5   She Gave Me the Moon 44
Chapter 6   Grenada at the Wrong Time 50
Chapter 7   Visiting El Salvador, Turkey and Haiti During Curfew . . 62
Chapter 8   Trip to the Philippines that Bombed 69
Chapter 9   Finding Myself, the Early Years 76
Chapter 10   On My Way to Me at Murray State 80
Chapter 11   Emerging in a Big Way in a Small Town 87
Chapter 12   A Midwest Wedding and Hearts on Police Cars 96
Chapter 13   The Revival, a Renewal of Faith 106
Chapter 14   Looking for God in all the Wrong Places. 116
Chapter 15   Religious Experiences Here and Abroad. 122
Chapter 16   Transition Time at Murray State 138
Chapter 17   Jo and Friends Imagining Our Way to Mexico 144
Chapter 18   Success Sours as I Undermine Myself 173
Chapter 19   Australia: Long Way to Go for a Favorite Stop. 179
Chapter 20   From Brooklyn to Jamaica and Back 189
Chapter 21   Spain: I Should Have Learned the Language. 201
Chapter 22   Jazz and Reindeer in Finland 207

Chapter 23   Trading a Pair of Jeans in Russia 213

Chapter 24   Amsterdam: Smoking Weed and the Red-Light District . . 219

Chapter 25   Mexico or Canada: Do We Go South or North? 223

Chapter 26   Alaska and the Case of the Disappearing Glacier 228

Chapter 27   Around the World in the Caribbean 237

Chapter 28   Korea: the Soul of Asia 267

Chapter 29   Tahiti: Where Everyone Works for Something. 272

Chapter 30   Brooklyn: A City Within the City 277

Chapter 31   I Love New York 289

Chapter 32   Around the US, It's All Home to Me 305

Chapter 33   Cruising, a True Escape from Reality 320

Chapter 34   Ireland: John Wayne, Ronald Reagan and
All Americans 324

Chapter 35   Time Catches Up. 332

Countries Visited 335

CHAPTER ONE

ESCAPE FROM CHINA

I'm tryin' to tell you somethin' 'bout my life
Maybe give me insight between black and white
And the best thing you've ever done for me
Is to help me take my life less seriously
It's only life after all.

• • • • • • •

"Closer to Fine" by E. Saliers, sung by Indigo Girls

The year was 1983; the first US space shuttle *Challenger* was launched, Microsoft launched its word processing system called Word, Cabbage Patch dolls were the rage and parents raged to purchase them, the *MASH* final episode drew 125 million viewers, and I went to China to help the Chinese learn how to welcome tourists.

In 1972 President Richard Nixon visited China marking the beginning of a renewed relationship with the communist world. However, the growth of these new friendly relations was slow to materialize, in part because of the mistrust that festered within the closed walls of China. Ten years later, China decided that it needed to open its doors and let visitors see what their world was all about behind the Bamboo Curtain.

I was one of the privileged to be invited to help begin this exercise. I was requested by the Chinese government to attend a symposium on travel and tourism in Beijing in January 1983.

At that time in my life and career, I was Editor in Chief of *The Travel Agent*, a twice-weekly news magazine often called the *Time Magazine* of the travel and tourism industry. Along with two weekly destination supplements, we published four magazines a week and had the distinction of producing more editorial pages than any other magazine in the world. Our biggest competitor was *Travel Weekly*, which was called the "newspaper" of the travel industry.

We had forty-five editorial staff including reporters and copy desk editors. As editor, one of my roles was to be the face of the publication at travel industry meetings and conferences. Public speaking was one of the things I liked best so I jumped at every chance and traveled around the world making speeches at seminars and conferences.

In 1983, the flow of tourists to China was still very small, but this was an opportunity to make a mark for democracy and freedom of travel by helping to open the market for visitors to China. My colleague and friend, Alan Fredericks, editor at *Travel Weekly* had also received an invitation. We were going to one of the most closed and secretive countries, but with an all-expense paid invitation from the government itself. This was going to be fun and interesting.

As I prepared myself for this long trip—not only in days as we would be gone for nearly two weeks—but in length of actual flying with a six-hour domestic flight followed by a three-hour layover in San Francisco and a 10-hour international flight to Beijing—I began to feel nervous. I had a premonition that something was going to go wrong. After all, China was still very secretive and despite the fact that they had begun to accept tourists in 1978, the opportunity to travel independently didn't yet exist. Travelers to China at this still early stage were required to go as an officially sanctioned group with every move under scrutiny and control of the Chinese government. You saw what they wanted you to see and nothing more.

Despite this still stilted atmosphere, I was looking forward to going and seeing for myself and shared this excited anticipation with several friends. One of my industry friends, a public relations executive with Hill & Knowlton, mentioned their colleague who represented Kodak and was very interested in my trip to China. He called me and asked if I would carry one of Kodak's new disc cameras to China for him. Suddenly, fear struck. Was

I being asked to smuggle something into China? Was I crazy enough to do that? What was the payoff? Would I be rich after that and be able to retire?

But all he was asking me to do was take this very new and very small disposable disc camera to China and take some photos of Chinese people holding and using this camera in very recognizable locations such as Tiananmen Square and the Great Wall. I would then provide him with photos of these Chinese taken with my fancy Minolta SRL camera as well as the disc camera photos and he would do a PR campaign showing that the newly released Kodak disc camera was seen as far away as China, "So get yours now and be the first on your block to own one."

The task seemed simple enough, even for me. I packed my camera and lots of film and added the very-easy-to-operate disc camera to my protective lead-lined camera bag and off I went on what would be one of the most memorable trips in my lifetime.

Upon arrival in China in the early 1980s all visitors had to fill out extensive multi-page declaration documents that asked, not only for your personal particulars and your reason for visiting China, but also for a detailed list of what valuables you were carrying; including all jewelry, cameras and any other possessions that could possibly be used to bribe the Chinese officials. Even though we were invited guests of the Chinese government, we were all treated as if we were spies for the US imperialist regime.

I filled out my documents listing valuables as two rings on my fingers, one watch, a Citizen's watch, and two cameras. I also listed a gold chain around my neck and $800 in American Express Travelers Cheques which were mostly worthless because you really couldn't purchase much in China and US dollars were not really welcome at that time.

And finally, I listed the fifty ball-point pens that I brought with me, primarily to give out as tips and thank you gifts to the Chinese people. Local officials in New York told me to do that as the Chinese could not accept tips of US cash because they could not use or exchange US dollars, but they could accept ballpoint pens which were not common in China even in the 1980s. Ballpoint pens were the bribery choice of the day and easy to carry. And since they were not considered really valuable by the Chinese officials, as long as we listed them, we were safe and allowed to bring them and distribute them as gifts and tips to the people of the Peoples Republic of China.

Soon after our arrival in Beijing we began our introduction into the scenic history of this fascinating country that dates back long before most of our recorded Western civilizations. We toured the Forbidden City and the Palace with its gold laced statues, walked through the parks observing Chinese, both at play and exercising, doing their Tai Chi. And we sat in the middle of this immense plaza called Tiananmen Square where the Chinese gathered. As we watched the Chinese, they watched us as if we were expecting the other to do something of interest. It resulted in a lot of staring at one another.

I found everything interesting and loved watching the children interact with their parents. The only thing of interest to the Chinese was this six-foot, three-inch tall, bearded editor (me!), asking Chinese men and women to "take my picture with this disc camera while I take your picture with my camera." Most simply smiled and obliged, not really knowing what I was asking. Many just held up the disc camera for me to photograph and that was okay too. Upon completion of this simple task, I handed my Chinese accomplices a nice shiny blue ballpoint pen and thanked them. We bowed and parted and I went on to find my next Chinese photo assistant.

We were a small group of American and British journalists who were invited to this symposium, but there were more than 2,000 delegates from around the world in attendance. We were split into our own groups for touring and, with the exception of Beijing, the Forbidden City and the Great Wall, we all ended up going to different locations across the vast China countryside.

Like their Russian neighbors, the Chinese like to toast using small shot glasses filled with a clear, strong alcoholic beverage that reminded me of the white lightening we used to drink in Murray, Kentucky. I was one of the few who actually liked the taste. The problem was that every one of the Chinese officials felt obligated to toast us, their guests, and we, in turn, had to make a toast to them. There were a lot of Chinese officials and a lot of toasting. Drinking went on throughout the meals and into the late night hours. The good thing is that it killed any possible bacteria that these strange foods we were eating might have harbored.

I was very impressed with the drinking capability of the Chinese. They and my colleagues were equally impressed with my drinking capabilities as I was always stable as we moved away from the table.

During the day I continued to take photos of more and more Chinese people holding the Kodak disc camera. I had men, women, boys, girls, and even one very young child. When we were walking up the steep incline along the Great Wall of China, I had a variety of Chinese people come up to me to take my photograph as we Caucasians were as rare to them as my disc camera was. But a few of them ran from me when I offered the disc camera as they must have feared that it was some sort of evil trick. And by the way, the walk along most parts of the Great Wall is very steep as it climbs a mountainside and it makes its way along the China countryside.

THE INCIDENT

After a week of touring and taking pictures we were back in Beijing for the actual two-day symposium and our final banquet. We were staying in the Peking Hotel, a hotel built in 1900 that had been recently restored, but still had the feeling of a very old and musty hotel. High ceilings were everywhere. The lobby was opulent. The rooms were small, European style, with beds that were far too soft unless you like to sink into the mattress and disappear for the night. Hallways and rooms were dark and the overall feeling I had was that I was suddenly living in the past which was in line with everything else in China.

I spoke on the first morning, telling the audience how important travel agents and tour wholesalers were in promoting and selling destinations. I explained that there are some useless travel agents looking only for free fam trips where they are wined and dined by the destination and hotels. But I also noted that there were many more retail travel agents that took their business seriously and could be an important partner for China as it opened up to more visitors.

I closed my remarks with a humorous story. I could never tell jokes, but I could sometimes relate something that, to me, was funny. I didn't count on there being a different sense of humor in China.

The story I told them was about my first encounter with travel agents during a European destination trade show gathering at the New York Hilton Ballroom. While I and other reporters waited to eat at the dinner tables, there was a long line of waiters carrying trays of shrimp that never made it to the table because the travel agent locusts surrounded them and consumed the shrimp off the waiters' trays. But as I finished this story, there was silence in the room and a lot of stares from the Chinese delegates. They either didn't understand or were sympathetic to the travel agents because they too had a passion for shrimp and a reverence for locusts. No one laughed. After a very long moment of silence, I heard one lone person laughing and clapping (maybe laughing because of the silent treatment I was receiving). That was followed by a short burst of applause from the audience which enabled me to quickly leave the stage.

The next day I had my morning free so I took a long walk down the main avenue in the opposite direction from prior excursions. I even wandered into a department store and ended up buying a tan colored suede sport coat for $90 (they accepted my Travelers Cheques) that would have cost $500 in New York.

I walked through many of the shopping streets taking photos of the stores, the people and even the few billboards advertising TVs, clothing and baby formula. I also continued to have Chinese people hold the Kodak disc camera while I photographed them.

I was on my way back to the hotel and saw a couple of interesting billboards that I wanted to photograph. Just as I was taking pictures, three teenage boys came up to me and asked me if I wanted them to take my picture. Aha, I thought, one more photo for Kodak. I gave them the disc camera and instructed them to take my picture while I took one of them. We did the mutual photo shoot with the billboards in the background and I retrieved the disc camera from them and placed it in the side pocket of the light jacket I was wearing.

I then reached into my inside pocket to get three pens to give them for their kindness. As I handed one of them a pen, a second one of them went behind me and crouched on hands and knees while the third one pushed me backwards over him. As I fell to the ground, the first one, reached into my side pocket and grabbed the disc camera. The second one tried to grab the Minolta, but it was on a strap around my neck and fortunately neither it nor my neck gave way. Then all three ran. It all happened so fast that I lay there stunned, but not hurt.

Still on the ground, I watched all three jump on the number 68 bus and disappear into the traffic. Literally hundreds of Chinese people were walking by. A few dozen stopped to look at me, this Caucasian lying on the ground. One Chinese man and two women came over to help me up and check on me without saying anything. They quickly walked away as soon as I stood up. I stood there totally stunned. I had been mugged in Beijing at noon on a busy street with hundreds of people around—this does not happen in China.

"Did anyone see what happened?" I yelled. "Is there a policeman around?" I said to no one in particular. No one answered.

I thought to myself that I was not hurt, other than my feelings, and I had only lost a disc camera that was meaningless to me and worthless to them. And, I had already completed my objective for Kodak of taking pictures during my touring; many pictures of Chinese people holding the disc camera. I was sure that they did not need the actual disc camera back. So, I walked back to the Peking Hotel, had lunch, and went to my room to pack. We had a farewell banquet planned for that night as we were leaving at seven o'clock the next morning for home. I wanted to get the packing done before dinner so I could just go to sleep after what I expected to be a long dinner with lots of toasting.

That's when I discovered that I had a potential problem. I saw the papers on the dressing table which I had signed upon entering China. I quickly re-read them to see what they had to say about the valuables that I had listed, including the Kodak disc camera which I no longer had in my possession. The papers were very clear: I had to show customs officials that I still had in my possession each of the valuables listed upon entry before I would be allowed to depart. Failure to do so could result in detention and even jail.

I quickly called the Chinese attaché who was in charge of our small group of journalists and told him what had happened. Halfway through my telephone call he cut me off and told me he would meet me in my room in minutes. He was there knocking on my door in less than two minutes. He was very nervous and kept asking me to repeat my story about what happened. "This does not happen in China" he kept saying to me. But I think he believed that it did just happen. He took my papers and said that he would speak with authorities and take care of everything. And he left with my entry papers and passport, without which I could not leave China.

I kept thinking over and over again, the line in bold lettering in those papers which read: "Failure to produce all valuables upon departure would result in detention and possibly fines and imprisonment."

The rest of the afternoon was spent in my room, hiding and worrying. However, I didn't have long before I had to return to reality as we were having our final banquet and it was going to be an early dinner since we were all leaving very early in the morning. Our bus was leaving at seven o'clock in the morning for the airport which meant that I had to be up by six o'clock to shower, get dressed and down for a quick breakfast.

I finished packing, sat around for a while and then got dressed and went down for dinner. It was 6:15 p.m. and I was beginning to relax as I was met by several other journalists that I had become friendly with during the two weeks we had been in China.

Dinner was another formal banquet in which we all sat around a large round table and toasted one another. I only took sips that night because I was still concerned about my stolen camera and the implications from the attaché that I might have used this for some ill-gotten benefit. Our media attaché had told me just before we went in for dinner that we would discuss this after dinner when we had more time. So, I just sipped each time a toast was offered and drank a lot of water instead.

After dinner, four of us went into one of the lounges in the Peking Hotel that was extremely large and opulent. We each sat in a huge red leather easy chair with a high back. Normally these chairs can be hard and uncomfortable. But these may have been the original chairs from 1900 and had become soft and pliable over nearly 90 years of use; I imagined by portly Chinese politicians.

Alan Fredericks, my colleague from *Travel Weekly*, sat to my left and sipped some wine. Across from me sat an Australian business writer who had fully toasted everyone during our dinner. He was wasted and slurred his words as he slumped in the chair. A British political writer sat to my right. He looked a lot like Humphrey Bogart in Casablanca as he sipped on cognac from a large brandy sniffer and smoked cigarettes without taking them from his lips. The cigarette just dangled there as he spoke and ashes went flying when they got to a breaking point. He was eloquent with his clipped British accent and fascinating with his stories.

The Interrogation

This wonderfully dramatic scene out of an old movie came to an abrupt end around ten o'clock when two police officers in red and brown dress uniforms came beside me asking: "Are you Richard Kahn?" which I answered yes. This was followed by: "Can you come with us; we need to talk with you about the incident?" At which time, my Humphrey Bogart look-alike dropped his jaw, (but not the cigarette which held to his bottom lip like it was glued there) as my colleague Alan Fredericks asked me "What incident?"

I turned to my drinking mates as I put my brandy down and said, "I will tell you about it later, it's really nothing" and then turned to the policemen and said "Where shall we talk?" They only moved to either side of me and pointed, saying nothing more as they escorted me down one hallway, left at the end and down another hallway before descending down a narrow staircase into what looked like a basement or cellar area.

We walked down one more hard concrete walkway painted the same pale green as the walls of an old hospital and stopped in front of a door. They knocked on the door and it was opened by our attaché who greeted me with: "I told them everything you told me and they want to interrogate you, please sit down."

First of all, I didn't like the word "interrogate" and there were more than a dozen Chinese officials, most of them in either police uniforms or soldier uniforms or uniforms that I didn't recognize. We were in a very narrow room that must have been fifty feet long, but only about eight feet wide. Most of the officers sat on one side of the room. I sat with our attaché and the two officers that brought me down on the other side of the room. It was very uncomfortable and I was immediately nervous. No, I was actually scared, really scared. I was in China and it was 1983. They could do anything they wanted. I did not have the protection of our democratic way of life and government. I was frightened and began to shiver.

Our attaché noticed that I was nervous and told me "Don't be nervous, just tell them what happened." So I did. Then one of the more official looking officers in a solid brown uniform began asking me specific questions about where and when this happened. When I answered, he apparently translated everything into Chinese and several of them discussed my answers in Chinese. Then this one official would ask me another question.

At one point I remember beginning to sweat. Then I began to feel the urge to urinate. This could have been a dual result of all the water I drank during dinner and the nervous interrogation I was now experiencing. After a while, a woman in a solid green uniform interrupted the official that was questioning me and asked me a direct question in the best English I had heard all night. I realized that she understood everything I said all along. I wondered how many others understood English. Then it was back and forth between the two officials interrogating me. They wanted details that I could not provide about the individuals who mugged me. They repeated questions even though I had already answered that same question. I think they were trying to trip me up.

Suddenly, I realized that they did not believe me and they thought that I was hiding something and that I had committed a crime myself because this never happens in China. I really had to pee now and asked if I could go to the restroom. They hesitated, said something in Chinese to each other and finally nodded "yes."

As I got up, the two heavily armed guards, carrying both sidearms and machine guns over their shoulders, stood up and walked on either side of me as escorts to the restroom. Down the hall and to the right they guided me, as if I were a prisoner, to the restroom. One of them opened the door, held up his hand as a stop sign and walked in while I waited, legs crossed, for him to see if the restroom was clear. We were in the basement of the hotel and there was no one around, especially at this late hour. It was now past eleven o'clock and they had been interrogating me for more than an hour.

He reopened the door and nodded for me to enter. They both followed me and stood behind me while I went to the urinal. Normally I would not be able to piss with anyone watching me, let alone two armed guards watching intently. I really had to go and felt great relief, even some chills, as I stood there and urinated for what seemed like forever. I then turned and smiled at them and we left the restroom. I forgot to wash my hands, but I did remember to zipper my pants.

Once back in the interrogation room, they continued to ask me over and over again for details of the "incident" which is what they called it as they kept referring to the robbery rather than calling it a mugging—which they repeatedly told me does not happen in China. I gave them all the details, telling them about the spot where it happened, the billboards behind the three kids when I took their pictures and the bus they jumped on to escape.

Suddenly, one of them realized what I had said and asked in perfect English: "You have pictures of these three kids?"

And then, I too realized that I should have mentioned this important fact, but was too frightened by the whole interrogation procedure to think clearly.

"Yes," I blurted, "I have many pictures of these three kids taken with the billboards in the background just before they knocked me down and stole my disc camera. I can process the photos and send them to you."

"Where are these pictures?" one of the army-looking officers asked. Suddenly everyone was speaking in English. I then explained: "I have taken more than forty rolls of slides and have packed them away in my bags because we are leaving early tomorrow morning, but I will get them developed and get the pictures of the three kids who mugged me to you as soon as I get back home."

This was not good enough for them as they conferred in Chinese and one said: "We will develop the pictures for you and then you can identify the ones you said created the incident. You will stay here as our guest until we solve this incident."

I turned to him and looked across at all of them and said, "I'm sorry, I have to get back to work, but I will get the pictures to you immediately."

"We will decide when you return to America. We need to solve this incident first to protect our image with your media," said one of the officials as they dropped the ruse of not understanding me and all of them now seemed to be conversing in English with me.

I pleaded in a non-stop run-of-the-mouth: "But I have to get back to work. I have been here nearly two weeks. I promise to get the pictures to you as soon as I get back. I can't stay here any longer."

"We will see," was all that he countered with.

Another one of the officials said: "We are proud of our country and want to show the world that we are a safe place to visit."

I pleaded: "I've had a wonderful time and will only report about the great time I have had here and all the wonderful sights I have seen. I would never report about this incident."

Then, one of the police officers asked: "Can you show us where this incident took place? Do you remember exactly where this incident took place?" I said "yes" and within minutes we were on our way out of the basement through a side door of the hotel normally used for deliveries.

I was escorted into the back seat of a police van with an armed guard on either side of me. Two police officers sat in front. Others from the interrogation room climbed into two other vans, one an army van. Then all three vans pulled out along the main avenue, a large six lane boulevard just south of Tiananmen Square and the Forbidden City.

While I did not remember the exact street that the mugging took place, I clearly remembered the billboards that I photographed. I described the one particular billboard to the police during the interrogation and they knew exactly where I was talking about. However, I think they tried to trick me by stopping at a different sight where there were other billboards. I told them, "This is not where the incident took place." I had previously refused to refer to this as "the incident" as they kept doing and had insisted on calling it what it was—a mugging, but I was now fearing that I had no control of my future and was trying to do everything I could to appease them, including calling the mugging an "incident."

Finally, we slowly rolled up to the corner where the incident took place. While it was dark, I could clearly see the billboards, one with a women's face holding up something that looked like a make-up case and brush. "That's the spot," I blurted, "Stop here please, this is it."

All three cars stopped and we all got out. I pointed to the billboards and detailed what had happened, using the two armed guards to position them in front and back of me to show how they knocked me down and took the camera. I then pointed to the corner where the bus stood and told them the number of the bus was 68, which should help them narrow down where the kids were heading when they left.

They thanked me and we all reboarded the vans to return to the hotel.

When we got there, I was escorted back to my room. More than three hours had passed since I was abruptly removed from my colleagues to be interrogated. It was now one o'clock in the morning. I asked our attaché that was overseeing our group if I could have my passport back. He had taken it from me with my papers when I first brought the incident to his attention in the afternoon. He said he would see me at seven o'clock when we were supposed to board the bus and explained that higher officials had my passport with them. I didn't like the sound of that, but there was nothing I could do.

I was exhausted and entered my room hoping to get a good night sleep. I immediately discovered that someone had been in my room during my absence and had opened my luggage that was sitting closed on my bed when I left for dinner. I could see that the camera bag was opened and I looked in to see if they had taken my forty rolls of film. They had repeatedly asked for my film and I repeatedly told them I did not know which roll had the pictures of the incident and that I needed my film to return with me to New York.

I didn't know if they would let me leave China. They said they would let me know in the morning. I was in China and the Chinese officials could do whatever they wanted. My options were their choices. They were in control. They could take my film, but they didn't. They left all forty rolls sitting there after rummaging through my bags and finding the film I told them about. They could detain me until they processed my film or detain me indefinitely until they solved this crime which I doubted would be easily done. Or they could let me return to New York, fearing the adverse impact of detaining a reporter because he was "mugged." But no one knew anything about this incident. I had feared telling anyone because I didn't want to create a bigger incident.

Suddenly I realized I had to tell someone what was happening. Up to this point I hadn't told anyone except our Chinese attaché. Even the group I was sitting with when they came to get me for the interrogation had no idea what was happening.

I called Alan Fredericks and woke him up. "Alan, are you awake?" I asked. "I am now," he retorted. I didn't have anyone else I could call and we were friendly colleagues traveling together. I needed a friend I could trust.

"I have a favor to ask, please don't leave this hotel or China without me tomorrow morning," I pleaded. "What in the world did you do?" he queried.

"I can't talk about it now. Just don't leave without me."

"Okay," he assured me. But even then, I didn't think he could do anything to help me. At least someone else knew something was happening, even if he didn't know what.

I then laid down and tried to sleep. I didn't even get undressed fearing the possibility of more interrogation in the middle of the night. I didn't really sleep anyway, thinking that I was really in trouble in a foreign country that could do anything they wished with me including throwing me in jail for using my camera for ill-gotten gains. I was terrified and continued to shiver uncontrollably on and off all night long.

The next morning, I waited by the lobby door of the hotel as everyone was boarding the bus for the airport. I couldn't leave without my passport and papers so I just waited for the attaché to show up. Everyone else was on board waiting to leave. Alan came back off the bus and asked me what was going on. I told him: "I can't talk about it now. Just don't leave without me." He returned to the bus, but I knew that when they were ready to leave, they would leave without me.

Then our attaché showed up with one of the police officers from the interrogation the night before. He handed me my passport and papers and told me to board the bus. The police officer said nothing, but he followed me on board the bus and directed me to sit in the back. The attaché followed and told the bus driver to leave for the airport. We were on our way, but I could tell that I was not done with this controversy.

Arriving at the airport our luggage was tagged and taken and we all stood on a long line to clear immigration to leave the country. There were two lines and our attaché stood at the front, making sure that everyone cleared without incident. The police officer stood by my side and moved slowly along with me as we progressed along the line. My colleagues just looked at me and then at the police officer and then back at me. While they asked many questions with their eyes, they did not verbalize any questions.

When I got up to the front of the line, I handed my passport to the immigration officer, the attaché handed my airline tickets and paperwork to the immigration officer, and the immigration officer began to read the paperwork which now indicated that my second camera was no longer in my possession. The explanation was in Chinese so I was not quite sure of what it said. I decided to tell the truth if asked anything. And that's what I began to do when the immigration officer asked me to explain what happened to my other camera.

I didn't have much opportunity to talk as the police officer standing there with me began arguing with the immigration officer in Chinese and there was much back and forth as I stood there in silence and everyone on both lines behind me looked on in horror. I asked our attaché what they were arguing about and he said, "You." Then he smiled, "They are arguing over you. The policeman explained what happened to the camera, but immigration wants to hear it from you before he decides to let you pass or not. They are arguing over who has more authority and I think it will be immigration since we are at the airport."

And he was right. The immigration officer won out and I had to go through another lengthy interrogation with two other immigration officers. It took so long that they moved everyone off of my line and onto the other line. In the end, I was standing there alone, with the police officer by my side, now an allied friend in support of my plea to leave, while three immigration officers interrogated me over and over again about the details of what happened to my disc camera. Every time the police officer tried to speak, he was ordered to shut up (I assumed) in Chinese by the immigration officers. My attaché was long gone with the rest of the group to ensure that they got on their flight back to San Francisco.

I was slowly getting very nervous again as the interrogations continued and all other passengers disappeared. I watched the time and pleaded with these officers that my flight was about to take off and I would miss my flight. They were unmoved by my concerns and continued to question me over and over again and comment to each other in Chinese. Then, suddenly, with no explanation, they were okay with my story and stamped my papers and passport and waved me through. Having the police officer at my side was now a benefit as he ushered me along and got me to the airline entrance just before they closed the gangway. He even wished me well. Our attaché told me that I would be contacted on Monday by someone from the Chinese embassy about the pictures.

I boarded the Boeing 747 filled with hundreds of passengers waiting for their last passenger—me. (This wouldn't be the only time I was the last person to board an airplane as all the other passengers waited.) As I walked down the aisle to my seat, several of my colleagues asked me what was going on. "Not now," was all that I could say, still fearing that I was in China and the wrong comment could get me disembarked and detained. I sat in my seat, silent and sweating. We took off and I still kept silent. We were on a Chinese airline and I was concerned that I was not yet back in the USA and therefore not safe from the whims of the Chinese authorities.

Once we landed in San Francisco and had disembarked the airplane I almost cried out of relief. I was back on home soil, safe from fear of eternal incarceration in a Chinese prison. I answered all their questions, almost in a press conference like setting as a dozen reporters gathered around me to ask what had been going on back in Beijing. We had an hour or more before our separate flights to our final destinations and I was now relaxed for the first time in more than twenty-four hours, but still on edge following the long ordeal and multiple interrogations. I kept the story simple, not wanting to make our Chinese hosts look bad. I did tell of the interrogations, but not about my fears or their threats to detain me. I didn't want any of them reporting that.

HOME AT LAST

The flight back to New York and that weekend was uneventful. Monday morning, I went to work and called over to Advance Camera to pick up my forty rolls of film for developing. I requested the film processing to be expedited by the next day and went about my normal routine at work.

It was around eleven o'clock in the morning that I got an intercom call from our receptionist: "There is a young man from the Chinese embassy out front who says he is here to pick up some pictures from you, but I have nothing up front for him. Do you have the pictures he is looking for?" I just said, "Send him back, I'll take care of him."

I greeted him with a warm smile as he stood stoic and said, "I have been instructed to pick up the pictures." I quickly explained that the pictures were being developed at the camera store across the street and they would be back sometime tomorrow. Without hesitation he said, "Can I wait for them?" I smiled and again explained that the pictures would not be ready until tomorrow. He asked if he could use the telephone to call the embassy. I let him use the phone at my desk.

He spoke quickly in Chinese and again turned to me and asked, "Can I wait for pictures to be returned?" I tried once more to explain that the pictures were being developed from negatives and that they would not be ready until tomorrow and that he could not sleep in our office as the office closes overnight. I also offered to bring them to the embassy tomorrow as soon as they arrive here. He repeated that, I think, in Chinese over the telephone and hung up.

He then handed me a bent and soiled card with the address and phone number of the Chinese embassy, which at that time was on 12th Avenue and 42nd Street. I thanked him, tried to return the much-overused card to him, but he pushed the card back to me. I escorted him to the door, promising over and over again to bring the pictures sometime the next afternoon.

The next day, the forty boxes of slides were delivered around noon and immediately after lunch I quickly looked through them, found those showing the three kids that stole my camera and brought them back to Advance Camera to have prints made so I could bring them over to the Chinese embassy. I arrived at the embassy just before four o'clock and left the pictures with a receptionist. When I got back to my office our receptionist told me that the same young Chinese man was back in our office looking for the pictures again. He waited about an hour and left. I called over to the embassy to make sure that they got the pictures and I was told "yes." I considered the case closed.

I finally began to relax. I had delivered on my promise to provide the pictures, I was not going to make a big deal of this in our magazine and I didn't need the disc camera. I had what my Kodak friend needed—plenty of photos with Chinese people in China holding the disc camera as if they were using it in China. I called over to the guy at the PR agency and told them I was sending the photos I took, but I did not have the disc camera because it was stolen in China. There was silence at the other end of the telephone.

Then the questions began flying. I recounted the story to him, not in the detail that I just did, but suffice it to say that I covered the essentials. He was intrigued and said he would be back to me because this may be even better than what he originally planned. He was envisioning a PR campaign around the fact that the new disc camera was so much in demand, that even Chinese were lifting it off of unsuspecting tourists. I objected because I did not want the Chinese to come after me for creating a bad impression of their country. Even though I was back on US soil, the fear of retribution from the Chinese government hung over me like a dark red cloud about to smother me if I make a quick move.

It was merely eleven days later that I got a call from the Chinese embassy. They wanted me to come into their office. They had a package from

China to give me. At first, I feared going into their office. I thought they might be kidnapping me. Part of me realized that was absurd, but part of me did not put anything past them, especially after the three-hour interrogation I faced in China. But this was America so I should be okay, even in their embassy—or so I thought. I made sure that my colleagues knew where I was going and left the office for the long walk across town from 5th Avenue and 46th Street to 12th Avenue and 42nd Street.

I was greeted by one of the embassy officials who invited me into his office, smiling all the way. Once there, his face turned serious and he spoke slowly and carefully, watching all of his word choices as he told me that the Chinese "authorities captured the three boys who had mistakenly taken my camera and they will be punished accordingly." I wondered what the punishment would be and asked my host that question. "They will never be able to make that mistake again," was all he said.

I pictured them standing in front of a firing squad being executed. And, from what I had heard and read, that was to be expected for the embarrassment they had caused their country. They really made a big mistake that day they took that disc camera; a camera that was useless in China because the disc technology hadn't reached there yet. I felt bad for them. Even though I went through a horrendous ordeal because of them, I felt sick that they may have faced an even more horrific experience as a result of their mistake. I wanted them punished, but not put to death. I never found out their fate.

Then, the Chinese consul handed me a large vanilla envelope with currier stamps all over the package which was addressed to me c/o the Chinese embassy. I opened the envelope and took out the disc camera that I had carried all across China. It was clearly my camera, but it was damaged by someone who tried to pry open the case where the film was contained on the disc. My tiny disc camera was returned to me thousands of miles from where it was stolen less than two weeks earlier.

As I walked back to my office, I marveled at the fact that my little one-ounce camera had been found in Beijing, a city of nine million people and a 4,000-pound car could disappear in New York, a similar city of nine million people and never be found. There was something positive to be said for the Chinese authorities. And I decided to tell that story, over and over again. First to Barry Farber, my dear friend who hosted an all-night radio talk show on WOR, a major radio station in New York City. Then to *New York Magazine* which featured the story complete with my picture of the boys on page 12 on April 4, 1983. Then to *Photography Magazine* which also featured the story and on and on.

It was a good story with a positive ending, at least for me, but surely not for those three kids. However, their pictures were featured in several major US magazines so they went out more famous than they could ever have imagined. For me, it was fifteen minutes of fame. For Kodak, it ultimately meant nothing since the disc camera never amounted to a successful venture for the company and lasted only a short time on the market.

For the longest time I wondered why the Chinese authorities decided to let me go home that morning, especially when several officers were insisting that I be detained and they had the ability to do that legally based on the documents I had signed that indicated I did not have all my possessions I entered the country with. I tried to reach the attaché who had escorted our group, but repeated attempts were all unsuccessful. Case closed.

CHAPTER TWO

IT'S NOW REALLY ABOUT TIME, AND ABOUT TIME

I wish that I could stay forever this young,
not afraid to close my eyes
Life's a game made for everyone,
and love is a prize
•••••••

"Wake Me Up" sung by Avicii

Standing at the urinal, the old man struggled to find the opening in his boxer shorts so he could relieve himself. He pushed and pulled at his shorts through the unzipped opening in his jeans, but could find no opening in the shorts. Frustrated, and nearing the painful point of no return, he un-buckled his belt and pulled his pants down. It was at that point he found that he had donned his boxer shorts backwards, leaving no exit for relief in front. It had been a long trip and he was tired.

I was not really sure of the direction I was going. I always knew where I wanted to be, but often got lost in pursuit. Today was no different. It was an overcast day in the beginning of summer 2016. I was 72 years old, but still living a vibrant life. I loved telling people my age as the inevitable response was "Wow, you don't look 72." And except for the occasional back spasms and knee pain, I was blessed with a healthy body and outlook on life.

I pulled into the gas station at the traffic circle where Routes 29 and 40 meet in Greenwich, New York, just south of Cossayuna Lake. As was true to my nature, I had gotten lost on country roads several times along the way. It had been a life-long trip that brought me to this small lake community in Upstate New York. After leaving the crowded streets of Brooklyn in 1962 for the softer roads of Murray, Kentucky, now many long, winding highways later, I found myself on another country road enjoying the sharp curves, the canopy of trees and the unexpected vistas beyond the turns.

Remembering the love of long drives on country roads, especially in the Catskill Mountains of New York back in the 1950s, when the big heavy Oldsmobile my older friend Stuart had let me drive would hug the winding roads, speeding up as I would come out of the turns. I always loved the canopy of trees that turned open roads into country caverns. Savoring the memory of being carried by the car as our bodies shifted back and forth with each turn through the countryside.

The first time Stuart turned the wheel over to me he just said, "Rich, grab the wheel and steer, and keep this baby on the road." I leaned over from the passenger side and took the wheel with my left hand. The big boat of a car veered sharply to the right as I pulled the steering wheel toward me. Stuart laughed as he regained control before we sailed off the side of the road.

"Try again," he urged, "and this time keep your eye on the center of the road and use two hands." He then leaned back, lit a cigarette, clasped his hands behind his head and stepped on the gas. He was controlling the gas and brakes and I just steered around one bend and into another. It was like floating on air and I really enjoyed the experience. After several similar rides over several weeks, Stuart threw the keys at me and said, "You're ready to take full control, let's go for a ride." I was thirteen years old at that time.

Driving experiences were one of my cherished memories. I enjoyed the power, the swaying car along the country roads, the freedom that invaded every pore of my skin with both strength and excitement. It paved the way for future fascination with cars and love of driving across country and the many adventures that enabled me to entertain listeners over the radio years later.

Today, the car slowed coming through the small village of Cossayuna with its tiny post office, a lone country store and the volunteer firehouse.

Two minutes later, back at the house on Cossayuna Lake, I parked the car in the gravel driveway, checked to see if Linda had returned from berry picking, and made myself a cup of flavored coffee. I then grabbed the homemade muffin bought earlier at the Lakeside Country Store and sat down in one of the Adirondack chairs on the deck overlooking the lake. I was completely at peace in this setting and knew that I was blessed with good fortune for getting to this place on the lake and in life. I sipped the coffee, enjoyed the warm summer breeze and watched the ducks move about on the lake.

Sitting there in peace, yes, but there were still too many thoughts bombarding my mind for answers. I needed to make decisions on what to do with the rest of my life. Ironically, I had reached this late stage in life without making too many decisions. Life had a funny way and moving people along a road with no need for decisions. I had just navigated life like it was automatic steering on a winding country road through twists and turns that brought me here. Now, however, I needed to decide the next turn on my own.

Thoughts wandered in as many directions as I had driven. One thought, in particular, came back to my four-year-old granddaughter Elora who, in a normally inquisitive manner for a four-year-old, had repeatedly asked: "Grandpa, why are you working again?" followed by "Grandpa what do you do?" Two-year-old Emilia smiled in agreement, "Wat Ganpa?" (Our third grandchild, Ronan, would not be born until later that year.)

I had only smiled at her, not prepared to answer either question, realizing that she was probably too young to understand anyway. I had also avoided that first question of "why are you working?" when presented by my three sons many years earlier. But the question of "what did I do?" was one that I attempted to provide many times over the years including to my parents, siblings and wife. My brother Ed still insists that I secretly worked for the CIA while traveling around the world. (I can't comment on that.) However, I now wanted to find the right answers for my grandchildren so they could understand why their grandfather took the many roads he did during his long trip of a lifetime.

I was very immature when leaving Brooklyn for Murray State University. Some might argue that I never matured. Others may find my slight immaturity as a quirky endearment (I like those people). I left home for school in

Kentucky more to get away than to get educated. I was not happy at home, couldn't afford to move out and had stopped talking with my father for more than a year. Murray, Kentucky offered a new beginning; one that I would embrace as one of the best times of my life, remembering even now how much I loved the atmosphere, despite the stifling religious-based rules. I loved the people, the friends I met and growing up, gaining confidence and starting on the road to becoming the person I wanted to be.

I left the three-room apartment shared with mother, father, brother and sister, fully expecting that this would be the last time I set foot in that place. I had packed a few of memories in a bag, but most of my cherished writings, letters, paintings and photos were left behind, later to be tossed by my mother when they finally, after living for 17 years in a tiny one-bedroom, three-room apartment, moved to a large six-room apartment around the corner. I never understood why they waited for me to get out to move into a comfortable apartment.

For five days before departure I packed for this move to Kentucky, methodically thinking about what I would take. In retrospect, I now often think of those hurricane victims in New Orleans and fire storm evacuees in California or those that lived through the tornados and floods that swept through the South and Midwest. Those people had only precious minutes at most to think about what they should take with them, fearing that they would never see the rest of their possessions again.

What did they take? What was really important? These were possessions, some accumulated over a lifetime, some even from the previous lifetimes of relatives and friends. Some of these possessions were part of a family history. There were stories along those walls. Not the walls themselves, but the material things that hung on the walls, sat in the drawers and hung in the closets.

Television reporters are always asking those unfortunate people, evacuees, escapees and survivors of devastating hurricanes, fires, floods, and tornados: "What did you take with you as you left, knowing that you may never see your possessions again?" And often, through tears, these people told of photos, letters, lucky charms, and just things that were linked to cherished memories.

How insensitive are these reporters asking foolish questions such as "How do you feel having lost everything?" What in the world could they expect these people who had just suffered a major tragedy to say other than "utterly horrible." If I were in their shoes it would be difficult for me to say anything other than "Get the Fuck out of my face."

My thoughts returned to the moment at hand sitting on the deck overlooking the lake. I had many possessions, but these were only possessions collected and gathered over time. They were not living things. But they did tell a story and if read correctly, would reveal a lot about my life.

I had traveled to more than 120 countries over this lifetime and had collected valuable memorabilia. Most of it had been stored in boxes. Many of these boxes had been thrown out when Linda and I moved into a smaller ranch house a few years ago. There were only a few photos of family and friends and memories—memories of everything experienced and collected throughout the years.

At 72 years old, the memories were vivid and in bright colors. Everything else was just something to possess. One of the most poignant memories was of the time I had no possessions and was free of stress and free to travel the world. I was in my mid-twenties then and life was different for everyone. That was more than 50 years ago and experienced in an earlier century. It was truly a different lifetime, but one that is worth sharing.

I began to reflect on what life really meant. I was questioning once again, as I had done frequently over the years. I moved in multiple social circles of friends and family and had a wide variety of friends that never mixed with each other, or even met. Many people who met me along the way had expressed that I was a great mystery. Even those who thought they knew me were really in the dark.

From the streets of Brooklyn, to Murray State University and back to New York where I eventually earned a Lifetime Achievement Award for Journalism and Public Relations, I remained an enigma to most including my "friends." I often saw myself as leading multiple lives with very different groups of friends, most of which never crossed paths. But all of them had a major impact on my growth as a person and I thank them for their contribution in helping me become me.

Even in that small community of 3,000 students at Murray State in the 1960s, I flitted from one group of friends to another, including journalism colleagues Jay Divine and Marty Kady, Alpha Phi Omega (the service fraternity) friends, coffee house friends John Juriga, John Barlow, Al Horkey,

Claude the Canadian and a great guitarist Danny Rowland. And there were my close friends and roommates Jerry Weitzen, Steve Jaffee, Ray, Pete the Bug, Phil the Pickle and especially my poet pal Henry Paul (Ebbie) Woolley. Not to forget the girls, Pam Reddick, another girl I called Princess, and Joanne Gomes.

Back home in Brooklyn, I left my friends the twins Allan and Sherman Pollack, Mary, Beverly, Bob Lyons, Morgan, Harvey, Sheldon, another set of twins Phil and Sammy and my girlfriend Geri. It took me far too long to reconnect with them when I returned to New York and got caught up in life of traveling and writing for work. There are also my Cossayuna friends such as Rob Haren and David Bassani, who have shown us that gay relationships are no different from heterosexual ones, including ups and downs as they married each other three times, in Vermont, Canada and finally New York. They are surely cemented together for life.

And finally, there were my business friends, Jim and Barbara Furey, Barbara Mitchell Raskin, Steve Hicks, Peter Warren, Hugh Riley, James Shillinglaw, Bill Cancellare, Bill Moore, Kathie & Frank Stapleton and so many others. Years later I would question whether they were real friends or just friends out of convenience for business. And then there was Taryn who crossed over from business to become a special friend along with her friends Kenny and Brenda who would remain my friends for life.

The interesting question was: Would I ever hear from any of them if I didn't make the call? In most cases the answer was no. But then why wouldn't I make the call. I'm no different from others if I don't put myself forward and make the call.

It was now about time that I did this. I needed to move on before time completely caught up. And I needed to tell my grandchildren what it was all about. If no one else cared, maybe they would. After all, they did ask questions. And I thought I may have found some of the answers along the way. Maybe my insights from my journey and my travels would be helpful—maybe not.

CHAPTER THREE

ON MY WAY TO PARIS

I believe, yes I do,
That everything we lose
Will be a gift in time
But the hardest part is leaving love behind
• • • • • • •

"Leaving Love Behind" by Zac Brown Band

I stepped off the Boeing 747, walked down the gangway and out into the airport. Everything was in French. I was in Paris. It was my first press trip as a journalist and I was covering the inaugural flight of Air France's first wide-bodied 747 jet. It was 1970, but this chapter started two years earlier.

I had left Kentucky after nearly six years, leaving my three jobs including a daily news reporter for the Murray Democrat, a swim coach and pool attendant at the local country club and a local radio news reporter and talk show host on WNBS "Home of the Radio" (where Nathan B. Stubblefield, a local Kentucky farmer, invented the radio before Marconi). I needed to find myself and become the real news reporter I wanted to be so I headed home to Brooklyn, New York.

New York City was, and still is, the Mecca for media. I scoured the newspaper ads, contacted each of the local news headquarters and found that despite my experience in Kentucky, I was not qualified to work at New York newspapers as a reporter. Interestingly, a good friend of mine who graduated from Erasmus Hall at the same time I did in 1961, skipped college and went straight to work for the New York Daily News. I went to college in Kentucky. Seven years later he was the Education Editor for the Daily News making a great salary and I was being turned down as not qualified for anything other than a non-paid internship. So much for the importance of going to college. Murray State may have helped me grow and mature, but graduating college did not help me land a job.

Weeks of searching resulted in nothing. I needed a job or would run out of money. I had just moved into a basement apartment in Sheepshead Bay at the south end of Brooklyn and had to pay two months' rent plus security. I also had to pay hundreds of dollars to get my car fixed and almost got caught in a scam perpetrated by the local repair shop I thought I could trust.

Allow me to digress. It all began when I was preparing to leave Kentucky. My wheels at that time numbered only two. It was a Jawa 625cc motorcycle. I thought about returning to New York with the motorcycle but remembered my good friend Allan Pollack taking a spill on the Queensboro Bridge and almost getting killed by a taxi cab when riding his motorcycle in New York.

So, I traded my friend Mike and gave him my motorcycle for his 1961 Chevy. My 1966 Jawa was probably worth more than Mike's '61 Chevy. The year was 1968 and his Chevy was beat up. But I owed him ever since I took him along on a test drive six years earlier in a 1949 Oldsmobile which I was thinking of buying as my first-ever car. Mike and I left the dealer parking lot in the old Oldsmobile, went up the road to the cemetery (possibly a bad omen of a mistaken drive) and then turned around to head back into town. Coming back down the cemetery road, I went to step on the brakes to slow down and discovered I had no brakes. I pumped and pumped furiously, then realizing we weren't going to stop, I stepped on the gas and prayed.

We sailed right through the stop sign, hit another car passing in front of us and careened straight into a tree. Mike ended up with a concussion. I almost lost my upper lip. We both ended up in the hospital. The driver of the other car and his small child were unhurt. I had to pay for everything and I couldn't shave for more than a month because of the stitches across my upper lip. So, I grew a beard which I still have today, more than fifty years later.

Fast forward to 1968 when I was planning on trading my motorcycle for Mike's Chevy, but the radio in Mike's car wouldn't shut down causing the battery to keep dying. Before we traded, I asked him to fix it. He disconnected the radio. I thought that disconnecting it fixed the problem. But on my trip from Kentucky to New York I had gotten as far as Indiana where I stopped for lunch and found the car dead when I went to resume my trip. I got a jump start and went to a mechanic who told me that the alternator was dead. I paid him $100 to replace it, charge the battery and get me back on the road.

Later, on the Pennsylvania Turnpike, the car died again when I turned it off while getting gas. A mechanic at that service station on the turnpike told me it was the regulator. Another $150 later and I was back on the road inching closer to home. But a pause at a toll booth a short distance later caused the car to stall once again. This time I just got another jump start and continued on, vowing not to stop ever again. This almost got me a ticket on the Delaware Bridge when I pulled into the toll booth, kept the car in gear (it was a four in the floor manual drive) with the clutch in and my foot on the gas revving up the engine so the battery would not die. I can still hear the toll booth attendant coughing and yelling at me for running the engine and smoking up his booth. When I finally arrived in Brooklyn, New York I parked the car near a local mechanic and let it die once more.

The next day he examined the car, did some diagnostic tests and said the radio was so poorly rewired that it was shorting out the entire electric system and repeatedly killing the battery. There was nothing wrong with the regulator, nothing wrong with the alternator and nothing wrong with the battery. He fixed the wiring and told me he would check out the rest of the car.

When I returned a couple of days later, he told me that my ball joints on all four tires were gone. He even pressed down on the fender so I could see the car bounce up and down. He said it would cost $200 per tire to replace the ball joints, plus the $250 for the wiring. With taxes I was looking at a $1,200 bill. After paying the rent, I had only a few hundred dollars left in my wallet and no savings. I gave him $200, told him I would pay him each month until it got paid off. He agreed and I drove away with my car.

The very next morning (yes, one day later, really), I was reading the New York Post and there was a big story inside about the latest scam in and around New York called the "Ball Joint Scam." The story read like a script for a live play I had played a part in the day before. I never paid the rest of that bill and the mechanic stopped calling after I threatened to expose him.

Now back to my job search. I went to McGraw Hill, met with the Human Resources Department and took some tests. They called me back and said that they had a job opening in which I would be a proofreader on a copy desk for one or more of their business magazines. I took the job and ended up spending half my time at Williams Press in Albany, New York where the two top McGraw Hill weekly magazines the prestigious *Business Week* and *Aviation Week & Space Technology* were printed. My job was doing the final proofreading before they went to press for printing. I would spend Tuesday to Thursday there and get Friday off. But I was a long way from becoming the reporter I desired to be.

One afternoon, I was sent over to the United Nations to pick up some reports that were being issued about plans for the US and Russia to cooperate on satellite communications. The problem they were having is how this new deal would be orchestrated. Enter the Indian Ambassador who comes with permits for these new Comsat satellites to be placed in orbit over the Indian peninsula.

I was gathering the papers just after this historic agreement was brokered by the Indian government and the Indian Ambassador, whose name I had trouble pronouncing or even spelling (and by now have long forgotten), was passing close to me. I asked him for some comments, took some quick notes and walked briskly across town back to my office.

Walking along 42nd Street from First Avenue to Eighth Avenue I had plenty of time to daydream. I imagined that I had just met with the Secretary General of the United Nations and got him to agree to a peace plan that would force both the US and Russia to stop nuclear proliferation. I was then imagining returning to my office at *The New York Times* to write the story. A block closer to my office and I was accepting the *Pulitzer Prize* for my coverage that resulted in this historic agreement. Another block closer I won the coveted *Nobel Peace Prize*.

On the last block before I reached my real office, I was imagining myself thirty years down the line with a bookshelf filled with awards from my coverage of major stories. At this point, however, I had yet to write anything important besides a cover story in the *Murray Democrat* newspaper following a tornado that hit just outside of town. The three-line headline for my story dominated the entire front page of the paper that morning and read:

TOR
NADO
HITS

Finally, back in my office at McGraw Hill I told the managing editor of *Aviation Week & Space Technology* what had happened. He told me to write the story. I did. But just as I knew nothing about car engines, regulators, alternators or ball joints, I knew nothing of the technical aspects of this agreement. I read the papers, inserted my notes from my quick interview with the Indian Ambassador and had a great copy desk editor who helped me fix the technical stuff. It ran with my byline. I was a real reporter, at least for the moment.

The following week I got called into the office of Bob Holtz, editor in chief of *Aviation Week & Space Technology*. I had never met him, but he wanted me to become part of his editorial staff as a reporter. I should have been happy, but I was devastated. There I was sitting in Albany each week within reach of a possible job on *Business Week*. How could I pass out a business card with the title of reporter for *Aviation Week & Space Technology*? Would it even fit on a business card?

I went home that night, visited with my parents to have dinner, and told them of the dilemma that I now had. I was being offered a job as a reporter, but it wasn't on *Business Week*, it was on *Aviation Week & Space Technology*. I knew that I knew nothing about that. Yes, I had produced a good story, but I had been at the right place at the right time and had a great editor to help me through the tech language. I could not rely on this for a regular job.

My father gave me some sage advice: "Don't quit your job until you have something else. You are a stronger, more viable job candidate if you are employed. You may be seen as undesirable if you are unemployed." Aside from that it would have been undesirable for my small bank account and my large credit card debt if I were unemployed.

I took the job. Soon after I learned that *Aviation Week & Space Technology* was, and still is today, one of the most respected and honored business publications in the world. I had, despite myself, ended up on a prestigious publication. When they realized that I had no technical background or understanding they assigned me to the soft stories such as the coming introduction of the wide-bodied 747 aircraft—another lucky draw for me. This was in 1969. Everyone was talking about the new Boeing 747 that Pan Am would be introducing in January 1970.

Instead of the normal 100 passengers on many of the current aircraft at that time, the 747 would carry over 300 passengers. Some people were skeptical about the size and shape of the plane. I was sent out to John F. Kennedy International Airport to interview some Pan Am executives and see the prototype live.

A Pan Am public relations executive named James Airey took me aside and began educating me on everything I needed to know about the Boeing 747. I listened, watched, photographed and recorded everything as they built the interior of a 747 in front of me. I had a rare insider look and was there for the inaugural on that cold January day in 1970.

Celebrities from various businesses and the world of entertainment were all on hand for the inaugural of the first wide-bodied jet ever to carry so many passengers. The flight was scheduled for a five o'clock evening departure from JFK to London. Camera crews were all over the Pan Am terminal. Interviews were being done everywhere I looked.

David Susskind, one of the top talk show hosts of the day, was making a big deal of this with his camera crew. He was one of the privileged going on this inaugural. But he was also one of the skeptical ones that had publicly questioned how this extra-large aircraft was going to safely carry so many people. Since I had been covering this story for nearly a year, I too was among the VIPs on hand. But as the aircraft backed away from the gate, something went wrong. Suddenly there were screams from some of the passengers on the aircraft. An engine on the right wing had flared up and was on fire.

The fire was quickly extinguished, the plane pushed back to the gate and all passengers were deplaned to wait as a new engine was being installed to replace the burnt one. Cameras rolled into action again and David Susskind commanded the center of attention as he declared: "This is like the Hindenburg. That plane is too big. It will never fly. I will not get back on that plane."

The plane took off a few hours later and returned from London the next morning. It continued to fly back and forth to London daily without further incidents for as long as I know. And I had my first cover story complete with my photos on the cover of *Aviation Week and Space Technology*.

Just a few months later Air France was inaugurating its own initial 747 between New York and Paris. This time I would get to spend four days enjoying Paris as part of my first press trip courtesy of Ed Tourtellotte, public relations with Air France.

Upon arrival in Paris we took taxis to the George V Hotel (pronounced Zhorge Sanct). There were four other reporters on the press junket. I didn't know any of them. The George V Hotel was considered a five-star hotel and one of the best in Europe. Service was outstanding. The rooms were small. So small that I had to shimmy past the dresser to get to the other side of the bed. I soon discovered that this was normal in Europe.

I took my first walk along the Champs de Elyse and marveled at the McDonalds copycat hamburger restaurant on one street in the midst of everything else that was strictly French. That evening after dinner I stopped into a gift shoppe to purchase something for my brother Ed. His birthday was coming up and I thought this would be a unique opportunity to get something special from Europe for him.

It was almost closing time and I was having difficulty finding something. A young, very pretty dark eyed girl working there said something in French to me. I tried to explain that I did not speak French. Another customer, a French lady, began translating what the girl was saying to me and also what I was saying to her. Between that gracious lady's help and some crude sign language, we communicated, we laughed, and we were able to find a nicely polished wooden game called Solo Noble or peg solitaire with stainless steel marbles. I purchased this and she began to wrap it. The store had closed by that time and we no longer had our translator, but we were still communicating and laughing with each other, mostly because we had no idea of what the other was saying.

As she finished wrapping and preparing the gift to be mailed to my brother, the store manager was getting ready to lock up, I was saying goodbye and thanking both the manager and Bridget (somewhere along the line I learned her name) for all their help. I stood there staring at Bridget. She was about 5 ft. 5 inches tall with very dark brown hair cut in a boyish pixie style; her smile exposed two wonderfully cute dimples. Her large round dark brown eyes definitely had a sparkle. Her voice was slightly husky. She called me Rishy.

I don't know what came over me or where I got the courage to speak up, as I tended to be a shy person around girls that I didn't know, but I suddenly asked Bridget if she would like to go have some coffee. Once again, I had turned to sign language. The manager said something in French to Bridget and she turned to me with a fantastic smile shaking her head up and down quickly several times which I understood as "yes, yes."

Bridget then directed me to a nearby cafe where we sat mostly smiling at each other. I tried talking to her, telling her all about myself. She said some things that I, of course, did not understand. We laughed often, especially after one of us said something. We didn't know what else to do. We drank coffee, ate some fruit-filled croissants and sat in silence smiling at each other.

She indicated it was time to go and I walked her home. She handed me a note with her name and phone number and, with sign language, asked me to call her the next day (I think). I leaned over to kiss her and she was very receptive. We stood there in an embrace for an unusually long time. It was almost as if we were both afraid this wonderful moment would disappear forever if we let go of each other. We kissed again, a long kiss. And then she kissed me on the cheek and turned to go up the stairs to her apartment. I walked slowly back to the George V.

The next day was Saturday. I was supposed to go on a tour. I called Bridget. She said in broken English that she would meet me at George V at ten o'clock. She had another couple with her (Sean and Cherrie) and they both spoke English well enough to translate for us. We spent the next two days seeing Paris. They seemed to really enjoy showing me Paris and I would rather be with Bridget than with a bunch of reporters that I really didn't know. And I got to see Paris from a local insider's view rather than the typical tourist route.

We crisscrossed the many bridges over to the River Seine that winds through the center of Paris and spent a good deal of time on the Left Bank, the more artsy area of Paris; similar to Greenwich Village in New York. The streets were busy with people going somewhere, nowhere or just talking with one another. This was not crazy busy like it is in New York. This was a relaxed busy. No one was rushing anywhere. There were just a lot of people. Many students lived, worked, and went to the universities on the Left Bank. We walked past the Sorbonne, the French university. I felt instantly at home.

We stopped at one of the many, and I mean many coffee shops—cafes—that line the streets of Paris. They all had at least one or two small tables on the sidewalk where Parisians sat, had coffee, and talked. Everybody was talking. Unlike New York where people whizzed by on the busy streets without looking at each other never talking to one another. In Paris, the sidewalk tables were full of coffee and pastries and the chairs were filled with talking people, most of them very animated.

We commandeered a table in front of one small cafe with the sign that read simply "Cafe." There were only three chairs surrounding the small round table and Sean asked a couple at the adjacent, and only other table out there, if we could have their extra chair. The man stood, picked up the chair and brought it over for Sean. An unnecessary gesture, but typical of the interactions I was to observe over and over again. This was Paris in 1970. Years later I would hear tales about Parisian snobbery, but all I would ever see is a very friendly city with an overwhelming number of young people in their 20s and 30s.

I had a very dark and bitter, small cup of coffee with a croissant that was so buttery it didn't need butter. The coffee was too small and too bitter, but I was beginning to like black coffee and it was a lot healthier than the cup of milk and sugar I used to have with a touch of coffee back in college. My friends would sit and drink coffee at the Student Union at Murray State as I poured a cup of milk into my coffee and then turned the sugar dispenser upside down as a steady stream of white powder flowed into the cup. It took a while and many turns of the spoon to get all that sugar to dissolve into the coffee. It was light and sweet and it took me several years to grow out of that very bad habit.

MEETING PEOPLE, THE ULTIMATE TRIP

Sitting there at the cafe in Paris we talked for nearly an hour. I was enjoying the moments and getting to know Bridget. There was no reason to rush. It was a beautiful spring day in Paris and I was enjoying what I would come to enjoy most about traveling around the world—meeting and getting to know people from different countries and very different cultures. Time had stopped for a brief moment. I was relaxed and enjoying a wonderful experience with three interesting people.

The church bells around Paris began to signal the noon hour and Bridget suggested we walk over to see Notre-Dame Cathedral. It was a short walk back over to the Seine and across another one of the many bridges and we were standing between two branches of the River Seine in front of this magnificent structure. Notre-Dame was grey and dark in spots from age, like an old woman who stood over her children, grandchildren and maybe great-grandchildren protecting them from anything that would betray them.

The Cathedral doors were large and stood open welcoming visitors inside. People flowed through the entrance in small groups. Inside there were hushed tones of dialogue that almost echoed from the cavernous mouth of the church. You could hear the soft chatter in many different languages.

Mass was underway and the pews in the front and rear were filled with mostly older people. They looked like locals, not tourists. We walked around in silence. I had questions, but held them out of respect for the Mass and for the grand Notre Dame. The church was all that you would expect. Magnificent. And yet, even that superlative does not do justice to Notre-Dame. The power of the moment, of being surrounded by its history, its knowledge, its mystical being, gave me chills. I was really in Paris and she was the grand dame.

Exiting into the sunlight we walked down cobblestoned streets that twisted my ankles in directions that no ankles should go. We took a taxi to the Louvre, which to this day remains one of the top art museums in the world. The Louvre walls were lined with some of the great Renaissance painters as well as modern art from the likes of Pablo Picasso. And while I was never blown away with the Mona Lisa, it was great seeing her smiling down at me in real life. I enjoyed the hours we spent in the Louvre, not knowing it was to be the only time I would get inside her walls despite the many subsequent times I would be in Paris. Every other time I was in Paris there was a workers' strike and the Louvre was closed. Strikes are common in Paris.

Since I had skipped the tours, I felt I needed to go to the press dinner that evening and asked if I could bring Bridget with me. Bridget looked fantastic and she seemed to have a great time. At the end of the evening I used sign language to ask her up to my room. She said yes and laughed along with me as she saw how small the room was. But the bed was big enough for the two of us and we spent the night together. I was in love.

The next day was our last in Paris. Bridget and her friends spent the day with me. But we had our last dinner together alone. It was probably not a good idea because we had very little to say without translators. We sat there looking at each other. Her eyes were so expressive. They were speaking to me without words. They glowed, they shined, they sparkled. I smiled back at her and my eyes just watered up. Then, as a response, her eyes watered up. We went back to her apartment and spent one more night together. We held each other all night. I did not want to leave in the morning, but I had to go pack and she had to go to work. I gave her my address and telephone number. We kissed and hugged and I left.

I did call her once from New York, but it was difficult since we did not understand what either of us was saying. I wrote her a letter including some phrases in French that Penny (a secretary in my office) helped me with, but I did not hear back. We had a most fantastic weekend together, but we were separated by words that neither of us understood.

Words, normally my best friends, failed to cross language barriers. Words, the life-like lava that flowed through my mind and onto the pages of magazines and newspapers expressing important truths for all to read. Those precious words failed me in Paris. I am glad I have the memory of Bridget and of those moments we spent together. And I think my brother Ed still has that Solo Noble I bought him in Paris. I hope he had as much fun with it as I had purchasing it.

CHAPTER FOUR

FINDING THE MYTHICAL GODS OF GREECE

Sometimes dreams get lost, sometimes love takes time
But the greatest things are worth standing in line
It's never a race as long as you get where you're goin'
Sometimes the heart, it takes the long way home
• • • • • • •

"Long Way Home" by Ryan Innes

Having found myself in the pilot's seat of my life, I couldn't have been happier as I traveled around the world for *Aviation Week & Space Technology* magazine covering the airline industry during its expansion into the wide-bodied jet era. Pan Am may have flown the first Boeing 747 from New York to London, but every major airline in the world was watching and stood in the wings ready to purchase one of those mega-carriers, virtually doubling the number of potential passengers per flight.

I was invited on one inaugural 747 flight after another. American Airlines took me from New York to Los Angeles on a flight in which more than 300 passengers experienced what was inadvertently a forerunner to virtual reality movies. After a great dinner and a couple of glasses of wine, they started the scheduled movie for the flight—"Krakatoa, East of Java." It was a vivid depiction of the huge volcano eruption that destroyed a South Pacific island. The movie was less than great, but on this, American Airlines' 747 inaugural, their new multi-something entertainment system turned this movie into one of the most exciting experiential shows ever seen in flight.

Just as the mountain began to erupt on screen, the lights throughout the 747 cabin began to flash in sequence with the eruption. At the same time, the booming explosions on screen were heard clearly throughout the cabin with or without headphones. And then, coincidentally, came the air turbulence, as if it was on schedule and in sequence with the movie.

Anyone who has ever flown has surely experienced some air turbulence. Normally there are a few bounces and bumps and eventual smooth sailing. But add some bumpy air turbulence to the flashing lights and exploding sounds from the movie and you have everyone experiencing "Krakatoa, East of Java" in their own seats complete with special effects not even dreamed of by the film producers. Add the screams from passengers to the screams from the people in the film and you have a very special event. It was a thrilling ride and one I will never forget.

Not all inaugurals were as special as that one. But the one I was most excited about and wanted to go on more than any other trip was the Olympic Airways inaugural. I didn't know or care so much about Olympic Airways; it was the destination with which I was enthralled. Olympic Airways was the national airline of Greece. Greece was one of two destinations that I dreamed of visiting. (More on the second dream vacation in another chapter.) Greece was the home of ancient history and of Greek Mythology, both of which fascinated me as a child and later as a student of history and literature.

The invitation to the inaugural arrived in the office at *Aviation Week* and was addressed to Bob Holtz, the editor. He didn't take many of these trips and passed them around to various staff reporters. I knew it was coming and put my desire out there for all to hear. He turned the invitation over to me. Greece here I come.

However, everything is not always that simple. Greece in 1970 was ruled by a military junta and there were some strict regulations that were enforced on all visitors. One of these rules required all men to be clean shaven. I had a long beard that had been with me since college days and long shoulder-length hair along with the beard. I may have had a respectable job, but I still played the part of the rebellious, long-haired, bearded hippie that I had evolved into in the 60s. I was just the type of person that Greece did not want at that time.

The Greek junta regime was staunchly anti-communists. I too was an anti-communist and had belonged to the Young Conservatives Club back on campus, but I looked more like one of those socialist rebels that supported the communist movement and that was all they needed to reject me for entry into their country. I filled out the visa and application for the press trip in conjunction with the Olympic Airways 747 inaugural. I had to submit a passport photo with the visa application. I couldn't hide my long hair and beard. It was hanging out there for all to see along with my big, silly grin.

One of the airline executives that was my contact at Olympic Airways called me on the phone and said: "Rich, we can process your visa and get it approved here because we know you, but I am fearful that you will be rejected by Greek immigration personnel in Athens when you arrive. If they reject you, you will be held in a room at the airport until the next flight back to the US. I can do nothing. Your hair and beard will be found offensive based on current Greek law."

Several people in my office suggested that I just cut my hair and shave my beard for this trip and grow them back on my return. I was still the rebel at heart and therefore I rejected the Greek rejection of me. I knew I was a good person and wanted them to look beyond my facade. I didn't believe in judging by one's looks and I did not want to be held accountable based on my looks. "Not going to happen." was my answer. I gave the Olympic Airways inaugural to one of the other staffers at *Aviation Week* and pouted for weeks after.

Several years, and one job later, I got my chance to go to Greece. My shoulder-length hair was gone, but the beard, while trimmed, was still full. I jumped on a press trip going to several of the Greek islands. I was really excited. Anticipation was enormous. I was like a child waiting for my birthday. I wanted the time to come, but also loved the days leading up to it as I anticipated the gifts.

Greece finally came to me, or rather I finally went to Greece. We arrived in Athens at night, went to our hotel, the Athens Palace Hotel which was centrally located in the city. After a welcome dinner in the hotel, most of the guests on the press trip retired to their rooms to sleep. It was a long trip, a long day and everyone was tired. I had a nightcap of Hennessy brandy with one of my colleagues and also went to bed.

Sleep did not come easy, however, as I was so excited. I was in Greece with so much of the world's history surrounding me. I could almost hear the Greek gods as they joked among themselves about this mortal man and his childhood visions. Apollo was my favorite god and he just sat there amused by me while the others including Venus and Zeus laughed loud and long. The thunder and lightning from the storm outside my window rolled on through the night along with the laughter of the gods.

In the morning, the first thing I did was go to my window, pull the curtains aside and look to my left. There, almost within reach of my touch, was the Acropolis and the Parthenon, standing proud with its missing columns, a tribute to the warriors of ancient Greece. I stood with eyes fixed on this beautiful sight as the morning sun highlighted selected sections of this magnificent structure that has stood for more than a thousand years. I was finally there looking at this temple to the gods on the hillside overlooking all of Athens. I stood motionless in my undershorts staring at ancient history and began to cry. It was a wonderful cry of joy in reaching this destination, this destiny. I was finally in Greece.

Regaining my composure, I showered, dressed and joined my group for a quick trip up the hill to the Acropolis and the Parthenon. Following that touchy, feeling, hugging at the Parthenon we visited the Athens Museum with its golden treasures, the Temple of Zeus and the Market of Monastiraki with open air food stalls and a huge shopping area with old-style trading stalls mixed with modern stores and restaurants.

After lunch we went to the Plaka where we first visited one of the oldest churches in Greece, the Byzantine church and then the Jewish Museum. The Plaka is a sub-village in Athens with shops and museums and an abundance of restaurants and nightclubs. The Plaka is a hilly, winding section of the city with cobblestone streets and hidden treasures found tucked away as offshoots of these many tiny avenues. This is where the Greeks go to play at night and welcome visitors to join in the nightly festivities.

For dinner that evening we went to one of the larger tavernas with an open-air courtyard for dining. It was both a tourist stop and one that local Greeks frequented because of the good food and nightly music. We were told there are many of these restaurants in the Plaka. They all rise to the occasion each night with lively music and dancing.

Dancing is highlighted by the Kalamatianos, a traditional ancient Greek line dance of sorts lead by one of the Greek men, followed by a long line of men and women holding hands, sometimes connected by handkerchiefs, napkins or towels and moving in a circle shouting "opa".

It is an easy line dance, in which tourists can learn instantly and join in for a memorable event. The music and dancing go deep into the night and often includes the famous plate smashing that Greeks have been known to do for good luck. The ancient Greeks began smashing plates as part of a mourning ceremony. Now it is commonly done as part of a joyous ceremony and in the local tavernas in the Greek islands, where Greeks celebrate everything including just being alive. We drank a lot of ouzo, a Greek white wine, danced and smashed plates while dancing and shouting "opa" until our throats were horse. I think they supply cheap plates for this nightly exercise. I slept well that night.

The next day we were scheduled to leave on a cruise, but first we were going on some more sightseeing outside Athens for a look at more treasures from ancient Greece. We were instructed to pack our bags, leave them outside our doors and board a bus for our tour. Our bags would be taken directly to the ship which we would join later in the day.

I was so in love with Greece that I had to take some souvenir home with me. As I was packing that morning, I remembered the extra unused brilliant white towel hanging in the bathroom. It had a Greek emblem on the towel with the words Athens Palace Hotel embroidered. I packed the towel in my bag, left the luggage outside my room, went to breakfast, and then to the bus for the excursion outside Athens. We ended up joining the cruise ship after lunch. I went to my assigned cabin, opened my luggage to unpack and found my souvenir towel was missing. Instead, I found this hand-written note:

"Dear Mr. Kahn, We took the liberty of retrieving the hotel towel that inadvertently found its way into your luggage. In this way, you will not have to go to any expense to return the towel to us at a later date. We hope this does not inconvenience you in any way." It was signed by the General Manager.

I looked out my verandah and saw that the ship was moving. We had left on a cruise of the Greek islands. First stop Mykonos.

Mykonos is where the Greeks go on vacation. It is also where many of the rich and famous hideaway in the "white" hills dotted with stark white-washed houses. The streets wind along the steep hillsides climbing their way up from the sea towards the gods that overlook the Greek islands and their ancient history. It is a beautiful island and a walk up the steep cobblestoned streets connect one to a past that has never quite caught up with today.

Sitting in one of the outdoor cafes of an old fishing village on the shore-line of Mykonos, we sip ouzo, eat figs, and watch Pete the Pelican (or one of his descendants) sitting lazily on one of the posts sticking out of the water, a remnant of an old dock long gone except for Pete's Post. If you are lucky, he will spread his wings and go fishing with an ease and perfection that is gained over many years. Otherwise, Pete the Pelican just sits there watching the tourists watching him. It's a Greek standoff. At night Mykonos moves to the beat of the DJs as clubs draw locals and tourists to all-night dance parties that rival Miami's South Beach for glitz and glamour. It is an island that never sleeps. We didn't.

I could have sat in the seaside cafes all day, every day. Sipping coffee or ouzo, eating figs and olives along with warm pita. I was in heaven and the gods were looking over my shoulder.

A few days later we got one step closer to the Greek gods as we landed in Santorini. That first day we went to visit some local churches and the ancient ruins of Thera. The next day we traveled up to the Monastery of Profitis Illias (Prophet Elias) built on the highest peak of Santorini. Built in 1712, it is one of the oldest active monasteries in Santorini and it was a privilege to walk the hallways and outside corridors with the still active Monks tending to gardens and wine vineyards. We did so in complete silence to show respect for their vows.

The Monastery of Prophet Elias is built on the highest peak of Santorini and provides indescribable views of the island and Aegean Sea that sur-rounds it. Words cannot paint the picture or feelings that accompany the view from the Monastery. I felt a kinship to the Monks as we passed along the outside corridors that overlooked the island. It was only natural that I stopped for more than an hour to just gaze across the island at the distant sea and the connected sky in search of answers from Apollo or Zeus. The tour guide had to come looking for me as I was lost in thought somewhere with the ancient gods of Greece.

Our final stop that day was for sunset in Oia. Everyone loves a good sunset and there are many legendary tales of sunsets followed by the green flash that shoots out across the horizon just as the sun disappears below sight. I have been lucky enough to have seen the green flash twice. The first time was at Mallory Square in Key West where hundreds of people gather every evening to watch street performers and then, at the right moment, turn to face the horizon as the sun moves slowly into the sea.

The second time I witnessed the amazing green flash was at sunset in Oia on Santorini sitting with a small quiet group that reminded me of the Monks I had seen earlier in the day. The sun hung just on top of the Aegean Sea for what seemed like forever as it moved imperceptivity lower until it touched the sea. Then, as if a time clock was suddenly turned on, the sun began to lower itself beneath the horizon in one steady slow motion until that moment of truth as Neptune, the god of the sea, looked down with appreciation at all that was good on earth and spread his hands revealing the green flash across the horizon. The sun was gone and with it the momentary green flash like the wink of a god's eye. If you blinked, you missed it. I can still see that moment in my mind.

We also stopped in Ephesus which is in the Aegean Sea, but part of Turkey, not Greece. Ephesus is known for its 5,000-year-old ruins which have been under slow and methodical excavation by Austrian archeologists since 1954. A museum was planned when we first visited and excavations were accelerated in 1980. We got to walk around and watch the digs and look at some of the artifacts that had been recently discovered at that time. It was like watching history unfold.

I left Greece with a feeling of great accomplishment. I had finally gone to my intellectual birthplace. I had seen and touched ancient historical sites and walked the cobblestoned streets that Aristotle and Plato had walked. I now felt a closer connection with these great philosophers and vowed to re-read their writings upon returning home. I also had seen the green flash, surely the product of none other than the gods themselves.

CHAPTER FIVE

SHE GAVE ME THE MOON

Memories they can't be bought
They can't be won at carnivals for free
Well it took me years
To get those souvenirs
And I don't know how they slipped away from me
• • • • • • •

"Souvenirs" by John Prine

My days at *Aviation Week & Space Technology* magazine, beginning in 1968 and until 1973 when I started at *The Travel Agent Magazine*, was a period in which I grew as a journalist and continued to mature as a person. I was definitely not there yet. I struggled with early success and failed often producing weak articles that didn't make the pages of the magazine.

One success that I was proud about was the cover feature on the magazine including photos that I took of the first Pan Am Boeing 747 to ever fly. Another successful article was an investigative exposé which resulted in a major investigation into cargo operations at Kennedy International Airport by the Civil Aeronautics Board (CAB) and which subsequently won me an award from the Business Writer's Association. However, I almost ended up in jail on the way to write that story.

It began with a theory I had that cargo security was very lax at Kennedy Airport. I had discovered this during the time I spent at the airport watching the preparation for the first Pan Am Boeing 747 flight including the detailed education I received from my Pan Am friends. There were rumors of rampant theft and multiple rings of racketeers that were operating in the cargo areas and moving merchandise around like they ran a wholesale department store.

I convinced Robert (name changed to protect the guilty), a college friend, whose father owned a trucking company in New Jersey, to help me with a scheme that would demonstrate the lack of security. He drove this fairly large truck to Kennedy one evening with me riding shotgun with my camera in hand. We stopped at three different cargo terminals including United, Delta and one shared by foreign carriers. At each terminal we backed up to the loading docks. I got out and took pictures and then loaded a number of boxes on our truck. I then took more pictures. There were cargo handlers all around watching us, but not really paying attention to us. Maybe they thought we were part of the theft ring and we were supposed to be there stealing merchandise.

After stopping at three cargo terminals, stealing quite a few boxes and loading them on our truck, we drove from the airport, past security and went directly to the local police precinct in South Jamaica, Queens. We parked out front, I left my buddy at the wheel of the truck and went inside to identify myself and tell the police what I had done.

I also asked the police to call the Civil Aeronautics Board because it should be their jurisdiction and they would want to investigate. The front desk sergeant looked at me and said: "Is this a college prank? Are you pledging for a fraternity? What's really going on?" When I persisted, he seemed to get annoyed: "I don't have time for this crap, we've got a lot of shit happening out here in our streets and no time for your fantasy world. Now get out before I just lock you up for the night."

I went out to Robert and told him what the police said. With concern rising from his voice, he asked: "What are you going to do now? I've got to get this truck back tonight and I am not going to keep all those stolen boxes with me. My father will kill me." I went over to a pay phone (outdoor phones available for anyone with change to use in the 1970s) to call my contact at the Civil Aeronautics Board. It was now nearly ten o'clock at night. I was standing outside a police precinct on a pay phone (long before cell phones). I left a message for the CAB telling them what

I had done and advising them where I was and the telephone number of the police precinct.

I hung up and stood there by the pay phone not knowing what to do next. There were too many boxes of unidentified stolen things. I didn't look to see what I was stealing. It didn't matter. But now I became fearful that I may have stolen some major items and could go to jail for this.

I then told Robert to pull the truck into the police parking lot, lock it up and go home to Brooklyn with me. It would be safe in a police parking lot. We would come back first thing in the morning and by that time I hoped the CAB Director would have called the precinct and an investigation would be underway. He really didn't want to do this, but agreed. We parked the truck and found a taxi to drive us back to my apartment in Sheepshead Bay, Brooklyn where Robert called his father to tell him that he would be late for work in the morning but it was for a good cause that he would explain later.

The next morning, I called the Civil Aeronautics Board and found that they had already called the police precinct, but no one there knew anything. I explained what we did and he told me that a couple of CAB agents would meet us at the precinct at ten o'clock. We drove in my car back out to Queens, met with the CAB officials, showed them the truck and its materials (which they transferred into a van) and told them I would have the photos to them within 24 hours. I then went into the city to my office at the magazine to write the story and get the photos developed.

A major investigation had begun even before my story appeared in print on October 26, 1970, under the headline: "Air Cargo at the Crossroads: Pressure Rising for Tightened Security." The result was tighter security at the cargo terminals at Kennedy Airport which, unfortunately, only lasted a few years. The word on the street is that I could re-enact my scheme today with the same results I had in 1970.

I had several mentors at *Aviation Week*, particularly Bill Gregory, the managing editor, who taught me how to edit copy which made me a much better reporter and writer. Then there was Aura (Aury) Marrero, the all-knowing librarian, who took me under her wings and guided me like a mother eagle teaches its fledgling eaglet. She will never know how important and how much she meant to me in my education as a journalist and a person.

A Break from the Office

It was going to be a hot weekend in July. Aury suggested that we drive up to the Cape for the weekend to get out of the sticky hot streets of New York City. I had never been to Cape Cod. Aury had been there many times. Aury had been lots of places. She was a few years older than me and was the cool, sophisticated woman that had everything the young girls lacked. I was only twenty-five.

Aury was smart. She was funny and she knew everything and everybody. She was the librarian in charge of research at *Aviation Week & Space Technology* and I was a cub reporter. She was a tiny, 5 foot 2 inches tall (so she claimed) cute Puerto Rican girl that made herself successful despite early hardships. She was a respected editor and she told me that I had writing ability, but had not realized my potential. She promised me that I would be great. I liked her optimism. We soon were going out to dinner to restaurants that served an eclectic and diverse cuisine. She introduced me to good wine and I put down the beer bottle in favor of a wine goblet.

She also introduced me to many interesting people, artists, writers, photographers, musicians. Thanks to her I had entered the elite creative community in New York. I even met her ex, a tall handsome famous artist that illustrated some of the bestselling children's books on the market. Despite their breakup, they remained best of friends and I became part of her circle of friends. I was suddenly thrust into a life that seemed more like a grade B movie than my own existence. But I was loving every minute of it and falling in love with Aury and this sophisticated, fast pace world.

Most of the people I met were Aury's friends and friends of her friends and they were all older than me. Fortunately, that was nothing new to me. Ever since I was 14 and my mother told the owners at Ashley Country Club in Spring Valley, New York that I was sixteen so I could get a job as a life guard, I was living an ageless lie that surrounded me with friends that were two or more years older. Graduating from High School early also help perpetuate this lie and continued as I went to college with friends that were older. But this was different. These were not kids. They were adults; some in their thirties and forties and I was still just twenty-five.

During the week, I spent most nights at Aury's apartment on 53rd Street and Third Avenue in Manhattan, right next door to Governor Rockefeller's office. She had four cats and I quickly found out that cats are nocturnal. While we were at work, they slept most of the day and came to life at night playing with each other; sometimes wrecking the place as they jumped from shelf to shelf knocking over anything that was on display. I kept my own apartment and my dark blue Volkswagen Beatle back in Sheepshead Bay, Brooklyn.

With plans set to go away with Aury for the weekend, I had picked up my car the night before and we headed out early Friday morning to beat the weekend traffic to Provincetown on Cape Cod. We were headed to Woody Allen's house for the weekend, but he wouldn't be there. His soon-to-be ex-wife would be our host for the weekend. The house was filled with a load of guests, none of whom I knew, but they talked about movies they were either in or filming. After dinner we decided to find somewhere where we could get away from the crowds. That meant getting out of Provincetown. We ended up in Dennisport.

The weekend was hot and sunny and we enjoyed great meals and meeting some new and very interesting people that we would never see again. It was magical.

Sunday morning we decided that we should head back to Manhattan after a late breakfast—once again, designed to beat the traffic. It never happened. It was such a beautiful day that we lingered too long and by the late afternoon when we got onto the road we ended up sitting in long lines of cars moving very slowly, or sometimes not at all, as we worked our way on the single lane road that leads on and off the Cape.

It had been a hot and sunny day, but most people, including Aury and I, were calm and relaxed, even when we sat stagnant waiting for the traffic to move. We sat at one point for nearly an hour while they apparently cleaned up an accident several miles ahead of us.

The day disappeared into night, but the heat remained along with the long summer daylight as we continued our slow climb up the Cape towards Connecticut. Most people were listening to their radios and suddenly the music was interrupted with a news break. It was after we had been on the road for nearly five hours at that time and still moving slowly.

The announcer came on very excited about what was about to happen. And then we listened intently as we heard the radio broadcast from Apollo 11 as it touched down on the moon. We looked up to the sky to see the moon as if we would be able to see what was happening. It looked no different than any other night. It just sat there in the sky, a magnificent glowing yellow ball, sometimes, full and fat, other times just a sliver of its former self. But this was different as we heard Neil Armstrong say, "That's one small step for man, one giant leap for mankind." But honestly, we could hardly understand what he was saying through the garbled and noisy broadcast.

We knew this was a special moment. Everyone knew it and suddenly we were no longer just a bunch of impatient drivers in a long line of traffic. We were all together in a celebration of everything that was good. Aury and I hugged each other and watched others embracing one another. Everyone began honking their horns. It was a traffic party celebrating a magnificent moment in time. Some people got out of their cars and shouted. Others danced. Aury and I hugged and honked the horn. We smiled at the moon. And somehow, it really looked like the moon was smiling back on us.

Aury and I didn't last as lovers. But we remained friends for many years after our brief romance. She was a smart, sweet women. I was not ready for her.

CHAPTER SIX

GRENADA AT THE WRONG TIME

If you're going through Hell, keep on going, don't slow down,
If you're scared, don't show it,
You might get out before the devil even knows you're there.

• • • • • • •

"If You're Going Through Hell" sung by Rodney Atkins

After nearly five years as a reporter covering the travel industry at *Aviation Week & Space Technology*, I was courted by the owner and publisher of *The Travel Agent*, a twice-weekly travel industry news magazine. The year was 1973 and the travel industry was booming with the growth of both the wide-bodied jets and charter operators that made mass travel vacations to Europe and the Caribbean very affordable. He was expanding the magazine and needed someone who understood the travel industry to manage day-to-day operations. I took the job.

Over the next decade I went from managing editor to Editor in Chief and Associate Publisher and traveled extensively to represent the magazine making speeches and presentations as well as volunteering on a variety of travel industry associations as a mentor to help hoteliers, destinations, travel agents and tour operators grow their business in the marketplace.

Sitting at my desk at *The Travel Agent* magazine editing some boring copy about destinations few people would ever visit, I got a call from Jim Furey, a media rep I worked closely with on Caribbean projects. I would write articles for special travel sections in magazines like *Business Week* and *US News & World Report* and Jim would sell advertising to support the sections. This time Jim called to ask if I would be interested in joining him on a trip to Grenada to do an assessment of the destination's tourism product and, at the same time, advise the hoteliers and the director of tourism what they needed to do to make a comeback into the competitive Caribbean marketplace. We had performed this service as volunteers for the Caribbean Hotel Association for many other Caribbean islands and were well prepared to help. This request came from Prime Minister Maurice Bishop.

The year was 1983, and Grenada at that time had been shunned by American tourists because the Grenada government was aligned with communist Cuba. A few months prior to Jim calling me, I had met Grenada Prime Minister Maurice Bishop at a Caribbean conference where I had been on stage doing a humorous education seminar for hoteliers and travel agents. Bishop was introduced to us by Grenada hotelier Royston Hopkin, later to be knighted by the Queen of England to become Sir Royston, the first and still the only hotelier in the Caribbean to have that distinction.

Maurice Bishop was a tall, dignified and charismatic man. One could easily see why he was chosen to lead Grenada after so many years under control of a dictator. But the fact that he had turned to communist Cuba for his alliance was not very popular with US officials. However, we were being urged by the Caribbean Hotel Association to help the hoteliers in Grenada; something we did regularly across the Caribbean.

The call came about three months after we returned home from a conference in Aruba and just prior to my leaving for an annual ASTA (travel agent) World Travel Conference taking place in Korea. Jim and I planned to meet up with Tony Mack in Grenada and set the date for mid-October to give me a couple of weeks after our biggest conference of the year scheduled to take place in Korea (more about that almost ill-fated event later).

Tony worked on education and training for the Caribbean Hotel Association and was one of our regular crew on these volunteer assistance ventures. None of us got paid for this work. We did this because we all had a vested interest in seeing Caribbean tourism grow and succeed. Sometimes our air tickets were "comped" by American Airlines and always our hotel accommodations were provided free by the local hotel association.

All other travel costs for this trip were being funded by the Organization of American States (OAS) which was trying to help Grenada not be so dependent on Cuba. A quiet unassuming man named Ambrose was our contact and would be meeting us at the old airport on the industrial south shore of Grenada and driving us across the island to the tourist section where we would be accommodated at Spice Island Beach Resort, one of the more upscale hotels on the island, and not coincidentally, run by Sir Royston Hopkin and his family.

There were no direct flights from New York, so we took American Airlines to Barbados and waited for our puddle jumping connection on LIAT which would stop in St. Vincent on its way to Grenada. The airplane carried about twenty passengers and rocked and rolled across the Caribbean, rarely on time, but rather dependable as one might expect an intra-Caribbean carrier to be.

However, on this warm October 14, 1983 afternoon in Barbados, we waited at the airport for our LIAT connection for a very long time. We were supposed to be on a two o'clock flight and at three o'clock we were told that the two o'clock flight was cancelled and that the three o'clock flight was delayed. That flight too, got cancelled and the last flight of the day, the four o'clock departure, was also delayed. We began to worry that we would have to overnight in Barbados when at six o'clock we were told to board the four o'clock flight—four hours after our original scheduled departure.

The small plane, as I mentioned, carried about twenty passengers. And since the two previous flights that day had been cancelled, and Jim and I were two of only three passengers on the flight, we began to wonder why no one else was flying. How unusual I thought. We took off and landed twenty minutes later in St. Vincent, where the one other passenger on board got off. No one got on. Now it was just Jim and I and we were on our way to Grenada.

Another twenty minutes and we were landing at Pearls Airport, an old, small airport on the industrial side of the island with one runway and a small house-like building that served as passenger terminal and maintenance facility. A new mega-airport was being built on the tourist side of the island by the Cuban government and our intelligence reports indicated that it would serve as both a passenger terminal and an army base for the Cubans.

We walked into and out of the tiny building in less than ten seconds and were outside on the road looking for Ambrose or anyone holding a sign with our names. No one was there to greet us. We waited just a few minutes as it was getting dark and the airport was closing up since they did not have the capability for night flights. We assumed that since we were so late, whoever was supposed to pick us up gave up and left. After all, the drive across the mountain was an hour and a half and we were four hours later than expected. We asked the lone taxi driver sitting there to take us across the island to Spice Island Beach Resort.

The driver hesitated at first, spoke to one of the airport workers who was locking up and gave us a price which seemed exorbitant, but we really had no choice. We didn't want to be stranded at the airport on the other side of the island. Cell phones did not exist at this time and we had no one to call. There was no other way to get to where we were going and night was approaching.

This was my first time to Grenada, and I could not appreciate the true beauty of the island as we traveled across the twisting, turning mountain roads in the dark that had descended upon us. We did marvel at the festive mood of the local residents that we found lining the dark roads and streets as we crossed the mountain. I noted to Jim that this was very encouraging to see so many people out celebrating on a Friday evening. I just figured this was their way of welcoming the weekend as was the custom on many of the Caribbean islands. We had just come from Barbados where the Friday night "fish fry" was a weekly dining festival at Oistin's and other spots across the island.

We arrived at Spice Island Beach Resort and was greeted at the front desk by a shocked Royston. "What are you doing here," he asked as if we were not supposed to be there. Jim and I both reacted with, "I thought you knew we were coming this weekend." Still in shock that we were there he said: "Yes, of course I did, but there was a coup this morning and the prime minister is under house arrest and the airport is closed. How did you get here?"

"We took LIAT over from Barbados, but had to wait because they kept canceling flights. . ." And suddenly a light bulb went on in our minds and we began to get a brighter picture of what had just happened. We later found out that LIAT had canceled all flights, but operated that one flight we were on just to pick up some of their employees and fly them off the island and back to St. Vincent. The airport, was indeed shut down and there were no aircraft coming or going. We were stuck on the island of Grenada in the middle of a coup.

Royston told us not worry, that he would accommodate us and hopefully things would settle down quickly and we would get out in a day or so. Naturally, he did not expect the original planned meetings and seminars we were supposed to conduct to go on as scheduled. Tony could not get to Grenada because flights out of Puerto Rico were cancelled from the morning on. Everyone knew that there was a coup other than Jim and me. That's why all the local residents of Grenada were lining the streets. They were out there, not celebrating the weekend, but rather celebrating the coup.

Ambrose, from the OAS, came over to Spice and met with us to discuss our options. He did not think the airport would be open in the morning, but he said there might be an option to leave by boat and sail over to St. Vincent to catch a LIAT flight back to Barbados. The sailing would only take a few hours and we could easily connect and get back home. He would check on that option in the morning, but for now, he wanted to take us out to dinner at one of the local restaurants in St. Georges, the main city in Grenada, only a short drive from Spice Island Beach Resort.

As we left the resort driveway, Ambrose pointed out the Cuban barracks complex just across the road from our hotel. It was a huge army barracks complex. As we drove down the road adjacent to Grand Anse Beach he pointed out the Medical school where many American students were in attendance.

We got to the restaurant and everyone was buzzing about what was happening. The place was filled with local residents and the radio was blaring news and chatter about the coup that had taken place. At one point the "Revolutionary Government of Grenada" got on the air and explained: "We have placed Prime Minister Maurice Bishop under house arrest because he is courting American interests and bringing them down to our island which will destroy our way of living." Jim and I looked at each other. Were we those American interests they were talking about? We were asked by the prime minister to come to Grenada. We were now the enemy of the people. Would we be arrested next?

Just then some local comic decided to play *God Bless America*. Jim said, "Don't stand up, it's a trick to get us to reveal ourselves. Act like a Canadian." I'm not sure I know how a Canadian acts "A", but I did my best to hide my New York accent and tried my best to revert to my Kentucky dialect; as poor as that was. We ate dinner—the food was rather good—then Ambrose drove us back to Spice. We went to our beachfront accommodations and I said goodnight to Jim and walked down the beach path and entered what should have been, under any other circumstances, a dream of a hotel room.

Spice Island Beach Resort, at that time, had forty-eight rooms, many of which were sitting right on Grand Anse Beach in the middle of the sand only steps away from the Caribbean Sea. This is how a Caribbean resort should be. I walked along a winding path, lit for the night by foot-high globes which provided just enough light to illuminate the lush surroundings. The path ended in the sand and I then walked past several stand-alone units that sit on the beach. My unit was two down from Jim's and the third from the end of Spice Island's section of the beach. Grand Anse Beach was a huge horseshoe shaped beach with power-white sand that faced the capital city of St. George's across a moon-lit bay. It is perennially listed as one of the top ten beaches in the Caribbean.

There was a foot bath that sat in front of the door so you could wash your feet when you come in from the beach during the day. I wiped my shoes on the mat and unlocked the floor-to-ceiling sliding glass door and entered the one-room accommodation where my bed sat in the middle of the room. At the far end was another sliding glass door which went out to an open-air garden followed by the dressing room, bathroom and shower.

I undressed and got into bed. The moon lit up the water and reflected a shimmering light across the beach and into my room. It was both beautiful and romantic. I lay in bed thinking what a wonderful place this was and what I could write about in my articles for the magazines. Then I heard gun shots. They seemed to be distant, but I could not really tell. I was not accustomed to hearing gun shots.

Then I heard more gun shots. I looked out the sliding glass doors in front of me and checked to make sure they were locked—not that being locked would stop a bullet. Then I lay back down, hoping to fall asleep. More gun shots that seemed closer. I turned away from the front sliding doors and was now facing the back sliding glass doors and realized—I had nothing but glass in front of me and glass behind me. I closed the curtains on both sides, but still had no peace of mind. I was vulnerable to attack. I lay in bed wondering if they knew I was there. They, the Revolutionary Government of Grenada, must have known we were there. Did the taxi driver tip them off? Would they come at me shooting through the glass doors? I was vulnerable. I was scared, shivering scared. I couldn't stop shivering.

I picked up my pillows and blanket and moved beyond the sliding doors in the rear of the room into the shower which was concrete. I snuggled in the protection of the corner of the shower and fell asleep to the sounds of gun shots.

The next day Royston suggested that we go over to the Holiday Inn where we were supposed to be making a presentation to the local hoteliers. I said that I doubted that anyone would be there, but he felt that we needed to do this just in case anyone was watching. It would be worse to avoid it in favor of giving in to the revolutionary government that had taken over. I pointed out that they have guns, but Ambrose agreed that we should try and act like nothing has happened and it doesn't matter to us.

We went with Royston to the Holiday Inn. The only person that showed up was Jillian, the executive director of the Grenada Hotel Association. Ambrose and his assistant, a lovely young lady that also seemed concerned that she was on this island in the midst of a coup, were also there. Jim had his relaxing comic nature going full blast, but I found very little to laugh about as gun fire could be heard in the air as the morning wore on.

As we were sitting around a long dining table on the outdoor patio waiting to have lunch (we did have to eat you know) a young Canadian reporter for the Toronto Sun came in. He was both excited and nervous as he explained that he just came back from downtown St. Georges and had witnessed a massacre during a rally at the old fort. He took out his tape recorder and played this horrifying noise with screams and lots of gun shots and more screaming. I got a chill sitting in this open-air restaurant in the Caribbean on a 90-degree day. This was the sound of chaos. It was close by and I was scared. He had just finished playing the tape a second time when two local Grenadian teenagers entered the restaurant.

They looked like any other teenagers dressed in tee-shirts, jeans and sandals. Except that both of them had rifles on their shoulders and they were not hunting deer. They came directly towards our table, as there was no one else in the dining room. As they approached, I discretely pushed my large professional-size camera to the floor along with my note pad and pen. I did not want them to know I was a journalist.

This turned out to be a brilliant move on my part as I discovered a short while later when they began questioning the Canadian journalist about what he was doing in Grenada. He, in turn, asked them for credentials. I thought to myself—those rifles on their shoulders are their credentials. But they did not hesitate and the two young soldiers handed their entire wallets to the Canadian with some sort of identification indicating they were members of the revolutionary government army.

They asked the reporter to pack his things as they were going to escort him off the island. He objected at first, but they insisted that this was an internal political issue and he, as outside media, must leave. The reporter left with them and I breathed in relief that I was safe—for the moment. Later we learned that this reporter was not escorted off the island, but rather taken to a mountainside prison dungeon where he remained for several weeks before being discovered and released.

After lunch we went back to Spice where life appeared to be normal with the exception of the fear that was centered in my gut. It was like a permanent case of indigestion or nausea that just sits there reminding you that nothing is normal and the fear is real. I had placed one call to my brother when I had first arrived, but could not get any calls through to the US since. I felt isolated in a third-world country that was going through a major internal crisis. I did not want to stay. And I knew that they, the Revolutionary Government of Grenada did not want me to stay.

That night, we were all carted off to the Cuban Ambassador's home for a cocktail party. The Grenadians were attempting to maintain calm in face of the chaos that surrounded them. In this way, they did not give in to the potential new reality of the coup that might disrupt their lives. Everyone at the party was jovial and very friendly. The Russian Ambassador, who's name I have forgotten, offered me his card with his private telephone number as he said: "Please call me if you are concerned about the in-fighting going on here in Grenada. I will offer protection for you in my home."

That statement came just prior to my close friend Jim telling the Russian Ambassador that he has Russian heritage and names all his dogs

Nikolai. The Russian Ambassador stared back at Jim and softly said, "My son's name is Nikolai." I quickly walked away.

We had a nice time that night and on my way back to Spice Island Beach Resort I was brought back to reality as I heard more gun shots in the distance. Once again, I took my pillows and blanket and slept in the confines of the shower.

One of the reasons for my heightened fear was the growing cadre of Cuban soldiers that were filling the barracks just across the road from Spice Island Beach Resort. At first, I thought that these were airport workers that were brought in to build this magnificent airport facility that we were briefly shown. But when I saw the hangers and maintenance facility, I quickly realized that this was not a commercial airport for a small Caribbean island, but an army base to use as a staging point in the strategically located Eastern Caribbean.

We were also told that the prime minister and his followers were massacred in the fort on Saturday which was witnessed by the Canadian reporter. Chaos was now elevated to crisis for me.

Several days of this half charade and half reality went by and Ambrose assured me that we were close to getting resolution and we would be able to get home. I was concerned that my family was at home in the dark because communications to and from the island were sporadic at best and news reports on television offered a dire picture of an island in turmoil with people being shot and killed. Ambrose said that if things became escalated and we were in any real danger he would have a motorboat take us out to a sailboat anchored in the harbor. He even pointed out the specific boat. I felt little comfort in that, knowing that I was very prone to seasickness, especially on sailboats. But I would gladly welcome a four-hour sail to get away from the perennial fear-based nausea I was currently experiencing.

A few days later, while leisurely eating breakfast—everything was done leisurely since there was little we could do—I was suddenly told to go get packed, I was leaving in thirty minutes.

I was quickly escorted from the restaurant and taken back to my room to pack. Less than thirty minutes later I was ushered into a waiting unmarked black car. In the front was a driver and a guard literally running shotgun with a rifle in his lap. Waiting in front of this car was another car with several men inside. Quickly with no fanfare the two cars were off on our 90-minute trek across the island. Jim decided to stay in Grenada for the moment. He left the next day.

As we drove up the twisting, turning mountainside we passed several Cuban army truck convoys coming down the mountain. Seeing them passing caused me to be concerned at first, but as no one stopped us, I began to relax just a little as I could begin to foresee the end of this terrifying experience.

We arrived at Pearls Airport that had been closed for the past week and found no activity. I was escorted inside and found four other people waiting to board a LIAT flight to Barbados. There was no aircraft on the tarmac and no one at the ticket counter. I didn't have a ticket anyway. My armed guard left me there with the other four waiting—waiting in silence. I became concerned again. Nearly an hour went by with none of us talking with each other. I felt I needed to ask: "Does anyone know when the plane is coming? Does anyone have a ticket?" No one actually answered but three of the four shook their heads indicating "no."

We continued to wait in silence until a very tall women in a dark blue suit came in to the small airport building that served as ticket counter and waiting room. Suddenly a plane landed and we were immediately hustled out on the tarmac and boarded the plane. No flight attendants, no one took our luggage, no one asked for tickets. We just hurried out, carried our luggage ourselves and boarded the plane. We took off almost immediately and I finally began to relax.

We stopped briefly in St. Vincent where two of the four others that boarded with me got off and several others got on. Next, and last stop for me, was Barbados. When we landed and I got off the plane, I actually got down on my knees and came very close to kissing the ground. Tears rolled down my face. The nervous energy that was pent up for the week had turned to a relief cry. No one stopped to see if I was okay. I was ignored and left alone on the tarmac crying softly to myself. A minute or so passed and I composed myself, stood and walked off the tarmac to the transit area and to the American Airlines counter where I handed them my original roundtrip ticket. Ambrose told me that American would honor it knowing what had happened in Grenada. I was skeptical.

The American Airlines flight attendant looked at my tear-stained eyes and explained that the flight was full, but she would see what she could do.

I just had to wait on the side while everyone else boarded. Once again, I became nervous that I would be delayed and have to find accommodations on Barbados. For nearly fifteen minutes I watched 200 people board the American Airlines 747 before the flight attendant called me over to give me a boarding pass with a first-class seat. She smiled at me and said, "Have a nice flight, and welcome home."

I arrived home after midnight that night and went right to sleep. The next morning I awoke, turned on the TV news and began to nervously shake uncontrollably as I watched films of what happened the day I left as the US Marines attacked the Cubans in Grenada including one missile which came up short, hit and demolished one of the beach units at Spice Island Beach Resort — the second from the end—right next to where I had roomed until that morning.

Most of the ammunition was targeted at the Cuban barracks that sat across the road from Spice Island Beach Resort, but being precise was difficult in such close quarters and a good deal of Spice felt the impact of the barrage of gunfire. There also were bullet holes in many of the units at Spice as a result of the battle between the marines and the Cubans.

Fortunately, none of the hotel staff or Hopkin family were hurt. Ambrose had warned everyone and they had closed the hotel and moved the few guests (it was still the off-season) to their personal homes in the hills, far enough away from the shore where all the fighting was taking place. It ended quickly as the Cubans were not prepared for the US marines. No one expected the US to intervene in the politics of a Caribbean island. The US government used the excuse that there were hundreds of American students studying at the Grenada medical school which was (and still is) just a short walk down Grand Anse Beach from Spice Island Beach Resort.

After the battle was over and order was being restored, many of the medical school students were interviewed and all of them thanked the US government for saving them. I quietly thanked Ambrose for getting me off the island before the marines landed.

Two weeks later, I was back in Grenada meeting with hoteliers and tourism officials to begin the rebuilding of tourism which would become one of the central forces for the island's economy. The local reception for Americans was phenomenal. There were signs all over the place thanking the US Marines for freeing the island from the Cubans and the tyranny of dictators. Unfortunately, Maurice Bishop was dead, a casualty of his own desire to help his people. But many who followed his ideas and ideals would help rebuild the island with the pride that was truly Grenadian. It remains today, one of my favorite destinations, and one that I frequent for long weekend escapes just to relax away from the rest of the world.

And where do I stay? At Spice Island Beach Resort where Sir Royston along with his family operate what I feel is one of the best boutique resorts in the world.

CHAPTER SEVEN

VISITING EL SALVADOR, TURKEY AND HAITI DURING CURFEW

Some humans ain't human, Some people ain't kind
You open up their hearts, And here's what you'll find
A few frozen pizzas, Some ice cubes with hair
A broken Popsicle, You don't want to go there

•••••••

"Some Humans Ain't Human" by John Prine

Grenada was not my first coup experience. Several years before, I was on a press trip to El Salvador in late 1979. The press group arrived in the early evening and were swiftly escorted from a very chaotic scene at the airport, with armed guards all over the place, to a hotel in the center of San Salvador, the capital city. We were told that it was not safe to go out alone because the now-famous "Bloodless Coup" had taken place and a curfew had been issued for anybody on the streets after dark; for any reason whatsoever. This being a Latin American country, we knew to take those curfew orders very seriously or end up in jail or worse.

It reminded me of landing in Istanbul, Turkey a couple of years before. There too, our press group was greeted by machine-gun toting soldiers and a nine o'clock curfew. However, the difference was that Turkey did not experience a coup. This was just normal procedure enacted by a paranoid

Turkish government at that time. Istanbul by day seemed normal, except for the soldiers with machine guns on every street corner. But tensions were high as we experienced while shopping in the famous Grand Bazaar. We were being coerced into buying things and felt very threatened as we tried to walk away without making any purchases. Vendors made us uncomfortable by grabbing our arms and shouting at us if we didn't buy something.

On the El Salvador press trip there were several travel journalists and we had a welcome dinner that first night with the resident manager of the hotel. It was a strange "welcome" as the head of the tourist office could not attend as planned because of the curfew in place. After dinner the journalists settled down with after dinner drinks (naturally) to talk about all the possibilities facing them in the morning. None of us had ever experienced the effects of a coup before and we all were very apprehensive about what was happening in the dark, deserted streets outside our hotel. Some were even concerned about the impact on the hotel and whether or not we were safe at all. But they all expressed some minimal positive feelings because they were assured it was safe to visit at this time and we were all in this together. I guess the phrase "safety in numbers" was in their minds, despite the fact that a revolutionary army had taken over the government from a long-despised dictator.

One of my colleagues had actually been there during the coup a few weeks earlier and had assured me that we would be safe. That was good enough for me.

Drinks were in the bar adjacent to the lobby. This was not a big hotel. The lobby was small with two large front doors always opened by a well-dressed doorman. The center of the lobby had a couch facing the doors and four large easy chairs all surrounding a very large round Mexican-looking coffee table with Aztec designs embedded in the surface. The front desk was just behind the couch and the two elevators were on the left side when you entered the lobby. The lobby bar was through a large opening to the right opposite the elevators and the restaurant was situated past the bar through an ornate doorway.

While sitting in the lobby bar enjoying after dinner cognacs, tia maria and my choice of frangelico on ice, we talked about jobs as reporters and how we would now have a news scoop for our travel trade publications and maybe even get an opportunity to write for a major newspaper or magazine;

a dream that every trade paper reporter harbors inside their mind as a frustrated newsperson. We drank and talked late into the night, despite the fact that we were all exhausted from the flight down and the added tension of the coup, because no one wanted to leave to go to bed for fear of the unknown.

It was then, that I thought I saw an old friend walk through the front door of the hotel and straight to the bar for a drink. I saw him out of the corner of my eye. I thought it might have been Stuart, the man who let me to drive his car on those country roads when I was just 13 years old. The journalists were sitting at a semi-circular booth with a round table. I was sitting in one corner with a clear look at the bar across the room as well as the lobby including the front doors.

I watched the man at the bar with intent. "I think that man over there at the bar, the one with the white hat, is someone I know," I told my colleagues quietly. "I'm not sure since he has his back to us, but I thought he looked familiar when he first came into the bar a little while ago," I added. I could only see his back and waited a few minutes to see what he was up to, but he quickly downed a drink and went straight to the elevators and disappeared without giving me a chance to verify if it was who I thought it was.

With the idle chatter that was going on at the table between the other reporters and the combination of other conversations and soft Latin music in the bar area, I was not able to hear anything he said at the bar as I observed him talking with the bartender.

I excused myself from the press group, went over to the bar and asked the bartender if he knew who that man was by name. The bartender said he had no idea who that was, but I didn't buy it. They seemed to know each other and the bartender poured him a drink without him asking. I asked again and got the same answer. "Don't know who your friend is, not sure I know who you are referring to." It was a lie, but not unusual for a bartender protecting the interest of his customers. I turned back to the group of reporters and told them that I was going up to sleep.

The next morning, we had breakfast at the prescribed press itinerary time and were met at nine o'clock by the tourist office representative as well as a uniformed soldier from the El Salvadorian army. He had two open-air jeeps waiting in front of the hotel and said that we are going on a quick tour so he could show us the results of the bloodless coup that had taken place. He motioned for me to get in the first jeep in the front seat next to him and then motioned to two of the reporters to hop into the back seat. The tourist office representative and the other two reporters joined another uniformed soldier in the second jeep.

The city of San Salvador was bustling as is normal on a busy day in Central America. There was no appearance of anything that might have happened recently that would change the direction of this country forever. Everyone and everything looked perfectly normal as would be expected if there had not been a coup. We further understood when we arrived at the burnt-out police station ten minutes later when the lead soldier explained that this was a bloodless coup and that following the burning of the *Policia Nacional Civil* (Central Police Station), he exclaimed with pride: "The dictator vanished and a new government was installed. We are all safe." When asked about the curfew, he said it was "just to make sure that no one gets any ideas, if you know what I mean?"

I then wondered if that was my old friend at the bar last night and what he was doing out so late after curfew. . . and where was he all that time while the bloodless coup was happening. Was he involved in any way? It was a question I would never get answered. But for now, the news of El Salvador President Romero's overthrow was welcomed by youthful cheers everywhere. Unfortunately, after returning home to the US several days, and many wonderful experiences later, I began to hear about all the violent killings being undertaken by the newly established junta. One dictator had been disposed of, but the country was heading into a very long civil war in which many people on both sides would lose their life.

Dictators were not unusual in the Caribbean and Latin America. The US government often supported them, or at best, turned their back on the atrocities because these dictators supported the US versus our communist enemies in Russia. One such dictator was Baby Doc (Jean-Claude Duvalier), son of the long-time Haitian dictator Francois Duvalier known affectionately as Papa Doc because he led the Haitians on a populist and black nationalist reform movement. Baby Doc was just a dictator out to make sure that he remained in power and he often instituted a curfew to keep the population from exploding against him. He did so until a popular uprising overthrew his regime in 1986.

Meanwhile, on a press visit to Haiti around 1970 I had the pleasure of meeting Papa Doc. He was totally blind by that time, but nevertheless his mind was sharp. He recognized the voices of those in the room with the sole exception of mine. When referring to me, he was kind enough to address me as "Mr. Newsman." Years later when meeting his son Jean-Claude (Baby Doc), I did not find him to be the same welcoming charismatic individual. He was just plain rude.

Over the years, I visited a number of destinations which were run by either a dictator or some very strong president that had full control of the country. Many of these government leaders treated me with a reverence that I hardly deserved. I was nothing more than an editor of a travel industry trade magazine. Yes, it was an influential publication in a very important industry, but nevertheless, I was not reporting in *The New York Times* or *Time Magazine* and I knew that.

On one such trip, around 1985, I was on line passing through customs and immigration at the international airport near Lagos, Nigeria and was standing behind some US businessman who was being shaken down by the customs officials. He was asked to pay a $1,000 fee to qualify his visa to enter the country. He kept insisting that his visa was already qualified and all his papers were in order from the Nigerian consul in New York. He was entering the country to set up a working arrangement for his construction company with a Nigerian construction company. He was there to help a local Nigerian company. The customs official didn't care. He kept telling this man that he would spend the day in the airport and get back on the next TWA flight back to New York if he did not pay the $1,000 fee.

When the man finally agreed and took out his checkbook to write a check, the customs official held his hand up and said: "No checks. Only cash or Yankee go home." The man protested again and again pleading that he did not have that kind of cash. But the customs official didn't budge. Finally, the man reached into his jacket pocket, pulled out a billfold and counted out ten $100 bills into the customs official's hand, who then waived him through with a big toothy grin and a "have a nice day sir."

All this while, I stood no more than eight feet away watching, listening and sweating. I am not sure that the sweat came from the heat in the airport or the fear that I was next to be shaken down for cash. I did not have that sort of money on me. I didn't need much money because I was a guest of the tourist office and would be touring Lagos and its surroundings, possibly even having a meeting with Major-General Muhammadu Buhari, the president of Nigeria, who had taken over just two years prior to my visit in a coup d'état.

I stepped forward, handed my well-traveled, multi-stamped US passport and visa to the customs and immigration officer and he carefully turned every single page looking at all the places I have been. Several times while looking through my passport, he looked up at me and smiled. I smiled back through the sweat pouring down my face. "Hot in here," he said. I was not sure how to react so I just said, "Yes" softly. "What did you say?" he questioned. "Yes, it's very hot. I didn't expect it to be so hot," I answered. "What did you expect?" he queried with a bit of a frown now expanding on his face. "I had no idea. This is my first time to Nigeria. I am a travel writer here as a guest of the tourist office and your government," I offered in hope of some compassion for me. It worked. The big toothy grin returned and he welcomed me to his country.

I did get to see a great deal in the five busy days I spent in Nigeria including a really bustling city of Lagos, several museums and a beautiful beach area with luxury hotels. Nigeria is the most populous country in Africa and one of the top ten most populated countries in the world. It was a busy place with a wide diverse feel that few countries in Africa can claim.

I also did get my visit with the president. It was on my last day in Nigeria. I was invited for breakfast in a massive room used for Heads of State dinners. Major-General Muhammadu Buhari had a mixed reputation for his strong-arm control of the country. But he had clearly helped Nigeria become an economic force in Africa and the world. He was a gracious host to me, an insignificant journalist writing travel articles.

We were having some great conversations about our President Ronald Reagan. Somehow, he may have assumed I knew President Reagan personally. I never said that, but I did know a lot about our president and shared some of that very public knowledge in our conversation. He was fascinated and asked more and more questions. I began to watch the clock and, although I was having a great time, I tried to excuse myself because I had to catch a plane back to the US He told me not to worry and that he would provide his presidential car to drive me to the airport.

As conversations continued and time went by, I continued to remind him that I needed to leave to catch my plane. He called over one of his assistants, said something too softly for me to hear and turned back to me saying: "It will be okay. You will not miss your flight today."

Shortly after that I started to become alarmed as I knew that there was precious little time for me to get to the airport and I apologized, explaining that I was really enjoying the conversation but the plane would be leaving shortly without me.

He smiled as he leaned over the table and said: "The plane will not be leaving without you. I have made sure of that." And that he did. An hour or so later when I reached the airport, was escorted through customs and immigration, and reached the gate a full half hour after the scheduled departure time, I boarded to a round of applause from some of the not-so-patient passengers who knew that their plane was being held up for some late guest. I was embarrassed but had done nothing wrong other than witnessing the ultimate power that some heads of state possess.

CHAPTER EIGHT

TRIP TO THE PHILIPPINES THAT BOMBED

A woman is a mystery a man just can't understand
Sometimes all it takes to please her is a touch of your hand
And other times you've gotta take it slow and hold her all night long
Heaven knows there's so many ways a man can go wrong
·······

"Must Be Doing Somethin' Right" sung by Billy Currington

Then there was the failed coup in the Philippines by my friend Doris Baffrey who just happened to be the Director of Tourism for the Philippines in North America and daughter of a decorated Commander in the Philippines Navy. She had also become my friend as we at *The Travel Agent* magazine and thousands of travel industry delegates prepared to convene in the Philippines for the American Society of Travel Agents (ASTA) World Travel Congress.

But, on Sunday, Oct. 19, 1980, Doris Baffrey set off a bomb twenty rows from where Philippines President Ferdinand Marcos was sitting in the convention center in Manila. He was there to address the 6,000 travel industry personnel that had gathered for the annual ASTA conference. I had lunch with Doris in Manila just a few hours before.

Doris and I knew each other very well; or so I thought. We worked around the corner from one another in New York City and in the months leading up to the ASTA conference we had lunch or dinner many times. I was, at that time, chief editor of the magazine. We were reporting regularly about the upcoming annual conference which was taking place in the Philippines and I had gotten close to her as an important source of information on our biggest conference of the year. This annual conference drew most of the leading executives from all segments of the travel industry including the airlines, cruise lines, tour operators, destination tourist offices and travel agents from around the world.

I had interviewed Doris several times about the upcoming conference. This procedure was normal. But there were some controversial issues surrounding this conference. Nothing was normal in the Philippines. Ferdinand Marcos was an elected president, but he ruled the Philippines more like a dictator. His wife Imelda was famous for her collection of shoes which she proudly showed off. I once had the privilege of visiting the palace and seeing her shoe collection. There were several closets, actually rooms at the presidential palace that were turned into closets to hold the thousands of pairs of shoes that she owned. I cannot believe that she ever wore all those shoes.

Meanwhile, a large segment of the population of the Philippines were not happy with either Ferdinand or Imelda and they did not want the travel industry to come to the Philippines because they saw this as another way in which Marcos would get rich while the populace would remain poor. There were demonstrations in Manila months before we were set to travel and threats issued by the opposition party including some that warned the travel industry to "stay away or face the consequences." And while many of the previous ASTA conferences drew as many as 10,000 delegates, this South Pacific paradise managed to convince only 6,000 people to attend. That was still huge for the Philippines.

Doris and I got together in New York for dinner a week before the conference. She was too busy for lunch so I suggested dinner. We had grown close over the past year and going out to dinner was as much a social event as it was for business. We talked about her lengthy stay as director of tourism for the Philippines in North America and her desire to return to Manila in a new role. She opened up about her estranged relationship with her father, a high-ranking official in the Philippine Navy. We joked about our relationship. We had recently spent more time, more lunches and dinners, with each other than any of our real friends. At first, I didn't think anything about this because this was business. This was a big story for our magazine and I took it on as one of my personal projects.

I wasn't dating anyone at this time so I had the time to do this as needed, even in the evenings. But I never realized how close we had gotten and how much time we had spent together in the months leading up to the conference. I still dismissed this as nothing more than work. I often took my work home, or more accurately spent so much time in the office that it was more like home than my two-room apartment in Brooklyn. Maybe, in the back of my mind, I was growing more and more fond of Doris. She was the primary organizer for this major travel industry conference and I respected all that she was accomplishing.

I flew to the Philippines a day ahead of the conference as was my usual procedure which included carrying boxes of our magazines to be distributed to the delegates as they arrived and checked in for the conference. We produced a special issue with more than 120 pages of news and features about the travel industry and the conference to be distributed at the registration area where all attendees must pass through.

It was my habit to get there a day earlier with the magazines so I could set up and be ready when the first delegates began arriving. I could then personally hand them a copy of the magazine and, at the same time, talk with them, and catch up for a moment before everyone got too busy. This was especially helpful with the top executives from some of the airlines and cruise lines that would draw a lot of attention once all the travel agents arrived. They were more sought after than even shrimp at a cocktail party.

Shrimp, by the way, was an all-important ingredient in the lives of travel agents. I learned how important shrimp were to travel agents the first week I went to work at *The Travel Agent* magazine. (This is the story I told the Chinese at their symposium I mentioned in Chapter One that failed to get me any laughs.) The year was 1973, and I went with Jim, one of our veteran writers, to attend a European Travel Commission trade show event being held at the Hilton New York Ballroom on 6th Avenue and 54th Street. Jim pointed out that around the perimeter of the very large ballroom sat each of the European destinations and some of the tour operators who packaged vacation tours to Europe. They sat at table tops waiting for the travel agents and had their brochures for the taking as well as small gifts such as pens, tee-shirts, hats or key chains with their destination or company names imprinted so the travel agents would remember them and think of them when consulting with their clients, potential travelers planning their vacations.

I noticed there were a handful of travel agents sprinkled around the room and some of them were at the table tops talking with the European promoters. They were the serious, professional travel agents learning about opportunities for their clients. However, I also noticed there was an extra-large group of people surrounding something in the center of the ballroom, but the crowd was so large that I could not see what they surrounded. Jim told me that was an empty table on which the food would be placed and that the travel agents were waiting for the food to come out. Just then, as if on cue, doors at the far end of the ballroom opened and a line of waiters carrying trays of shrimp made their way across the empty floor towards the center of the room and the waiting travel agents. Only, the travel agents did not wait. They took off like a group of screaming girls chasing the Beatles or some other rock stars and swooped down on the unsuspecting waiters carrying trays of shrimp.

The waiters never had a chance. They never made it to the table in the center of the room. Within less than two minutes the locust-like travel agents had devoured six large trays of shrimp and left the waiters bewildered holding large empty silver trays.

Over the years I would see this scenario repeated in many ways at many venues — especially when shrimp were involved. We even put out a special April Fools Edition of The Shrimp Agent (only for internal pleasure) about a travel agent couple teaching their young children how to go after shrimp at a trade show and how to eat as many as possible in one night and where to find the next shrimp trade show extravaganza. There must be something in those shrimp.

Meanwhile, there I was on my way to Manila with thirty-five boxes of magazines to distribute at registration. But there was a hitch in this system. I did not ship those thirty-five heavy boxes by freight. Rather I spent extra money to carry them with me as luggage, ensuring that they would arrive with me at my destination. I learned this early on in my career as I was fortunate to have most of my boxes arrive at one of the conventions, only to see my competitor with no magazines because their freight shipment got lost somewhere between New York and Europe. After that conference I always kept the boxes with me at all times.

I would have the thirty-five boxes loaded into two taxi cabs in New York headed for JFK International Airport. One of my colleagues would ride in one taxi and I would take the other. However, as we arrived in Manila, we found that the taxis were too small to carry thirty-five boxes of magazines in just two cars. We had to get five taxis and one of the taxi drivers took the lead explaining to the others what we were doing and where we were going. They just wanted to make sure they were going to get paid for carrying all those boxes since they would not have a human being in the car with them. The porters loaded the five taxis, I got into the lead taxi and we took off for the convention center, our first stop, so I could leave the boxes and not have to do this again.

When we got there with our taxi train we found the convention center was closed for the day. We went on to the hotel with our thirty-five boxes; and these were big, heavy boxes. The doormen and the hotel bellmen didn't know what to do with this. I got them to bring all thirty-five boxes up to my room and had them stacked along the wall. The next morning I had to get the bellmen to bring them down and get another five taxis to take them to the convention center. I shelled out a lot of tips those two days moving all those boxes around. Once at the convention center, I set up a table in the registration area and began the process of meet and greet all day long.

I took a break to have lunch with Doris. She seemed distracted, but that seemed natural as this was a big event for her and her country. This could mean millions of dollars in tourist revenue over many years as was typical after a destination hosted the travel agent conference. Travel agents always heavily promoted the destinations that hosted their annual conference. The reason was simple; after they experienced the destination themselves, they could more freely talk about the destination and sell it to their clients with confidence that they were selling something good.

Doris may have been worried that someone would carry through on the much-publicized threat to disrupt the conference. She told me not to go to the opening ceremony for fear that something might happen because Ferdinand Marcos was the featured speaker and there could be demonstrations and angry mobs. I explained that I had to be there as editor to cover the event. She seemed overly worried about me being there even telling me that she would get me any speeches that I needed and suggested that I go to one of the many promotional dinners that were taking place instead of going to the opening ceremony. I thought that was odd, but then realized that she was genuinely concerned about my safety. She told me if I did have to attend the opening ceremony, I should stay in the back just in case something happened. I liked her concern for me. I thought to myself, that I would take her out for a nice social dinner when this was over and we got back to New York.

I arrived at the convention center as thousands of attendees were pouring in through the two large front doors with heavily armed guards spot checking everyone. I found a seat in the middle of the audience, in the center of the room, about twenty rows from the front which was already filled with delegates. There were another twenty-plus rows behind me that were quickly filling up. It was a packed house with nearly 4,000 attendees. The show started soon after I arrived with musical processions followed by speeches by ASTA officials. And then it was time for Ferdinand Marcos to speak. Before he got up on stage a film about Marcos was being broadcast with loud patriotic music and fireworks on the huge screen behind the podium where he would speak. That's when it happened.

At first, we thought it was part of the program. A loud explosion with fire and smoke coming from the center of the audience, just a few rows ahead of where I was seated. Then we heard the screams and saw people climbing over seatbacks to get out of their seats and away from the fire that had erupted.

It was a bomb and eighteen people including five Americans were seriously injured. After exiting the big hall with all the delegates, I went straight to the conference venue press room where we were set up to communicate our stories about the travel industry. There were telephones and fax machines to send stories to our publications. We were twelve hours ahead of New York where it was only seven o'clock in the morning so I could not call the office. I filed a quick story and then all communications went dead. The Philippines cut themselves off from the world as they anticipated a full-force coup may have been underway.

That night in the Philippines we journalists hovered about in the press room. Communications with the outside world came on and off again, but we were able to get a few telephone calls through to New York. We shared information as reporters tend to do in a war zone, but there were no further bombs, no guns in sight, no shootings. Only the aftermath complete with rumors of many dead and a possible insurgence by the Philippine people. It never happened. I don't remember if anyone of the injured died, but several were seriously hurt including two that lost limbs. After the initial explosion, it was discovered that there were at least three additional bombs placed in the auditorium including one in the row right behind me. None of them went off.

It was also soon discovered that Doris Baffrey was the mastermind of the plot against Marcos and his regime. Despite the fact that she worked for the government promoting tourism, she was part of a rebel team of opposition forces that wanted to free the Philippines from what they called "a tyranny of villains." My Doris Baffrey. The soft-spoken young lady with whom I had become so close. She almost had me killed. In retrospect I began to remember the clues she had given me. Yes, in retrospect. But I was lucky that I wasn't injured or killed by this person I had so trusted and liked. How could I be so blind to what she was all about? How did I not see the clues to her hatred of her parents and the Marcos regime?

Doris Baffrey became a major headline in news stories around the world. A terrorist that was my close friend. A traitor that I had interviewed multiple times. And a friend that I had socialized with for many months. She would be jailed immediately awaiting a future trial. Her father, the Philippines Naval Captain, was questioned, but he remained a close confident of President Marcos. I was never questioned, but I wrote my stories for *The Travel Agent* magazine and brooded about losing my good friend Doris.

Years later, having been back to the Philippines several uneventful times on press trips, and having reincarnated myself as a marketing and public relations specialist in the travel industry, we were hired by the Philippines Department of Tourism to represent and promote tourism to the destination. We worked for the Philippines for more than five years as their official public relations agency and then did ad hoc promotions for both the destination and Philippines Airlines.

However, I never saw Doris Baffrey again.

CHAPTER NINE

FINDING MYSELF, THE EARLY YEARS

There's more than one answer to these questions
Pointing me in a crooked line

·······

"Closer to Fine" by E. Saliers, sung by Indigo Girls

I was born in Brooklyn, technically part of New York City, but, with more than four million residents, Brooklyn is really a city unto itself. I lived with my parents, my brother Ed and sister Barbara in a three-room apartment. There was a small dining room when you entered the apartment and an even smaller kitchen directly off of that room. The living room (where we all lived together) was to the right of the dining room. The bedroom was the left of the dining room. And there was one small bathroom, also off of the dining room, where I sometimes hung out for privacy (more about that later). My parents slept on a convertible couch in the living room that opened into a full-size bed. My brother, sister and I slept in the large bedroom.

Our apartment was on the top floor of a six-floor building. There were eight apartments on each floor, forty eight in all, and we knew only about a dozen of the residents. My early years in Brooklyn were confined mostly to this building and the block the building sat on.

I grew up with a lot of fears based on things that happened in and around that apartment. First, there was a man in an apartment down the hall that turned on the gas on his stove and sat there in his kitchen until he was dead. We heard the commotion out in the hallway and when we looked out our door all we could see were a lot of policemen. And then they wheeled the dead man out and took him down in the elevator.

From that moment on I feared going near that end of the hall as well as the dark stairs leading up to the roof because I feared that his ghostly spirit might come down from the mysterious dark unknown hidden up on the roof, especially at night. When I would go downstairs to visit my best friend Michael (who lived in the apartment directly below ours), before returning to our apartment, I had to have him stand at the bottom of the stairs while my Mom kept the door wide open to our apartment upstairs. I would then run, at top speed, up one flight of stairs and past the evil black darkness looming above me on the roof.

Then, to make matters worse, our next-door neighbor's apartment was broken into. The thieves came down from the roof using the fire escape and came through their bedroom window which leads onto the fire escape. Now I had more proof that there was evil on the roof plus an added fear that our fire escape was vulnerable to intruders.

And finally, my childhood fears were made worse when I got stuck in the elevator and the door opened in between floors. There was nothing but solid dark red brick facing me. I rang the emergency alarm and pressed every button on the elevator panel. Suddenly the elevator jerked upward slightly and there was a space to crawl out onto the next floor. I waited to see if there would be any further movement and there was. The door closed and the elevator started smoothly going down, stopping on the next floor below. The door reopened and I jumped (really jumped) out.

I stopped taking the elevator that day and from that moment forward I was known as the boy who took the stairs. But I didn't just take the stairs, I ran up and down the six flights of stairs every day, sometimes several times a day. Running up six flights of stairs as often as I did helped build up my legs for latter use in track, on the football field and for basketball. I was not the best athlete, but I was fast. At night when I came up to the sixth floor where I lived, I leaped up the stairs and sprinted down the hall to my apartment. Yes, I was a child filled with fears.

Those fears kept me secluded and protected in the apartment. And spending so much time at home lead to creative games and an assortment of writing, drawing and painting. It was the early start on what would eventually become my profession. But I was also a very shy child and didn't have many friends beyond Michael Katz and some of his friends, all of which were two years older than me.

I did try to generate friends in some unusual ways. At ten years old and in the 6th grade of elementary school I made some very important school yard friends that protected me from the bullies like Randy, a small, rough kid who lived on the corner and loved to beat up bigger kids like me. My solution was to steal my father's condoms and sell them to kids in the school yard. I gave them away free to a couple of big kids like Jack who then protected me the rest of the year.

Those fears and shyness followed me until I moved to Kentucky to attend Murray State University. But I had begun to emerge from my cocoon when I turned fourteen and began hanging out with a group of boys and girls that would become my closest friends with some of those friendships lasting forever. (More about that later.)

Meanwhile, back at *The Travel Agent* magazine, I was extremely fortunate for the opportunity to use my writing and editing skills and immersed myself in my job and forgot about my dream of writing the great American novel.

I did not go looking for a job at *The Travel Agent* magazine. It landed in my lap after a short medical leave of absence from *Aviation Week & Space Technology*. I had met Eric Friedheim, publisher and editor of *The Travel Agent*, many times at travel industry lunches and somehow talked myself into an eventual job. He was expanding the magazine and going to a twice weekly schedule and was looking for a managing editor to replace the one who was planning on retiring. Friedheim wanted someone with a travel industry background. I was hired.

Interestingly, Friedheim hired me and Karen Rubin for the same job and when we both started work there on September 10, 1973, we both thought we were in charge. It only took three days before she and I were fighting. Friedheim sorted it out and put me in charge as Deputy Managing Editor, most likely because of my work on *Aviation Week* where I won a Business Writer's Award. But Karen was positive that it was a gender issue. It took a while before she and I became friendly co-workers and eventually life-long friends. She went on to become a well respected author and freelance contributor to many publications.

I spent sixteen years there from 1973 to 1989, eventually becoming Managing Editor, then Editor in Chief, and eventually Editor and Publisher. We published a travel industry news magazine twice a week as one of two main travel news publications and often published additional magazines focused on destinations or segments of the travel industry.

But it was at Murray State University in Murray, Kentucky, a small town tucked away in the far southwestern corner of Kentucky that I evolved from that shy kid growing up in Brooklyn into a journalist that would become an editor of a major travel industry publication and get the opportunity to travel around the world and enjoy the experiences that are shared in this memoir.

CHAPTER TEN

ON MY WAY TO ME AT MURRAY STATE

"All of my friends were strangers when we met."
•••••••

(apologies to David Bowie)

My first real travel experience was in 1962 when I left the hot August pavement of Brooklyn, New York for the green pastures of Kentucky. I was on my way in search of myself at Murray State University in the small town of Murray. I've been asked one particular question many times over the years: How did I end up in Murray, Kentucky? Actually, this move was no different from any major move I made before or after. I just followed those paths that Robert Frost had suggested in the *Road Not Taken* and often found myself growing stronger, more self confident and happy.

My choice of Murray State University was just another one of my non-choices that evolved out of convenience and an attractive path that was laid before me. It actually began a year prior without any knowledge that Murray State existed. I wanted to go away to college, but couldn't afford to pay tuition. My parents, with three jobs between them, and two other young children still at home, couldn't seem to find the extra money to pay for my college. The fact that my father and I were not talking to each other because of my insolence and also that I cut school for most of my junior year, didn't help my cause (that's another story in another chapter). We hadn't talked for nearly a year.

I graduated from Erasmus Hall High School, the oldest, and one of the largest high schools in the entire US. We had more than 8,000 students in the school and more than 2,000 in my graduating class. Many famous performers and athletes attended with me including Barbra Streisand and professional basketball Hall of Famer Billy Cunningham. But I was just one of the sticky pieces of chewing gum found under any one of the old wooden desks in a classroom on a campus surrounded by five-story red brick buildings. No one knew who I was or cared. With so many students, we were just numbers.

After exploring several small schools in New Jersey, Pennsylvania and upstate New York, and finding that I could not afford them, I settled on applying for Brooklyn College, a large, free institution normally reserved for those students that excelled in high school. To my parents' surprise, my grades were high enough despite the class cutting and other minor issues that kept me from attending the graduation services. Brooklyn College accepted me, even if my parents didn't.

Shortly after beginning classes at Brooklyn College, I was sitting in a history class when a student messenger came in and handed the professor a note. The professor read the note and then looked up and said something like: "Is number 785968407 here?" Most of the students began looking at their student ID cards to compare numbers. I hesitated, but took my card out of my wallet when the professor repeated the question and read the number again. I glanced at my card briefly, but did not scrutinize the numbers carefully. They looked similar. When the professor asked one last time if the number belonged to anyone in the class, I raised my hand, stood up, gathered my belongings, and followed the student messenger out of the classroom.

"Do you know what this is about?" I asked the messenger, still not knowing for sure that the ID number was mine. "Someone in the administration office needs to see you," he answered. On our way to the Administration Office, we passed one of the big double doors that provided access onto the campus. I never hesitated, turning suddenly and exiting into the fresh autumn air, briskly walking across the campus and heading home, never to return to Brooklyn College. I did not want to be a number again. I needed to find myself and it would not be underneath an ID number.

Without a college to attend, the battles between my father and I grew more frequent and more heated. I needed to get a job. Sheldon, one of my neighborhood friends, told me that Guardian Life Insurance Company was looking for people who were good in math to be loan calculators and approvers. I applied and got the job. I was a loan calculator and the first line of approval or denial for dozens of people each day as I would examine and analyze each loan application and calculate the risks as well as what interest we would charge if we approved the loan. I was instructed to approve only those with low risk factors based on established criteria and information provided in the application. If I approved an application it went to a higher level loan approver for final review. If I denied an application it only went to a higher level if the applicant requested another review. In this way we were the first line of defense, but not the last line of approval.

Shelly and I played pinochle every day at lunch with two other loan approvers. I was making and saving money and having fun. Winter turned to spring and spring became summer and I took the subway from Flatbush, Brooklyn all the way up to the Parkchester section of the Bronx to see my friend Steve and his sister Renee. We knew each other from summers spent at Ashley Country Club in Spring Valley, New York. I liked Steve, but really liked Renee. We had hung out together one summer, but I wasn't sure she really cared. When I got there, she was off somewhere else. That gave me the answer to my question of whether or not she cared. Steve and I spent the day together and he told me about this great college he had attended that past year. "Why don't you come to Kentucky with me for the fall semester and see what you think," Steve urged.

I went home that night, checked on my financial resources and Monday morning called the Murray State Registrar to talk about the possibility of registering for the fall semester—which, by the way, was starting in two weeks. She asked me a number of questions about my grades and what extracurricular activities I participated in. I told the truth because I knew she would ask for a copy of my transcripts. I had what would translate into a 3.5 grade point average, played a little basketball, was on the football team and swam competitively for Erasmus. Plus, I performed with the Erasmus Hall Men's Glee Club. I did not tell her I almost got expelled, had to report to the Dean's office before homeroom everyday because I had cut classes for more than six months straight, and was not permitted to attend graduation (more about that later).

That very day on the telephone, the registrar told me: "We are very interested in having y'all attend Murray State, but we have very little time and you will have to get us your transcripts from your high school and bring them with you. You will also have to find living accommodations on your own because we do not have any rooms left in the men's dormitory. We don't like to have freshman living off campus, but we will make an exception since we have no rooms. If this meets with your desires, then I will see y'all in Murray in two weeks." All I could say was "Yes, thank you, thank you very much." I called Steve and told him. He said that I could crash with him and his two roommates in their trailer until I could find someplace of my own.

I now had to get my act together in less than two weeks and I had to find someone at Erasmus Hall in the middle of August to get a copy of my transcripts. Somehow, I managed to get it all done and, on a Friday morning in late August Steve picked me up in his big dark green Buick and off we went to New Jersey to pick up his two roommates, Jack the Irishman and Phil the Pickle (everyone had nicknames in New Jersey). We were on our way. I was really going out of town to attend college. Even my father was happy and my parents threw me a quick going away party. I was on my first trip.

This trip, like so many others that followed, would not be uneventful. After a lunch break at a rest stop on the Pennsylvania Turnpike, Steve turned to me as we walked back towards the car and said, "Here's the keys, your turn to drive for awhile." I took the keys but failed to tell him that I really did not know how to drive, had very little driving experience, none on a highway and—did not have a driver's license.

I got into the driver's seat, turned on the car, put the gear stick into the reverse position and stepped on the gas. The car lurched backwards, scraping a car parked on the right side of me. I stepped on the brake, put the car in drive and lurched forward. I then tried to reverse it again, but once again scrapped the same car next me. Steve reached over and turned the key to off position, jumped out, ran around the car and told me to get out. He then jumped in the driver's seat, eased the car out of the parking space while I stood on the side.

For just a moment I thought he might drive off without me and my college days would be over before they had begun. He turned the car towards the exit and yelled for me to get in. Once back on the Pennsylvania Turnpike he pulled over on the shoulder and said. "Okay, now it's your turn to drive. I really need a break." This time all I had to do was get behind the steering wheel, put it in drive and step on the gas. I was okay. I was actually pretty good at keeping the car in the lane and even passed a couple of slower moving cars. I got us into West Virginia and Jack took over.

(Footnote: If you owned a car that was mysteriously swiped while you ate at a rest stop on the Pennsylvania Turnpike in August 1962, I sincerely apologize.)

Steve, Jack and the Pickle lived in a three-bedroom trailer just past Five Points intersection on the edge of the campus of Murray State University. It was walking distance to the campus and there were about a dozen trailers and one house in the trailer park. I was to sleep on the couch in the front room which served as kitchen, dining room and living room. The cost was nothing. I just had to contribute money for food. I lived there with them from late August through December when they asked me to either pay rent or move out. It was really too crowded. And I had amassed a bunch of dogs (seven in total) that had come to depend on me for food and lodging on cold nights (more about that later).

Two guys living in the house at the front of the trailer park had a spare bedroom. I figured, if I have to pay, I should have my own bedroom. I got the smallest room, but it had a door and that provided privacy enough.

One of my new roommates, Carl, was a farmer who was studying agricultural science so he could return to his family farm with new efficient ways to manage the property. He was a big guy at 6'5" and 250 pounds; all muscle from years of working on the farm. He was sweet on a tall, very pretty blond girl from Oklahoma. She rode horses competitively and they would talk about horses and farms and stuff. She was very pretty at 5'8" with sky blue eyes and long, silky blond hair most often kept in a ponytail. She was being courted by all of the guys on the basketball and football teams as well as the frat boys. She had no interest in any of them.

Carl was interested in taking their friendship to another level but didn't know how and was too shy to make a move. He came to me and asked for my advice. I suggested inviting her for dinner. Our other roommate agreed to help prepare the meal. I said that I would get dressed up and act as butler. I wore a dark suit with a white shirt and one of his bowties and looked the part. When she arrived, we welcomed her in, sat her down and began to pamper her with cheap Champagne.

Our farmer made a grand entrance dressed in jeans and fancy Western shirt with a new pair of Western boots. He looked the part. We finished cooking and I served the meal. Once they were done eating, we took off to get some coffee at the College Grille. We had set the stage. It was now up to him to draw the curtain. They had a great time and slowly began to develop a closer relationship. But it never became the romantic one that he had envisioned because she soon returned to Oklahoma to pursue a riding career.

We lost access to the house the following semester because the landlord needed it for relatives and I went searching again for somewhere to stay. I had joined Alpha Phi Omega, a service fraternity reportedly started by a group of Boy Scouts in 1925. Five of my Alpha Phi Omega brothers were rooming in a six-bedroom house. They offered me the sixth room if I would cook and clean for them. I didn't know anything about cooking, but I quickly found that you could put cheese on top of anything, including leftovers and it would become a great casserole. Breakfast was eggs and bacon in the mornings with lots of different leftovers that I could use for creative omelets. For dinner there was always hamburgers and hotdogs and my creative casseroles. I was a hit as a chef. I had no idea of what I was doing.

After a few months living there, my friend Jerry "the coach" Weitzen, also from Brooklyn, told me that he was moving into a garden apartment behind the College Grille. We became roommates there and for two more years after when we moved into a private home owned by Mr. and Mrs. Workman, an older couple that lived down the street from the campus.

While living at the garden apartments, Jerry and I got closer to our new next-door neighbors Ray and Ebbie, two of our friends from New Jersey and Pete the Bug, a tall, lanky guy who proudly called us all into his bathroom one day to show us the largest single lump of excrement that I have ever seen. This monster turd sat there clogging the toilet bowl as if someone had stuffed a small animal in head first and all you could see was the ass end. Another time, we were relaxing in our rooms when a gunshot rang out and we suddenly had a hole in one wall and a bullet in the wall across the room. Apparently, our next-door neighbor, a local resident, was playing with his guns. This was life off campus at Murray State in the 1960s.

Ebbie (Henry Paul Woolley) and I became close colleagues sharing our poetry, our thoughts, our words, enabling both of us to grow as thinkers and writers. We would often read each other's poetry and kindly critique what we read. His poetry and songs were always so insightful. Even then, he had the ability to observe the world as if he were a sage profit come down from the Tibetan mountainside.

After a lifetime pause, we resumed our collaboration nearly 50 years after we left Murray State. But it was really those early years in which we shared intimate thoughts about everything that helped pave the way for both of us to become better writers and to grow as people. Today Henry and I talk regularly and share ideas as we did back in college. Those moments together then and now are among my most cherished times.

CHAPTER ELEVEN

EMERGING IN A BIG WAY IN A SMALL TOWN

I cannot forget where it is that I come from
I cannot forget the people who love me
Yeah, I can be myself here in this small town
And people let me be just what I want to be
•••••••

"Small Town" by John Mellencamp

College, like high school, was of little interest. I spent more time in extra-curricular activities than in classes. I never studied and rarely did anything more than get by with a lot of Bs and Cs except in those classes that were really interesting, like "The French Revolution." It was more than a history class; it was like a twice weekly soap opera in which the teacher, Dr. T. Wayne Beasley, took us on a trip through a time in France made fascinating by the minutia he divulged each week. I even read some of the chapters in the book to better enjoy the stories that the professor told. I will never forget how Napoleon Bonaparte got captured when he stopped to take a leak in the woods and was recognized by a passing hunter. I always wondered, just what on Napoleon did the hunter recognize.

I immersed myself in the College News where I was the photo editor for a while, the assistant news editor and an all-around reporter. These positions on the newspaper landed me an assignment to pick up Doc Severinsen, the legendary trumpet player and band leader on the NBC

Tonight Show starring Johnny Carson. The Doc was the featured performer for the Murray State Homecoming game one year.

When I met him, his first question was "Where could we get a drink?" I explained that Murray, Kentucky was in a dry county and there was no drinking. Then I offered him a joint and took him to a room that was set up to be our version of the "green room" to provide comfort to any VIP coming to the college. Eventually, I took Doc to the stadium and handed him over to the college officials. In between the green room and the stadium drop off, I interviewed Doc Severinsen about what it meant to perform at Homecoming games and other college events. He gave a great interview and I got a fabulous story for the college newspaper. He also gave a great performance which resulted in a standing ovation in the football stadium.

I also pledged a fraternity, but not one of the social fraternities that stood for snobbery and made people feel inferior just because they didn't belong. Instead, I pledged for Alpha Phi Omega, the service fraternity that performed good deeds on campus. My big brother's name was Nasser, an Iranian exchange student. This would not be the last Iranian that I would become friends with. It would, however, stand in contrast to all that Iran stood for over the years and forever remind me that a country's political stance does not necessarily define its people. And it is always the people that really matter. I learned to separate the individuals from the prejudice I might have otherwise had for the country.

Later in life, I would meet Pascal Mahvi, the son of a Royal Prince of Iran and a confidant to the former Shah of Iran. We would work together to open and promote Jalousie Plantation, a luxury hotel in St. Lucia. I would fly off with him in his private jet and would become a trusted consultant on travel and hospitality matters for him. We would become business friends.

I would meet other Iranians, many good citizens of the United States. All these good people were trying to escape the political shadow of an oppressive Iran by referring to their native country as it was originally called—Persia. I liked the reference as it took me back to a time when Persia was a respected world leader, not the despised thorn in the Middle East it had become since the 1980s. Iran would become one of our most mistrusted foes in the Middle East, but, like anywhere else, prejudice against all the Iranians was not justified.

My chosen fraternity, Alpha Phi Omega, did good things. The fraternity brothers got together and created a Text Book Exchange so that students could bring in used text books that they no longer needed and, in exchange, get other text books for their current or future classes. It was very successful; so successful that the College Bookstore started a rival service on campus and put the Text Book Exchange out of business. In the end, the students benefitted and we had done a good deed.

The fraternity also took on the task of restoring and cleaning the face of the college library. A long, hard job, but one that won appreciation by the faculty and administration and helped me when I got in trouble. Appearing before the Dean for a campus infraction I committed, the Dean said to me: "So, you are a member of Alpha Phi Omega, huh? Did you have anything to do with the Library cleaning?" After a nod of my head, he said, "Nice job." I got just a slap on the wrist that time.

I was also active with the drama club. This resulted in several interesting performances. The best was when I appeared in a play based on the scriptures: *The Gospel According to Mark*. The director was another student, a friend named Charles Finnell. Young Mr. Finnell was an ordained Lutheran minister. He had been to seminary school and studied theology. He returned to college at Murray State to study speech, theater and English. He headed up the drama club and directed the play on the Gospel.

He also did some outrageous things to create more dialogue about religion on campus. First, he had me, a Jewish boy from Brooklyn, appearing in several rolls throughout the play, ending with the final scene in which this Jew looks up at Jesus who is dying on the cross and says, "He is the son of God, he truly is the son of God." Charles Finnell also did something that resulted in even more controversy in casting a very tall young lady with very long brown hair as Jesus. This was talked about long after the play had run it's two-night course.

Charles came to me one day at the Student Union Building, sat down with two cups of coffee, handed one to me and said, "I have a favor to ask of you." I took the coffee, took a sip and said, "The coffee is good. So okay, what do you need me to do now?"

Charles went on to explain that he, as a Lutheran minister was involved in the United Campus Ministry and they had this building at the far end of the campus that was underutilized. He said the ministers were hoping to create some regular weekly event to draw students into the United Campus

Ministry building, especially on Friday and Saturday evenings when many students normally went drinking.

Drinking anywhere in Murray was not an easy thing to do, especially for students at the college. Calloway County, where Murray was located, was still celebrating the laws of prohibition as a "dry county" allowing no liquor to be sold. Murray, as a city, didn't ease those limitations until 2012. But back in the 1960s, students would often drive the eighteen miles south on Highway 641 to Paris, Tennessee where they could enjoy a few beers in the local bars before returning to the campus—drunk. Unfortunately, sometimes they didn't make it back safely. The ministry wanted to do something to avert this weekly drunk drive by keeping the students happily occupied on campus.

Charles knew that I had come from New York where coffee houses were prevalent. Other big college campuses around the country were also homes to coffee houses where "beatnik" types would gather, drink coffee, share poetry and sing folk songs. Charles wanted to know if I knew about coffee houses. I told him about my years hanging out at the Cafe Wha in Greenwich Village.

My cousin Steve and I would often meet in the Village and hang out at Cafe Wha, one of the mainstays of the beatnik era in the 1950s. It was there that I met Richie Havens. Richie and I would often take the subway from the Village to our homes in Brooklyn together. He was a few years older than me and he looked after me on the subway which was often not a welcoming place to be late at night. Richie lived in Park Slope and I lived further along the subway line in Flatbush. We became good friends riding the subway together.

I was at Cafe Wha one night when the featured performer, Jerome MacMurray, didn't show up. Richie Havens was on the corner of the stage preparing to back up Jerome with his guitar and strumming with the "open E tuning" for which he was later to become famous. The manager asked him to move to the center of the stage and do that behind the microphone for a while. He was very shy, but when the manager offered him some money, he shuffled to the center of the stage, sat back down on a wooden chair and continued his strumming and humming as the audience began to clap in a rhythmic and melodic cadence. Suddenly, everyone was making music with Richie Havens and he began to sing. I'm pretty sure that it was his first solo performance. Two years and many club appearances later, he cut his first album and flew to success like a high-flying bird.

Years later, upon returning from college, I bought tickets to see Richie Havens at the Village Vanguard, an intimate setting for performers. I got there early enough to get a seat at a table near the front of the stage. During the performance Richie acknowledged, "It's nice to see old friends in the audience." After the performance I went up to the stage to say hello. He stepped off of the stage and we embraced. He also invited me and my friends, who came to the show with me, to join him at a party after the second show of the evening. I felt really great that Richie Havens, now a big star, recognized me from our past and wanted me to join him afterwards. We reconnected, and despite the fact that nearly fifteen years had evaporated since we hung out at Cafe Wha, it was like time had never passed.

At the after-hours party I met Richie Havens' manager, a tiny lady named Betty Sperber. This meant nothing to me until another ten years later when I was named to the Board of Directors of the Caribbean Hotel Association and re-met Betty Sperber, then owner of the King Christian Hotel in St. Croix, and one of the officers of the association. We reconnected the dots and recalled that we had previously met one another in a different time and place. It was just another example of the small world phenomenon that unites everyone.

Meanwhile, my story about the Cafe Wha was all that Charlie needed. "Could you please come and tell the other ministers all about the coffee houses and how kids would hang out there?" he pleaded. A meeting was set up for the following week. I arrived and was introduced to each of the ministers. There was the Methodist minister, the Lutheran minister, a Catholic Priest and an Episcopalian Priest along with ministers from the First Presbyterian Church, Church of Latter-day Saints, Church of Christ and, of course the Baptists which dominated the area. After proper introductions, Charles reiterated what we were all doing there to discuss what could be done to help keep students on campus over the weekends and how I would explain the concept of the coffee house to them.

It was then my turn. I went into a lengthy story about the growth of the coffee house movement in Greenwich Village and across the country. When asked by the eager Methodist minister whether the United Campus Ministry building could work as a coffee house, I looked around the room and nodded, "Sure." They asked what would be needed. I explained that the kitchen looked adequate and they would need to build a small stage at one end of the large downstairs room and get an assortment of small tables and chairs. They would need to create a dim light atmosphere and set up a microphone and speaker system. They were mostly nodding their heads in agreement and the Catholic Priest asked, "How much will this cost?" to which I answered, "I don't know, but I can research it for you."

Then the big question came from the Baptist minister: "Could you, would you run the coffee house for us?" With that several of them chimed in, "Yes, could you do this?" "We would be glad to pay you." "How fast can you build this coffee house." "When can we start?"

"Gentlemen, I am honored that you consider me worthy of your project and plans. I can help you put this all together, but I don't know if I can run this for you. Let me get together with Charlie, I mean Minister Finnell and we will get back to you as soon as we can with a detailed plan. Is that okay?" I then thanked them, shook hands with most of them and grabbed Charlie's arm as we exited.

Once outside I turned to Charlie and said: "We have to talk about this. This could be big, but it may be bigger than us. Let's go over this tomorrow." Charlie agreed and we both went off to sleep on it.

The next day, Charlie came with news about how excited the ministers were and that they were offering to spend whatever it would take to turn the downstairs into a real coffee house. And they are willing to offer me a weekly fee of $30 to run the coffee house on Friday and Saturday. That was a lot of money in 1965, but I would need help and they would have to get paid too. I went back Charles with a counter offer. "I want the guarantee of $50 a week and also need some money to pay my help out of the profits."

The ministry thought that they would host this coffee house for free. They were not looking for profits. I told them that no one attends a free concert. I was planning on bringing in talent to perform and students will pay to be there. We thought we would charge a couple of dollars as a contribution to get in. They would get coffee, donuts and entertainment and could sit there all night if they wished. The basement could easily fit as many as 90 students and that meant $150-200 a night minus costs for food, entertainment and promotion of the coffee house. I would earn a small weekly income as well as have some funds to pay my friends that would be helping to serve coffee and clean up.

Charlie transmitted the deal to the ministers and they agreed. I met with them and excitedly told them about specific plans. The Methodist minister was put in charge of overseeing everything. My first move was to name the coffee house. I called it **Nowhere Coffee House.** I then created flyers and posters which showed a girl and boy talking: The girl is saying: "What are you doing this weekend?" The boy answers: "Nothing." The girl then asks, "Where are you going?" and the boy says: "Nowhere," as he points to the coffee house in the picture.

I had friends, Al and Claude, Danny and others that would perform. They were good folk singers and Danny was a gifted guitarist. They were the first performers. I read some of my poetry. It was a start that drew a modest crowd. Word of mouth begat student interest. One student begat another, one folk singer begat another and one poet begat another poet. Word got around the campus and within seven short days we had built up a following. It was almost biblical. But we didn't rest. We went seeking additional talent to appear in our modest coffee house in the United Campus Ministry building.

Nowhere Coffee House took off when I went down to Nashville with one of my radio colleagues and convinced Chris Gantry, a singer songwriter famous for writing several of Glenn Campbell hits including *Dreams of the Everyday Housewife*, to come and appear at Nowhere.

I purposely did not announce the appearance of Chris in advance, but word spread quickly after Glenn Campbell's, song writer Chris Gantry had appeared at Nowhere and from that point on it became the place to be on Friday and Saturday nights just in case another famous singer might be there. And from time to time we were able to convince several other country and western performers (even some stars) to make the trip up from Nashville to try out their stuff on our small, but enthusiastic crowd in Murray. The only caveat was that we could not promote that they were there because they were not getting paid. Nowhere Coffee House was a hit and I was in my element, both on stage and running the show from backstage.

I had fully emerged from my shy shell and was now appearing before crowds of strangers with the same comfort level that I had with my close friends. I would remember these times years later when thrust upon the stage to make speeches and presentations to thousands in the travel industry. It was the formidable years at Murray State that provided the building blocks of my success years later.

This is also where I learned how to play the harmonica. You see, I could not play the guitar or any other instrument. And, I surely could not sing despite my years of practice with the Erasmus Hall Glee Club. I could not carry a tune. I wasn't even allowed to sing Happy Birthday at family birthday parties. One day, Danny took pity on me having to sit on the sideline while they all jammed and sang. He tossed me a harmonica and said, "Just blow in and out and try and stay with us." It didn't happen overnight, but Danny showed me how to play *Blowing in the Wind* and then how to jam with them on *San Francisco Bay Blues* where they let me have a harmonica solo on stage resulting in a shocked audience applauding. I don't think they knew whether to laugh or clap. I'm glad they clapped.

Audience appreciation was important to me. It may have been the classic need to replace the lack of attention and appreciation from my parents, especially my father, who from when I was 11 years old, worked two jobs, leaving the apartment after dinner and not getting home until morning after we had left for school. He slept all day and we only saw him on Sundays, which was not enough for me. My mother also worked part time including some evenings, leaving me to babysit my younger brother and sister.

I needed attention and at first I got it by offering unsolicited comments in school resulting in my fifth-grade teacher writing a note to my parents telling them that I was a bright student, "but acted like a buffoon." I didn't know what a buffoon was and thought at first that it was a compliment. I graduated into a full-fledged class clown in high school and carried that into my relationships with my local friends in Brooklyn and all the way down to Murray, Kentucky. Fortunately, my buffoonery morphed into humorous poetry and got me the attention I needed on stage as both the MC and resident poet of Nowhere Coffee House.

I also got attention doing a local radio show on WNBS, called the "home of radio" and named for Nathan B. Stubblefield, a local farmer who lived all his life in Murray, Kentucky. In January 1902, a month before Marconi's famous radio demonstration, Stubblefield publicly produced the first "radio" transmissions using a magnetic wireless telephone system he had developed. A few months later *Scientific American Magazine* reported the success of Stubblefield's radio demonstrations in Washington, D.C. Being a simple farmer, Stubblefield displayed a healthy mistrust of the Washington, D.C. politicians and failed to get the support he needed to expand his development. He did, however, receive a patent for his wireless system in 1908, but was unable to turn this into the huge success that Marconi did a few years later.

Meanwhile, I proudly sat in the studios of WNBS and performed a variety of roles including reading the early morning hog reports and news. I progressed to a DJ show as a fill-in for my friend Tony, but excelled as a talk show interviewer and host. That's where I got an opportunity to tell stories, including those about growing up in Brooklyn with the Amboy Dukes as my neighbors. And, while I never knew or experienced any of the gang fights the Amboy Dukes were famous for, I did often live in the shadows of fear from an invasion of the Baldies, a gang from the Bronx which were rumored to swoop down on junior high schools and shave the heads of both guys and girls just for fun.

Working at WNBS also helped prepare me for my Travel Talk show that I later hosted on a number of radio networks in New York City including ABC, WMCA and WEVD. Murray State was my coming out party. I can't say I worked hard at my studies, but I did work hard at everything else including a variety of jobs and my very important social life. And it was an active social life from beginning to end.

CHAPTER TWELVE

A MIDWEST WEDDING AND HEARTS ON POLICE CARS

Fifteen years old and smoking hand-rolled cigarettes
Running from the law through the backfields
and getting drunk with my friends
Had my first kiss on a Friday night, I don't reckon that I did it right
But I was younger then, take me back to when
•••••••
"Castle on the Hill" by Ed Sheeran

At one time, I contemplated leaving school and moving to Effingham, Illinois, a small Midwest town which proclaimed itself as the heart of America. This happened after going to a wedding there back in the 60s. It was a small city along Route 40, which at that time was the major East-West route from Pennsylvania through Ohio, Indianapolis and Illinois. It was later replaced by Interstate 70 which must have hurt thousands of businesses that lined Route 40. Interstate 40 was straight and flat and went through hundreds of small cities and towns that grew up along the highway. Flying over the Midwest you can see how these towns sprawled out in all directions with the center of the city overlaying the highway. It was no different for Effingham.

I drove up to Effingham with John, I think, to attend a mutual friend's wedding. It was a wedding to remember, which is why I forgot many of the details. John had a car. Nothing special, but it got him back and forth from wherever he had to go. He let me drive as usual despite the fact that at twenty years of age I still did not have a license and therefore couldn't buy a car.

We were on the way to Amanda and Pete's wedding in Effingham, Illinois. John and I arrived on Friday afternoon. The wedding was set for Saturday at noon at their local church with a reception to follow. They were staying at Amanda's mother's home. Her father had died years before and Amanda had gone off to college in Kentucky where she met Pete. Amanda had lived with her mother and two younger sisters, ages eighteen and twenty-one.

The first thing I saw as we entered town was a police car. Not just any police car. This one did not instill immediate fear shivering down my bones like the time, several years later, when my tail light was out and a cop pulled me over. I knew I did nothing wrong, but fear of police was so intense that I began to quiver and it came right out of my mouth as my voice quivered in sequence with my fear-induced shaking body.

"What is it I have done?" my voice squeaked in a much higher octave than normal so that even the police officer knew I was frightened. Ouch, I thought, now the tall imposing officer would become suspicious. Did I have any pot in the car? Would I be busted because I had one joint somewhere on the floor of the car? How many years would I be sentenced to?

"What do you think?" the officer tossed back determined to throw me off.

"Nothing that I know of," I cautiously countered gaining some modicum of order in my voice.

"Your tail light is out and that's worth a hefty ticket—license and registration please."

Relief came, but slowly, for as long as he stood there, I knew my entire past as a pot-smoking, anti-war protester (I marched with Conservatives Against the War) would suddenly unfold and the officer would search the car and find drugs, guns and explosives and I would spend the rest of my life in a cockroach infested jail cell with a seatless toilet bowl.

Of course, all of this was unfounded and untrue, except for the pot-smoking, anti-war protester part. But the fear of police was ever present – until Effingham, Illinois. It was there that the Effingham police car, complete with a big red heart painted on both sides, a loving symbol, welcomed the world to "Effingham, the Heart of America."

Indeed, I did feel welcome and wanted to stop the car and get out and hug this officer. Better judgment, and traffic, prevented me from doing that. But I promised myself that I would hug a cop the first chance I got—not just any cop, but one that had that big red heart symbol, not only on their police cars, but squarely on their shoulders in a bright red emblem. I was liking Effingham. This was going to be a great wedding.

John and I went to Amanda's house to check in with the bride and groom. Pete was there and welcomed us with hugs, saying: "I was waiting for you guys. Amanda and her mom are at the church or hall taking care of last-minute details. She'll be back shortly and we're going to take the traditional 'relationship drive', wanna come along?"

Neither John or I had ever taken a relationship drive. It was something that they do in small towns where the bride and groom grew up together and just before the wedding, they would take a drive past all the hot spots that they visited while dating. They had a number of hot spots that they frequented so there would be a relationship drive-by with everyone honking horns and waving arms and the whole town smiling.

John and I got in line right behind Amanda's convertible driven by the best man. Pete and Amanda sat on the top of the back seat and off everyone went with 11 other cars following. First stop was McDonald's, of course, because that's where the drive-thru was and where Amanda had worked during summers. Other cars got out of the way, even letting the entire parade of eleven autos and Amanda's convertible proceed straight through the drive-thru. Everyone cheered, honked horns and smiled. Even though most of them had no idea who Pete and Amanda were. That didn't matter, it was a tradition that everyone understood and cherished.

Then we drove past the local frat house, two bars, a local Italian restaurant, a drive-in movie theater and a couple of private homes where some of Amanda's best friends lived. Their best man, who may have been partying in advance, drove like he was at the Indy 500 and by the time they got back to the house that Amanda and Pete would be living in starting Sunday, they had lost everyone else. I was driving John's car and managed to stay close behind. I didn't think that this was the purpose of the relationship drive-by, but the best man made it a game. Apparently, he set out to see if he could lose everyone as he sped through town. He succeeded.

It didn't take long for everyone else to show up. The pre-wedding party then commenced complete with beer kegs, tequila and pot. It was the rehearsal party before the rehearsal dinner—which I didn't remember after the pot and tequila, but was told that it was quite a good time.

The wedding was Saturday and the church was Presbyterian (it was where Amanda grew up, but not on the relationship drive-by list). The ceremony was simple and fast (once the minister finished his sermon). Then everyone stood out on the church steps to throw rice and flowers. After that we all headed to the VFW hall for the reception. The reception was also simple and very sweet. Not like those over-the-top, too expensive and gaudy weddings back in New York City. This was down to earth, just enough good food, good music from a DJ and lots of mixing, even among locals who often didn't mix well with college students. All gifts, and there were many, were left on a large table near the door.

I always bristled at New York weddings and the tremendous waste of food that cost so much and did nothing but feed the pockets of the caterers. Many years later when Linda and I got married at Thatched Cottage on a wonderful sunny Sunday afternoon, the cocktail party in the gardens overlooking the Long Island Sound was another example of a decadent and wasteful affair. It was a wonderful, but over abundant display of food and drink during the cocktail hour which lasted nearly two hours. When it was over and everyone was being invited into the ballroom for dinner, our friends Ralph and Cathy from Barbados were ready to leave, thinking they just had one of the most plentiful wedding dinners ever. They didn't know that dinner was yet to come. This was Long Island, New York and wedding caterers tried to out-do one another, no matter how simple you asked it to be. And we paid for it.

Back in Effingham, I danced with one of Amanda's local friends, a very, very pretty black girl who reminded me of Princess from back at school in Murray, Kentucky. Princess (not her real name), was a very talented, creative writer and artist who happened to be black, but gravitated to the white crowd. This was not a common occurrence in the 1960s in Kentucky; a state still proud of its Confederate heritage. And while the good people of Murray were generally tolerant, they were not ready to fully integrate on all levels in the 1960s, especially the intimate social level which included dating.

Princess and I were just friends, good friends that shared creative moments, poetry, art, and some good times laughing together in the library and other such venues. But at social events, such as dances at the Student Union at Murray State University, it was an unwritten rule, fully accepted, that it was forbidden to mix. It was an unspoken law of the land that said, be friendly, be cordial, but then stay with your own kind. My kind was clearly white. Her kind was distinctively black. This was 1963, and desegregation had only just begun.

At one particular dance, during my freshman year, I strayed. I was warned by several friends not to do it, but wanted to dance with Princess. It was a fast dance so I felt that I was on safe ground. We would hardly touch, but would have some fun spinning and turning and laughing. She was a good dancer and so was I. When I approached her, she stared frozen in fear. Her head shook back and forth in disbelief. "No" she barely whispered. "No, don't ask me to dance," came from her mouth without her lips moving as fear enveloped her whole body.

I grabbed her hand, pulling gently, but steadily out into the dance floor in the center of the large ballroom at the Student Union Building. Looking on were horrified whites standing in disbelief of what was about happen. I couldn't see their faces, but she could and she continued to shake her head. The blacks standing behind her also had frozen stares turning a dark crimson with anger growing to rage. But many of these blacks were my teammates on the Murray State football team. I thought that they would understand. We played together, sweated together, had each other's backs out on the field. Why would this be different?

Before I could regain a sense of reality, I had escorted Princess, under protest, out into the center of the floor. The Kingsmen were wailing "Louie, Louie" and I was about to get an education with that dance. That actual "black and white dance" didn't last more than three minutes, but the damage was done. I walked Princess back to her table of friends and turned to walk back to the whiter side of the ballroom. One of the football players, grabbed me, put his extra large and muscular arm around my neck, pulled me close and talking softly, but directly into my ear, said he and some of the other football players were going to do me a favor.

The plan was to get me outside and beat me up in front of the white rednecks. This would save me from an even worse beating by the whites for crossing over and insulting them by dancing with a black girl. It appeared that neither the whites or blacks appreciated my feeble attempt at furthering the cause of integration. Everyone was happy with the status quo. The blacks were happy enough just being there and getting an equal opportunity for education, and in some cases at no cost. And the whites were happy with the blacks keeping to themselves in this newly integrated community. It was 1963, and I had crossed a line that wouldn't be crossed even in some northern cities for several years to come.

My friend from the football team held my shirt collar in a tight grip, stared deep into my eyes, demanding recognition of what I did and what was now going to happen. He tightened his grip resulting in my shirt choking me while he patiently waited until I acknowledged what he had said before he released his grip on my shirt. I walked back to my white friends and told them I was going out for a smoke. I then proceeded to walk out front and light up an unfiltered camel, my cigarette of choice at that time. It didn't take long for a group to exit behind me. Both whites and blacks filed out, almost together as if they were going to a new party. Unfortunately, I was the center of the party. Not a party that I wanted to attend.

The first to get to me was some guy I had never seen. He was about four inches taller and 100 pounds bigger than me and he told me in no uncertain terms that I had overstepped social barriers by dancing with Princess. He didn't use those words, but rather shouted in my face: "Y'all fucked up. Man, ya fucked up 'n I'll now fuck ya up." He then added: "Keep ya dirty white hands off ma gals." I then made my next mistake. Not knowing what to say, I just turned my back on this guy. The next thing I knew I was on the ground and the big guy was on top of me crushing me with his weight as he punched my back repeatedly. He was followed by maybe a dozen others, mostly kicking and some punching. I buried my head for protection, but got kicked pretty hard in the ribs and sides. And somebody stomped on my hands just missing my head.

Not one white person came to my aid. They stood there watching. The beating lasted only a few minutes as security guards for the dance came screaming at everyone to "break it up." Some kept kicking (probably thinking that "break it up" must have meant break me up) but this too quickly subsided. I lied there, actually more embarrassed then hurt, but definitely feeling like I had been tackled by the entire football team, over and over again for an entire game. I got up slowly. No one helped for fear that some-one from either the white or black side might retaliate. Finally, Jerry, my roommate from Connecticut and a fearless football player himself, came out, saw me and helped me up. He also proceeded to remind me, "You are absolutely crazy, totally insane and will get yourself killed if you attempt another stunt like that."

This never would have happened in Brooklyn, New York where I grew up on the streets in the 50s with a strong mixture of black, white, yellow and a variety of other colors, sexual preferences and more. I even remember playing football on Sunday mornings in East New York where I was often the only white boy on the field. My friend Clarence would refer to me as their token whitey and add, "if we lose the football we can always kick Moose (their nickname for me) around." But that was a long time ago and I was a long way from Brooklyn, then and now.

This time, however, I was in a very different place—this was Effingham. There were hearts on the sides of the police cars. I was going to dance with this black girl and intended to have a good time. I did. And no one beat me up. Life was improving.

After the wedding reception everyone went back to Amanda and Pete's new home spending the next two days partying like there was no tomorrow. For most of these kids tomorrow meant nothing. I didn't have to be back at school until Tuesday. Some of the kids at the party never had a schedule. Still others had no life at all. And others (there were numerous people at this never-ending party), they were so stoned that nothing mattered. This was the 60s and yes, "love-ins" did happen.

This was just another love-fest incorporating a group of young people, many of which came into Effingham for the first time and some that grew up there and would never leave. It was a group of people who would treat this wedding celebration as just another college party. Amanda and Pete were not leaving for their honeymoon in California until Monday and that meant we could toast their new union all day and all night Saturday and Sunday. We were still there on Monday when they left for the airport.

I found love that weekend on a mattress crowded with at least four oth-ers (which was not unusual), but John did not, so when Monday came and went, we went along with it on our way back to school in Murray, Kentucky.

Those days I loved traveling the open roads of the Midwest, stopping in local diners to eat breakfast any time of the day. I could eat breakfast for lunch and dinner as well. I loved the eggs, either scrambled or over easy. I loved the sausage and white gravy with biscuits. I knew it was not healthy, but it sure was tasty.

There were a lot of unhealthy things that I did in those days. Besides smoking pot, I smoked cigarettes and often smoked too many. Part of this heavy smoking was to keep my voice deep and resonant. I had smoked cigarettes as early as 11 years old, Parliaments (I don't know if they still exist and have not smoked cigarettes since 1969). My friend Michael and I would then hide the Parliaments in the lighting recess in the top of the elevator of our six-storey building. While I normally didn't take the elevators, I would get in and climb up just to get a cigarette and go out to the back yard of the building and smoke.

Smoking escalated when I was doing a radio talk show on campus at Murray State and my air time was changed from very early in the morning to eight o'clock at night. By nighttime, the deep resonant voice that listeners (and my three fans) had come to know was two octaves higher and not the same rich soothing voice they had enjoyed each morning as they dressed, ate breakfast and listened to the hog reports and the daily price of corn. I had to find a solution so I went to professor Bill Bonham, the speech teacher, who told me of a secret recipe for keeping voices resonant.

"Take a shot of Kentucky bourbon just before you go on air to ease your pipes and then continually take long puffs on your cigarette to allow the smoke to keep your vocal cords warm and relaxed. You will sound like you first woke up in the morning."

It worked. The voice was back and I was recognized once again. But I was now a chain smoker going through a pack or more during each show. When I walked across campus and stopped to talk with friends, others would stop because they recognized my voice from the radio. One time, a cute young co-ed stopped to say how much she enjoyed my radio show and the stories about growing up in Brooklyn, adding: "But y'all sound like ya out of breath." I smiled back at her. I couldn't tell her Bill Bonham's secret recipe for taking drags on cigarette after cigarette during the two-hour radio show. And I surely couldn't tell her I was drinking shots of bourbon since alcohol was outlawed in Calloway County.

It wasn't until 1969, when working as a reporter for *Aviation Week &*

Space Technology, that I gave up cigarettes. I must admit that I didn't intend to stop smoking. I loved smoking, especially when sitting at my desk banging away on a news story on the typewriter. I really did bang away. It was an old Smith Carona manual typewriter because I did not like the feel of the electric typewriters and didn't give up my banged up manual unit until forced to convert to computers in 1990, years after everyone else had discarded typewriters. I still keep the old manual typewriter somewhere in my basement just in case.

Meanwhile, back at the office in 1969, I came down with a bad case of bronchitis and every time I tried lighting up a cigarette and smoking, I would convulse in a coughing fit that would last for five to ten minutes resulting in pains in the chest and throat. Even weeks after the bronchitis was gone and the coughing spasms were only a faint memory, any attempt at smoking a cigarette brought instant reminders of the bronchitis as my body would begin to reverberate with a hacking cough that produced sharp, knife-like pains in my chest. So I was forced to temporarily, in my mind, give up smoking cigarettes.

Pot, on the other hand, was not as abrasive to the lungs and I was able to continue smoking the weed and even increase pot consumption. That too subsided, but only years later after an out-of-body experience that frightened me. I was on my way to a New York Knicks basketball playoff game. I was picking up a couple of friends along the way in Brooklyn. Before leaving my apartment in Sheepshead Bay, I smoked a couple of joints to relax. I then got in my dark blue Volkswagen Bug and drove down Ocean Avenue to pick up my friends. Ocean Avenue is a main avenue that goes nearly the entire length of Brooklyn. It is a four-lane avenue with two additional lanes for parked cars on both sides. There is always a steady stream of two lanes of traffic going each way. It was central Brooklyn.

The pot I had smoked before leaving home was very potent. I felt very relaxed. Somewhere along the way I had an out-of-body experience. I could see the road clearly and saw that I was driving okay, but my mind and body were not connected and I could not recognize my own hands on the steering wheel. I slowed the car down to a crawl because I was not sure if that was my foot on the gas pedal. Cars were passing on the right and others were blasting their horns at me from behind.

When I reached the building that my friends lived in, I stopped the car in the middle of the street, shut the engine, got out, closed the door, walked across the street, as cars whizzed by, and took the elevator up to the 5th floor where my friend Steve lived. Friends, Sherm and Alan (the twins) were already there. I asked one of them, "Could you please go down and park my car. I couldn't do it because I am no longer in control." I took them to the window to point out my little car sitting innocently in the middle of Ocean Avenue with other cars doing their best to avoid hitting it as traffic sped by both ways.

I then crawled up in the kitchen by the window and went to sleep. When I woke up, I had missed the playoff game (the Knicks lost that night, but won the championship that year) and vowed to cut out the pot — or at least cut down on the amount I was using.

Many years later, sitting in a bar having a drink with friends, I watched one of them light up a non-filtered cigarette and the pleasant memories of slowly taking a deep draw and feeling the warm smoke ease its way across the throat and fill up lungs wafted back into the front of my brain. I missed smoking. I wanted a cigarette. It had been more than 15 years, but the desire was still there. "Can I have one?" I asked reaching out for the cigarettes. "But you don't smoke" my friend said. "I used to," I countered still holding my hand out.

My friend smiled, almost like a pusher would as he gave a child some drugs and gladly handed me a cigarette. I took it, flicked the old Zippo lighter top, thumbed the wheel of the lighter and admired the resulting flame. I then tapped the cigarette on the bar to harden one end and placed that end in my mouth. I finally lit the cigarette simultaneously taking a deep draw of smoke and instantly unleashing a sudden body-shaking cough spasm that must of shook the entire bar. My body totally rejected this stupid move by me and was spitting out smoke. I haven't smoked cigarettes since.

Back in the 60s as we drove out of Effingham, I was still really enjoying smoking and while never liking the smell of stale cigarette smoke in a car, it didn't matter when traveling in a convertible. I leaned back, enjoying the fresh spring air as the convertible moved smoothly past corn fields of Southern Illinois. It was one of those memorable moments that would be re-lived many times as fresh air wafted towards the corridors of my memory. The wedding was great, the love was passionate, the hugs were real, the air was fresh, I had no deadlines and life was good. This was the 60s.

CHAPTER THIRTEEN

THE REVIVAL, A RENEWAL OF FAITH

"When you get where you're going,
don't forget turn back around and help the next one in line
and always stay humble and kind.

•••••••

"Humble and Kind" by Lori McKenna, sung by Tim McGraw

We were somewhere in southern Illinois on the way back to Murray, Kentucky when I veered off the main road. John was catching up on some long-needed sleep from partying too long and too much and didn't really pay attention. He trusted me with his life (not always a good judgment decision) and after a momentary glance out the window to confirm that we were now off the main road, he returned to a great dream about one of the young ladies he had met over the wedding weekend.

I had been drawn off road by a small road sign that said simply: "Revival." I made a decision to turn right in search of an old tent-style Revival, not for religious purposes, but more for the observation of the intricate relationships and interesting people that gather at a Revival. "There is passion at the end of this road," I said, abruptly waking John from an entertaining dream. But when we reached the end of the road where the Revival was supposed to have taken place, the tent was gone and the field was empty. We had missed this one.

We had both been to a Revival before, actually two. One on the campus of Murray State University another in nearby Mayfield, Kentucky in a farm field under a tent. Both of them included a fire-breathing, God-fearing preacher with enormous hands that healed the righteous believers in the audience, some of which were healed without ever coming forth to the stage or even being touched.

After seeing the Revival under the tent in Mayfield, I read up about faith healers in psychology books and found that there was a segment of scientists that agreed that people could be healed by forces other than medicine and operations. These scientists, including some doctors, believed that it was faith based on a person's complete belief in "their" God (whoever or whatever that God was) and the healing power of God which was sometimes stronger than modern medicines.

I always knew that the mind is a powerful force, but was now beginning to accept the fact that it had powers that went beyond what most people understood and that maybe there was some truth to the faith in this power. How else could the scientists and doctors explain the numerous cases of healing that went beyond medicine and science? How else could they explain the case of the young dancer who went off to war and returned with the lower part of his leg blown off, but refusing to give up, willed the regeneration and growth of his leg from just below the knee to what would be his ankle.

There were many cases in the books about unusual healings that could have been fodder for a sequel to the Bible. And there I was from New York, sitting in a cornfield in Kentucky, not far from Missouri and like they say in Missouri "Show me." During the Revival in Mayfield, I heard some great gospel singing which was entertainment enough. One of the singers reminded me of Ray Charles and I could have listened to him all night. But I also was entertained by the magic of Reverend Stillwater (name has been changed to protect the guilty). He was a local hero that had healed many of the area's sick people over the years. I watched as a young boy threw away his crutches and walked, supposedly for the first time in years. I watched as an old man allegedly regained his sight after years in the dark. I was still skeptical. I could not find anyone who knew these people and their alleged inflictions?

And there were other lesser miracles such as a cure for the hiccups, sniffles and a rash that was promised would disappear in two or three days. I also noticed that the good Reverend Stillwater did not touch the young girl with the rash on her arms, but that was probably because while he could heal others, he might not have been able to heal himself and he didn't want to take a chance of getting the rash or transferring it to others that he intended to touch and heal. Imagine going home and saying, "I can hear again, but now I have this awful rash all over my ears."

A few weeks after I had been to the Revival in Mayfield, Agnes, our cleaning lady that cleaned rooms for college students, came in one day very excited. Jerry and I were, at that time, living in a one-room apartment in a two-story garden building with ten apartments. Our good friends Ray and Ebbie along with Pete the Bug lived there as well. Most of the residents used Agnes, a little forty-year-old black lady, to clean our one-room apartments once a week. She did a little tidying up, but her main task was to clean the bathrooms, something guys never did, and to this day, probably never will do. The rationale for not cleaning the bathroom may stem from the fact that the bathroom is where we get clean and therefore it is hard to clean it and get clean yourself at the same time.

Hundreds of thousands, maybe millions, of women that are now reading this book are saying to themselves, and in some cases out loud to their friends, "This guy is ridiculous. He's just making excuses for being a slob."

Meanwhile, Agnes had a very large, noticeable goiter on the side of her neck. She had been to a number of doctors, but no one could figure out how to safely remove or diminish this goiter sitting on her neck just above her shoulder. It just appeared one day and, over time, grew to a fairly large grapefruit size goiter; and just sat there. There was no pain, just a large ugly goiter. Agnes wanted it gone. I had known Agnes for about seven months at that time and she had always had this goiter. It got to the point that I had forgotten about it because it was always there and I had stopped noticing it. But now she was excited and wanted us to know that by next week the goiter would be gone.

Jerry asked her how. Was she finally going to get that operation that she both feared and could not afford? "No" she told us. She was so excited that she almost didn't get it out as she stuttered: "The Reverend. The Reverend is coming. The Reverend Stillwater is coming. The. . . the. . . the. . . the Reverend Stillwater will lay his hands on me." She continued in an almost feverish pitch with her voice rising out of the Revival Tent that wasn't there as she declared for all across the campus to hear, "I will be healed. I will be healed."

She calmed down enough to explain that The Reverend Stillwater and his traveling Revival group was making a one-night appearance on campus at the Murray State University Auditorium and that she was one of the lucky local people that have been given tickets to attend in order to get healed. Jerry asked if she was sure that she would get called and healed. She took out a crumbled letter which indicated that she was one of the chosen few that Reverend Stillwater had heard about and he was going to use her, among a few others to "demonstrate the power and strength of God, when God, through the chosen hands of The Good Reverend Stillwater, would heal the evil that has invaded the sick and weak people of Murray, Kentucky."

As far as I was concerned there were a number of sick people in Murray, but despite the fact that Agnes had this large goiter on her neck, she was not one of them. She was a delightful lady that worked hard and was earning a decent living. But she did work very hard and she had a lot of mouths to feed at home with five children and no husband to help. Since Agnes was going to be among the featured participants, Jerry and I decided to attend the on-campus one-night stand of The Good Reverend Stillwater.

The auditorium was packed with a healthy mix of students, faculty and local residents that had come out, mostly because they believed in faith healers and the Reverend Stillwater was a regional hero. This was an audience much like that which we observed under the tent in Mayfield. This was a Revival audience and they were not to be denied their instincts and beliefs. They came ready with bibles in hand and children beside them so they could see and learn their faith, which is what this was really all about. A variety of religions were represented in that audience that evening. They had a lot of differences in their beliefs, but had one thing in common. They were all Christians and all believed, or professed belief that God could heal people on earth through the hands of someone like the Reverend Stillwater.

Several students spoke before the ceremonies began. They were mostly members of the United Campus Ministry, a group that I knew well. Jerry was bored and wanted to leave. I reminded him of his promise to Agnes. We would be here for her and pray for her to help her succeed in ridding herself of that ugly goiter.

Music began to play and singers came forth from the back of the auditorium, with a group of three or four coming down each of the four isles leading to the stage. They raised their arms and shouted out hosannas and hallelujahs as the audience began to chime in with their own versions of hosannas and hallelujahs.

Not everyone was singing. Jerry and I were not singing and there were many others that sat silent. But they were praying. Many throughout the audience had their heads hung down with eyes and lips shut tight in deep prayer. Still others had their heads turned up to the sky (actually the ceiling of the auditorium) with eyes bulging wide, jaw hung loose and silent as they hoped their prayers would rise from their outstretched hands up towards God. Others were not so silent filling the auditorium with an almost chaotic range of sound.

I really liked the entire scene as it depicted religion as a personal thing with everyone having the God-given right to express themselves and pray in their very own way. Each person in that audience firmly believed that their prayers had a shot at being answered. This was their collective faith, their honest belief. I even believed them. I saw it in their eyes, heard it in their voices and felt it in their earnest squeezing of their whole bodies whether they silently prayed or shouted out their thoughts, wishes, prayers and hosannas. The energy level was enormous and you could feel the heat in the air despite the dropping temperature that was so typical of a February night in southwest Kentucky.

It took me back to my youth in the bathroom of the apartment in which I grew up in Brooklyn. As a child I would stand on the toilet open the small window that was above the toilet and search the night sky for stars that would indicate that God was out there listening to prayers. Mine were mostly a rambling one directional dialogue. But I believed that God was listening.

The singing went on in the Murray State auditorium while the chorus came down the aisle and mounted the stage. It continued as others came out from behind the curtains to join them on stage. Suddenly there was an entire chorus of young people in purple and white robes across the stage being led by another man in purple and white with his back to us. They sang one gospel song after another and I was in all my glory. This was entertaining. Jerry, however, was asleep in the seat next to me. I nudged him because we were in the fifth row from the front and too many people could see him sleeping. The good news was that no one could have heard him snoring over the sensational sounds of the chorus.

I didn't know the gospel songs they were singing, but a lot of people in the audience did. I wanted to join them in singing and almost did twice, but it was Jerry's turn to nudge me, this time to keep me quiet as I was embarrassing him. That normally would not have stopped me, but we were in a public place and there were nearly a thousand people in the packed audience.

Finally, the chorus reached a crescendo, the man leading the group spun around and shouted "Do you want the Reverend Stillwater to come and help you find God?" The audience shouted back a collective "Yes." Everything from this moment on would be shouted out at the highest possible decibel level. The chorus leader did a full 360-degree spin around and shouted as loud as he could, "Do you want to see the Reverend Stillwater help the sick find God's help?" And the answer shouted back was "Yes." I think I even heard someone yell "Hell Yes." That would not have been unusual for this crowd and they wouldn't see or hear the incongruity of putting hell into this equation.

After another half dozen shouted questions, The Good Reverend Stillwater came down from the sky (he was actually on a swing that is used in theatrical productions and hoisted out of sight when not in use). He came out to center stage dressed in a white suit that reminded me of the Good Humor ice cream man without the hat. He also could have been Mr. Roarke from Fantasy Island. Jerry whispered "De Revrind, De Revrind."

He walked out to center stage in front of the podium that had been set for him. He put his hands together in prayer and looked up at the ceiling. Random shouts could be heard throughout the auditorium, but most people were silent and in awe of his presence before them. This was a television star. He had lead Revivals across Missouri, Arkansas, Tennessee and Kentucky. He now graced the stage where those in attendance could later walk upon. He was six-foot-four-inches tall and with his weight at only about 180 pounds he looked even taller.

He held his hands out palms facing the audience in silent request for silence. The audience was mostly quiet already. However, a few believers were working ahead of him and shouting for God to save them. It seemed like forever before he spoke. But as soon as he did, more people in the audience began shouting religious sounding things. No one could be sure of what they were saying. I was caught by the magnetism of this man and hung on his every word. Only Jerry poking my ribs brought me back to reality, or what was perceived to be reality. Jerry poked me again, this time because he had spotted Agnes, two rows ahead on the side. All of her children were sitting there with her, all dressed for Sunday church.

The chorus brought me back. And then the parade of sick people began. As usual, the first to take stage was a young boy in crutches. After hands had been laid on him by Reverend Stillwater, he walked off the stage without the crutches. He left by going behind the curtains so we never saw him again. He reminded me of the boy on the crutches that I saw in Mayfield. Most of the people that came to the stage initially went back stage and were not seen again. Some of them returned to their seats after they were cured or basically had the cure set in motion. Some, the audience was informed, wouldn't be fully cured of their ailment for a day or two. They were told to go home and do nothing other than pray to God and God would hear their prayers and cure them. My skepticism was kept alive by the staging of this procession.

More ailing people were called to the stage. Jerry whispered, "When is Agnes going? If she doesn't go up and get healed, YOU will need to get healed, as I will do some real damage to you for bringing me here."

I simply offered "Just wait and be patient."

But I too was becoming impatient and wondering if this was just another show and nothing more. We didn't have to wait much longer, however. While we were discussing the probability that this was really happening and we were there as witnesses, but not sure of what we were really witnessing, a man brought Agnes up on stage. Jerry stopped talking and we both concentrated on what was about to happen to our cleaning lady.

Agnes had a smile on her face like we had never seen before. She was always a happy and optimistic person, but today, she seemed especially radiant. As she approached the Reverend Stillwater she began to shake nervously. He took both her hands and began to talk with her softly. I couldn't fully hear what he was saying at first, but then, as he continued to hold her hands, he half turned to the audience and began to tell all about Agnes and her goiter. He asked the audience to begin to pray for her goiter to be gone.

He then turned to Agnes and shouted at her as she kneeled in front of him and the entire assembly, "Goiter be gone, goiter be gone." And the audience performing as his chorus said, "Goiter be gone, goiter be gone, goiter be gone." And the Reverend Stillwater said, "Agnes, do you believe in Jesus?" She shook her head yes.

He raised his voice, "Agnes, do you believe that Jesus will hear your prayers tonight?" She continued to shake her head in the affirmative.

He shouted louder, "Agnes, do you believe that Jesus will heal you tonight?"

She began to cry. (Anyone would have cried with this man standing over her and shouting at her.) I could see the tears coming down her cheeks as she whispered to the Reverend Stillwater "Yes, yes."

Then, as he already had done several times this evening, the Good Reverend Stillwater turned to the audience and began to ask for help in getting Jesus to heal this woman.

"Ladies and gentlemen, do you believe that Jesus can heal this woman?"

He waited for the audience affirmation and continued, getting louder with each question.

"Do you believe that Jesus should heal this woman?" Waiting for the "Yes Lord" from the audience.

"Do you believe that Agnes is a good woman and should be healed?" was his next plea. All the while as he shouted questions to the audience, he held Agnes two hands raising them up slightly higher each time.

As he got the audience into a near fever pitch, he turned his attention back to Agnes and asked her "Do you believe?" She shook her head yes.

"Do you believe in Jesus?" Another yes.

"Do you believe that Jesus will heal you here tonight?" Another yes.

"Let me hear you say it?" he asked.

"I believe" she said softly.

"Louder" he yelled at her.

"I believe," she said louder.

"Louder, tell the world, tell Jesus," he yelled.

"I believe in Jesus," she cried.

"Again," he shouted at her.

"I believe in Jesus, oh help me Jesus," she screamed.

At the same time, a variety of people in the audience began to scream and cry and ask Jesus to help her. Cries came from all around. Jerry and I were in the middle of a faith healing and the faith of the people all around us was amazingly strong. There was electricity in the air. I could feel it as it raised the hair on my skin. I could hear it in the singing and, I swear, I could smell it.

Suddenly, the Good Reverend Stillwater put his big hands on Agnes' neck, right on top of the goiter. There was silence for a very brief moment. Then he asked everyone to help.

"Help me ask Jesus to heal Agnes. Help me ask Jesus to heal this good God-fearing woman." This was followed by audience cries and prayers again.

"Oh Jesus, help this good woman," came from right behind our seats.

The audience frenzy was contagious. Shouts and cries came from all around. I too wanted to shout out for Jesus to help her. I was now sweating in this cold auditorium with the fever pitch that had risen throughout the audience. The fact that I knew Agnes must have been a part of what was now running through my body and electrifying my skin. I wondered if it was God's presence that was heating up the room with me included. I looked over at Jerry and he was totally fixated on the stage with pointed eyes waiting for an answer to the unasked question.

I turned my attention back to the Reverend and Agnes just in time to hear the Reverend scream at the top of his lungs "Thank you Jesus, thank you Jesus." And then he held up his hand to the quiet the audience. He waved his hand for silence again and slowly, the audience quieted down. He waited while there were a few more calls for Jesus from the rear of the auditorium.

And then he quietly began to chant "Thank you Jesus, thank you Jesus" getting louder all the time, "Thank you Jesus, thank you Jesus." All the while holding one hand on top of Agnes's goiter on her neck.

He continued getting louder until he was screaming "Thank you Jesus" with a chorus of "Thank you Jesus" coming from the audience.

Suddenly, he waived again for silence and slowly helped Agnes stand up. She was sobbing "Thank Jesus" over and over again. I could see that her face was wet with sweat and tears and she was trembling. The Reverend Stillwater held her in his arms to prevent her from falling. He whispered something in her ear and then turned her to the audience for all to see.

Chills still run down my body forming goosebumps on my arms as I remember that stunning moment. For there stood Agnes, sans goiter, for all the world to see.

A wave of hallelujahs erupted throughout the auditorium. People jumped out of their seats. Agnes's children ran to the stage to be with her. Jerry and I sat there in silence, not knowing what to think or do. We avoided looking at each other at first.

Jerry said, "I guess we can go now. She's done."

I countered, "So am I."

The following Tuesday, Agnes showed up with the biggest smile we had ever seen on her face. She knew we were there at the auditorium and proudly showed us her neck. You could clearly see where the goiter had been, but it was no longer there. All you could see was some shriveled up loose skin that had once held a mysterious goiter.

CHAPTER FOURTEEN

LOOKING FOR GOD IN ALL THE WRONG PLACES

"Faith is a knowledge within the heart, beyond the reach of proof."
•••••••
Khalil Gibran

Following that experience watching Agnes get healed I once again felt the need for religion. I knew that the healing really was not a miracle, but an act of "faith" which presumes that the person attempting to be healed believes that they are indeed, going to be healed. There are many recorded cases and examples of people being cured during a "faith healing," not necessarily by a specific religion, but by simple faith and belief that they will be healed. Remember the story I previously mentioned about the Korean War veteran who lost part of his leg from below the knee during the war. He was a dancer before the war and he told doctors that he would dance again and believed that his leg would grow back. It did, according to the report I read.

So, while I did not necessarily believe that Jesus or God or any other supreme being had a direct part in Agnes getting healed, I was certain that her belief was so strong that it created an internal healing mechanism that can't be explained by doctors. This faith in being healed is as real as the little pills of medicine for which the pharmaceutical companies charge hundreds of dollars. And, as I witnessed, this faith is sometimes stronger than those pills.

Nevertheless, this experience renewed my belief in a God. I was certain that the God that was force-fed to us as children, was not necessarily the ultimate appearance of the real God. Most, if not all religions, draw a picture of God as the one and only God; the soul and sole possession of that religion. He is often depicted as a larger-than-life head with long curly hair and a face that never smiles. Why, I wondered, did none of the pictures of God ever show him smiling?

I was sure that God was not the single possession of any one religion, but rather a supreme being that each religion painted to fit their own human creation. In this way, each religion could create a list of "dos" and "don'ts" that their God would condone and then look down from his lofty heights and smile at them. It justified the existence of each particular religion and it didn't matter if one God was slightly different from another religion's God.

I was very young when I realized that I believed in a higher authority, a supreme being called God. I don't recall why, but I had taken in all the conversations about there being a God, read about the different religious perspectives from Christianity and Judaism to Buddhism, Islam and Hinduism, and, in my mind, declared that everyone was right. There is a God and the different religious factions call him or her by different names, but, in my mind, "God" was one and the same no matter who called God what name they chose.

I was also sure that God did not care as long as you believed in him (or her) and lived a good life. Also, I did not think that being a good person had anything to do with going to church on Sunday. Over the years I've met too many ardent church goers that were not nice people.

I always felt that it was ironic that most wars were started and fought in the name of religion, almost as if God had played a joke on all of us. Over and over again in the history of the world we see wars where one religious faction started to quell the voice of a conflicting religion. Were these religions really conflicting? Were Christians so different from Jews? Were Muslims so different from Buddhists? Didn't each of the deities in these religions teach the golden rule? And wasn't tolerance of others an integral tenet of all of the religions?

The answer to all these questions is obvious. Yes, the teachings of the elders in each of the world's religions were basically the same. However, some of the rules—man-made rules—that followers are asked to obey are different and this creates an underlying separation of church and church leaving the frail humans to fight it out for their chosen religion; declaring with righteous indignation and demanding respect for their Bible, their Quran, their Bhagavad Gita, their Talmud and their Tripitakas, all of which are the word of God—translated by man.

Either God is playing a cosmic joke on us, or we just haven't seen the light as we continue to fight with each other in the name of religion; in the name of God. My God, with a giant ear in the nighttime sky, would hear nothing of that nonsense. He would just listen to everyone and sometimes help those that helped themselves. And sometimes not.

So, I began praying to God. In English. I called it talking to God rather than praying to God because most of the time I did not ask for anything. I just talked things through with God because I knew God had a sympathetic ear. As a matter of fact, I imagined this gigantic ear out in space just funneling all the chatter into a large container for translation and filing at a later time.

I would look up at the stars and know that God was out there listening to any and all that wished to talk with him. I would confess my sins (I could have been a good Catholic) and ask for forgiveness. I would talk about my choices, discuss the pros and cons of things that were happening or about to happen in my life and I would ask for guidance. Guidance was the only thing I usually asked of God. I needed a sign that I was making the right decisions in my life. And more often than not, a sign soon came which helped steer me in a positive direction.

I strongly believed that if I were a good person and helped others that were not as fortunate as I, then I would be favored by God. I tried to live by the Golden Rule which states: *Do unto others as you would have them do unto you.*

And while I flirted with religion from a young age, I can't say that I was ever a religious person. I studied the Bible in Hebrew school, learned my *"Haftorah"* lessons and was *bar mitzvah* at age thirteen. Joined Young Judea at age fourteen but only because of interest in meeting girls. Most of the others in the group I joined were sixteen or seventeen and looking for answers through their religion. I was a horny kid, when on a trip we took to a Young Judea conference in Atlantic City, I fell in love with an older girl in the group. We hid away on a hayride late at night and I returned home with poison ivy all over my body. Did God punish me for not taking the religious retreat seriously?

So, my temple, my church, was my small apartment bathroom I shared with my mother, father, sister and brother. The bathroom was small and narrow. On one side there was the sink and combined bathtub and shower. The other side was a wall with racks for towels. At the far end there was a toilet and above the toilet a small window. I always wondered why the bathroom window was so much smaller than the windows in the kitchen and bedroom. It would have made so much more sense to have this bathroom window the largest in the apartment since it was often the escape hatch for odors that were created from the bowels of overstuffed adults who downed strange smelling foods often created from recipes dredged up from Eastern Europe.

I escaped to the bathroom when I was upset and often cried there in solitude away from my family. I went there especially after getting a strong reprimand from my mother which included being hit by the yardstick that she wielded for extra punctuation. After crying for several minutes while sitting on the toilet (the only seat in the bathroom), I heard a whispering sound coming from the slightly open window behind me. I stood on the closed toilet seat and opened the window as wide as I could. The whispering sound abated. It must have been the wind, I thought—or was it something else?

Since I was there, I looked out at the night sky which was lighted by the moon and a symphony of white clouds dancing against a black backdrop. I watched the clouds slowly moving along and marveled at their almost-human appearances. One of the clouds even looked like a large head. I began talking to the night sky as if the clouds were the embodiment of God, just as we have all seen in paintings from the Renaissance period.

As I talked with God that night, the clouds slowed their travels as if to hear what I had to say. It was then that I first became sure that I understood the meaning of God and that God had heard and understood my feelings. After all, no one else did. I was ten years old at that time. I had been taught that God is omnipotent and that he would understand and hear all. I did not make any requests of God that night other than to be watched over. And to this day, I know that God heard and has watched over me.

Over the years I have been punished and rewarded. I have been treated fairly for what I have done and how I have lived. And the God that I believe in, participates in all religions and protects those that respect him no matter what book they read, or what building they pray or don't pray in. I have been fortunate and blessed throughout my life with rich experiences and much love from friends and family. I thank God for all of that.

These thoughts came rushing back to me as I examined Agnes and her neck. She believed in God and was a good person. Her good deeds were rewarded. The goiter was gone. I wouldn't ever go against those odds.

Life growing up in Brooklyn was not perfect. It had its moments. many of which were great moments building the sweet memories that still release endorphins when they are relived in my mind. Some were connected to religion, but with no religious significance, unless you consider dating a religious experience.

I clearly remember my first dance. I was twelve years old and terrified about going to the dance at the local temple. My best friend Michael was going to a dance at the synagogue with a bunch of his friends. They were all a year or two older, but I was taller than most of them so I looked older. Before going to this dance, we had to learn to dance. My mom asked a fifteen-year-old girl named Linda, who lived on the 2nd floor in our building, to teach us to dance. Linda was tall with dark, shoulder length hair cut in bangs. She was very fair and pretty with bright blue eyes. Three of us got to learn to dance that day. I watched every movement. And I embraced every moment, especially when I got to embrace her during the slow dances.

All too fast Saturday had come. I was not mentally prepared. We all met at the synagogue where the dance was being held. This being a place of worship was in itself weird. But this night at the synagogue would be different from all other nights. I followed the group and watched their every move hoping to find some pretty, dark eyed, dark haired girl to dance with. I pictured Linda and wanted to dance with her even though she was three years older than me. I had felt so comfortable in her arms.

Most of the guys got out on the dance floor pretty quickly. The music was fast and most of the kids were doing the lindy, a modern jitterbug or something similar. The age of the participants was limited to those from thirteen to seventeen. I was probably the only twelve-year-old. I danced one fast dance with a cute girl with long, dark, very curly hair. The DJ played mostly fast dances and the dance floor was packed.

Then came the time to slow things down. *"In the Still of the Night"* began to play and most of the kids on the dance floor stayed with their partners and began to slow dance together. I was standing on the sideline and remember looking away shyly. I could not bring myself to ask anyone to slow dance. There were several girls I had looked at, but none of them looked back at me so that was not a good sign. Instead I just chose to wait it out. But I never had a chance. There was Linda, my fifteen-year-old dance teacher from my building, taking my hand and leading me out on the dance floor. And I was slow dancing to *"In the Still of the Night"* with Linda, the tallest and most beautiful girl at the dance.

I was in heaven. I was having one of my most cherished moments. And, it was in a synagogue at a dance run by a religious organization. To me, at that time, it was a religious experience. God was good. I beamed. I was smiling so wide because I was dancing with the girl that most of the guys would have given their right leg to dance with (which would have made it difficult to dance).

When the music stopped, she smiled and kissed me on the cheek and whispered, "You must have had a good teacher, you dance so well." I smiled back. "Thanks. You made my night perfect." Later that night, I went to the bathroom, opened the window and thanked God for having Linda dance with me.

Many years, and what seemed like several lifetimes later, I met another Linda, a fair skinned, blue-eyed, blond in a ponytail. It was dancing at Club Getaway in Connecticut that brought us together. And I still thank God for that meeting which changed my life forever, resulting in the love of my life.

CHAPTER FIFTEEN

RELIGIOUS EXPERIENCES HERE AND ABROAD

"God made Truth with many doors
to welcome every believer who knocks on them."

•••••••

Khalil Gibran

Through the years, there were many moments that now line the corridors of my mind with vivid memories, especially mystical religious experiences I had while traveling. Here are few that stand out after fifty years and more than a hundred countries.

The Mystical Man of Mumbai

On my first trip to India, I met with the marketing director of the famous Taj Mahal Hotel. He was of the Sikh religion and wore a turban. Immediately upon meeting him I felt something special. There was a magnetism from the first handshake in which he held my hand firmly for an extra long time as he smiled and peered straight into my eyes. It was almost hypnotic.

We sat and talked about our respective travels. He wanted to know about my recent trip to Sri Lanka. As close as it was to India, he had never been there. He had traveled all over Europe and Canada, but had only been to New York as a stopover on a business trip to Los Angeles. He had a lot of questions about New York.

As we talked, it felt like I knew him forever. There was something very comfortable about him, his soft, deep voice, his piercing eyes, his worldly demeanor. He wore a turban and this identified him for everyone. We talked about how he felt when people would look at him and know something about him before they even met. He told me that it used to bother him. It was racial profiling. But he rose above it by communicating with God. He told me that he knew that I too communicated with God and wanted to know how I felt about my relationship with God.

I never asked him how he knew that about me. He just seemed to understand things unsaid and see things not present. He was truly charismatic and maybe a little bit of a mystery. He was a very special person. So when he asked if I would like to travel across India with him, I said yes. I called my office and told them that my return to New York would be delayed a few days.

We were in Delhi at the Taj Mahal Hotel in the northeast region of India just south of the Himalaya Mountains. The actual Taj Mahal was in Agra, India, just south of Delhi. It would be on our way as we were heading for Bombay on the southwest coast of India. Bombay was to later adopt its more traditional Indian name of Mumbai in the mid-90s.

We left Delhi for Agra which was a short ride and even shorter visit at the ancient Taj Mahal. Having seen the palace so many times on TV and in movies I immediately recognized it as if it were a familiar place that I had been before. The dramatic entrance that I expected was lost in the familiarity.

We traveled on to Kanpur where we could divert to make a stop for a view of the Ganges River, the lifeline of the Indian people, a polluted river that was known for spawning dysentery and other gastronomic diseases. I was too skittish to bath in the Ganges, but I watched the locals washing their clothing, their produce and their bodies. They lived with the river and it both protected them and infected them. They were used to it and treated it as both friend and foe.

We overnighted near Kahna National Park and the next day I was on safari, not in Africa, but in India with Elephants, tigers and many interesting animals that I had never seen before or after. At night it was just us, the clear sky full of stars and an eerie silence that left us with our thoughts. I learned to meditate in the dark nights in India and felt closer to God. My Sikh friend said to me: "I can tell that God sees and hears you like no other. That is a good thing. Never disappoint him." This both pleased and frightened me. Who was this man who seemed to know everything?

After that exhilarating experience we were off to Bombay, the coastal city of millions of Hindi speaking Indians. This was, at that time, the beginning of the growth of Bollywood, the Indian film industry. Bombay was, like Delhi, one of India's regional capital cities. It was densely populated and very poor. Bombay is on the water so the port business was thriving.

We then took a boat trip from Goa to Divar Island where we joined a retreat of people from Australia, Singapore and India who had gathered to get in touch with their inner self. I was in touch with my inner self, but it never hurt to remind myself who I was and remember my vow to God to be good to other people.

It was great to be a part of this retreat. I needed to get back to thinking and my personal writing. Thoughts and feelings were all pushed down by work. Work was getting in the way of life. It took a business trip to India to remind me that there was more to life than work. I returned from India, once again with renewed vigor and determination to write poetry again. And I did for a short while.

SMELL, HEAR AND TOUCH IN BIG SUR

The retreat on Divar Island took me back to my retreat at Esalen in Big Sur, California where I first learned to get in touch with my senses. It was 1967 and several of us from Murray State took a trip to Big Sur. I remember being in a large room with no windows. There had to be about thirty people in the room, most in their 20s or 30s, but a few in their 50s. We all sat on yoga mats that were spread out across the floor, giving us plenty of room between one another.

Soft music was playing and a soft, deep male voice came over the speaker system giving us hypnotic suggestions to relax. We closed our eyes as the lights in the room began to dim. We were told that the room would become totally dark. The absence of any light in a room without windows becomes completely dark. You cannot see your hand in front of your face.

The voice began to get softer as we were told to concentrate on sounds. At first there was the light tingling of bells which was a pretty sound. As the bells got louder, they began to annoy us. When they became too loud people began to complain. Then there was silence. We relaxed again. Now there was a distant train coming which was actually a soothing sound. But again, as the train got nearer and louder, the sound became irritating and then overwhelming when it seemed to be on top of us. This again was followed by silence. Several other sounds were played, including music and each time it was first received with relaxed pleasant feelings. But, each time as the soothing sounds became too loud, these same sounds irritated the senses.

Next came the smells. The first odor to be piped into the room was the smell of flowers. It too was relaxing and pleasant. It reminded me of beautiful roses. But as the room filled with the smell of more and more flowers, I felt that I would be overcome with the horrible odor of some old lady wearing too much perfume. Some people began to gag. I just buried my head to avoid the smell.

Cold air suddenly filled the room and the smell of the flowers were gone. This, however was followed by the sweet smell of something that I could not distinguish. I heard mumblings among the others who were also trying to fig-ure out what this nice, sweet odor was. As it got stronger, we could all tell that it was oil and once again we were becoming repulsed by the smell of too much oil in the room. More cold air and the oil smell was gone. Finally, another odor began to drift into the room. I thought it was very much like country air, but as it got stronger, I could tell it was either cow dung or fertilizer. Either way, it was becoming very unpleasant and not relaxing as it had been at first.

We were then treated to a combination of light sounds and smells sim-ilar to what we had just experienced, but in each case the sounds and odors were kept to a minimum and we did relax to the pleasant, almost musical sounds of bells and trains with the sweet smell of flowers. And we meditated and relaxed with our own silent thoughts and feelings.

The odors disappeared and the sounds changed to light music. The voice told us to stand up. We were told to put out our arms and hands and very slowly and carefully move forward until we touched someone else. It remained totally dark. Our eyes could not adjust to the absence of light. There was nothing to see. We were instructed that someone other than the person we were touching may end up touching us and that was okay.

We were then told to reach up and touch the other person's face, feel around to see with our hands whether they were a man or a woman and when we thought we knew we were to say "man" or "woman" and find out if we were right or wrong. They, in turn, were to answer "yes" or "no" with only one word spoken by each of us.

Next, we were asked to turn around in our places and walk a couple of paces until we found another person. This time we were instructed to couple with the new person we found and to begin exploring that person beginning with their face. We were told that we could touch any part of the body as we explored. We did what we were told. I thought it would become a sexual experience, but it did not. I was exploring a young woman, touching her breasts in the dark and I was not aroused. I was fascinated by the experience. I was blind and yet I could picture this woman and describe her better than if I had just seen her in the daylight. Seeing through my hands, hearing and smelling through my ears and nose without seeing, changed my perception of what I was looking at.

After we finished touching and exploring several people and were, in turn, touched by others, we were told to lay down and relax in the quiet, dark room. There were no sounds or odors being piped in. Only the breathing and occasional muffled cough. It was totally quiet. I could hear my own heart beat. I could smell myself. I felt truly in touch with myself.

That afternoon we went outside for some nature embracing exercises and experiences. We got close to the others in our group without knowing who they were or where they came from. There were no name tags, and no introductions. As we got closer to each other, we got closer to ourselves.

The only problem is that these feelings did not last. When I returned to school it was back to classes and studying. When I returned to work after my experience in India it was back to work and making money. I kept trying to remember the feeling and the look I received from my Sikh friend from the Taj Mahal Hotel. To this day, it remains one of the permanent memories etched in my mind's eye. I can recall these memories as vivid pictures and feelings, enjoying the relaxed experience as it triggers endorphins and happiness, even if only for a moment. It's one of those moments in time that make a difference.

Life is made up of moments. Some good, some not so good. Cherish the moments.

ANCIENT RITUALS IN NEW ZEALAND

A few years later I found myself on my way to Auckland, New Zealand for a convention where I would have to call upon my previous Sikh meditation to help me rise above a moment of crisis. I took a side trip to Maori country. The Maori people are the original settlers of New Zealand, similar to our American Indian population. They are a proud Polynesian people that continued to celebrate their ancient culture.

The small hotel I stopped at (more like a motel) had a full-service spa which I needed to help me unwind from the long twenty-seven-hour trip I had just completed coming across the world from New York. New Zealand sits down under Australia which is already down under.

I asked the young lady at the front desk what was the best therapy to ease the pain of traveling and rejuvenate me. She said an oil bath followed by a four-hand massage was the ideal treatment. I had never had either so I took her advice. The experience was memorable. I almost died and had a stunning rebirth. I will never forget either.

I first had to completely undress, take a shower, so I would not contaminate the oil and then put on a pair of tight rubber underwear to protect my most important parts. I then entered a small wooden frame structure that looked the size of a large outhouse, complete with a hole in the ground in the center of the room. A large and very, very strong Maori lifted me up by my armpits and slowly lowered me into the small round hole in the ground which was filled with a warm, almost hot, dark oil. There was a seat inside the hole which I was instructed to sit on. I did. Only my neck and head sat above the oil.

The warmth of the oil was very soothing. I relaxed immediately and got lost in wonderful thoughts, deep thoughts, expressive thoughts; thoughts that I would have loved to record and remember. But I either fell asleep or passed out. The next thing I knew I was being lifted out by the same very, very strong Maori that had put me in the oil. He told me not to try and stand and put me down on a large towel in which he rolled me back and forth to dry me. He then carried me outside and across the lawn to the main hall where he lay me down in a small room with a large circular bed that took up most of the space in the room. He handed me a thick colored beverage and instructed me to drink it slowly.

I took a drink and put the glass down. I lie there very relaxed at first. Then I tried to sit up, but couldn't. I became concerned; actually nervous. I took another small drink and tried again to sit up. I was unable to get up. I began to get very nervous. One of the young ladies I remembered from the front desk came in to see how I was doing, I said, "Not too well. I can't get up. This can't be right, is it?"

"Well no," she admitted. "You must have stayed in the oil too long," she added. "But we have a doctor coming to check you out." I am sure that was said to make me feel better, but it didn't. I only became more nervous.

Another lady in a long white coat came in and checked my blood pressure. "You are returning to us," she assured me. "Drink up," she said and handed me the thick beverage I had been sipping. I drank it all, laid back down and closed my eyes and began meditating. During my meditation I realized that I needed that hot oil. I needed that scare to bring me once again back to my true self. I kept getting lost in work with no purpose in life other than making money and once again I promised God that I would try harder not to do that anymore.

I'm not sure, but I think just a short time later, there were two young ladies sitting beside me. "How do you feel," they both asked almost simultaneously. I sat up, this time with no effort or distress. I started to touch my arms, legs, face, all of which had been numb before, and was thrilled to feel myself. "That's our job," one of the girls giggled. "We will bring you back to life," the other girl said, also with a giggle. It was then that I realized I was laying there completely naked.

They asked me to roll over on my stomach and almost immediately they began to massage me—lightly at first, then more deeply as they progressed. Each one of them sat on either side of me, kneeling on this huge round bed that sat on the floor. Their four hands moved in simultaneous rhythm on my shoulders, across my back, down my legs. They were like a machine with four hands. it was synchronized massage. I never felt anything like that before—or since. Every inch of my body was indeed coming back to life and more. It was like their hands were turning on electric impulses throughout my body. At one point they asked me to turn over but I was so into their touch I hardly heard them.

"Are you okay," one asked. I looked up and smiled. They just pushed me over onto my back and continued to do what they had done to my neck, shoulders, back and legs. This time to my chest, legs and stomach. As they neared my groin area, my penis stood up and took notice. So did they. They both giggled and without asking proceeded to give me a four hands "happy ending" to a both horrific and terrific experience. I could not stop smiling.

I fell asleep smiling and when I awoke, one of the girls was still there laying next to me to make sure I was okay. As I stirred, she quickly asked how I was. I continued to smile and told her I felt wonderful. She kissed my cheek and offered to help me shower and get dressed. I said nothing, but couldn't stop smiling and she kissed my cheek again and took my hand and led me to the shower. She washed me down, dried me off and helped me get dressed. A final kiss on the cheek and she said goodbye. I felt like I had died, been reborn and felt better than ever.

The convention I was there to attend was good too; I think.

ISRAEL, THE BIRTHPLACE OF RELIGION

I called upon these warm memories while riding an old school bus from Tel Aviv to Jerusalem one cold January morning several years later. I was on a press trip which included travel agents. There were about twenty-five of us and we boarded the old bus early in the morning for the trip over the desert mountains to Jerusalem.

As we passed the nomads in the middle of the desert I tried to imagine their life. They moved aimlessly across the vacant deserted desert encamping along the way for a day, a week, or even a month, but rarely longer. They seemed to drift in the same way that the desert sands moved with the wind. I was traveling all around the world, but I envied their freedom. I loved what I was doing, but I was not free. And it was rare that I stopped to think free thoughts.

When we crossed the mountains and approached Jerusalem, I was brought back to the live moment at hand as I began to shiver from the freezing cold. It was snowing outside. We were only a short drive from the desert, but here, just outside Jerusalem in January, it was snowing and the bus had no heat. There were no accumulations to record the snowfall, but we all watched and marveled at the spectacle of snow as the bus moved down the road towards the ancient city of Jerusalem.

I was unprepared for the snow and cold with just a light jacket. Everyone else on the bus had winter coats. Alan and Ina Rich, a couple of travel agents that I had just met, took pity on me and offered a scarf to help keep me warm. I took the scarf, began to meditate once again and warmed myself. This simple loan of a scarf also linked me to them in a bond of friendship that continued for many years.

Our main stop in Jerusalem was the Wailing Wall, an ancient section of the longer Jerusalem retaining wall that was connected to the Temple Mount; considered one of the great historic temples by both Christians and Jews. The Jewish people still pray at the Wailing Wall and it is considered an important rite of passage to kiss the wall. There was a bar mitzvah going on while we were there and we followed the mobile congregation into a nearby temple where the women sat in rows of sideways pews looking down on the congregation of men who mumbled their prayers. Every once in a while, the women would begin to shout out "lalalalalalalalalala" or something like that. I felt connected for a moment. Then I got lost in my thoughts. I was happy to be lost in my thoughts and once again promised myself and God (since I was in Jerusalem and so close to Bethlehem in proximity of the God of three prominent religions) that I would spend more time lost in thought.

I didn't. I went back to work editing the magazine, writing articles and editorials, directing reporters on what and how to cover stories about the travel industry and feeling that I was accomplishing something, but didn't yet know what it was.

And there was always another trip, another convention, another speaking engagement and, another flight above the clouds.

THAILAND, LAND OF TEMPLES AND MORE

Visiting Thailand was one of my early bucket-list stops that I knew I just had to do. With a travel industry convention being planned I took the opportunity to do some advance observations and surveillance. I booked Thai Airways because it had a great reputation for service. I was not disappointed. From the moment I got on board I was escorted to my seat in business class by a lovely flight attendant dressed in a typical airline suit. I mention her outfit because after takeoff she reappeared in traditional Thai cultural dress which made us feel we were already there. The food onboard was not airline food. It was gourmet Thai food. Passengers also had their choice of American dishes. I drank wine, ate dinner and went to sleep. Breakfast was great as well and then we washed and got refreshed for our arrival.

I passed easily through customs and immigration and then entered a welcome area where people were being greeted by tour guides, taxis and private cars. As I was staying at the Mandarin Oriental Hotel, I gravitated over to the Mandarin desk. The Mandarin Oriental Hotel chain was, at that time, and continues to be today, one of the best hotel chains in the world for accommodations and service.

There were more than 200 people who just got off that flight from New York. And while many were moving towards their respective welcome desks, I had not quite reached the Mandarin desk when a young Thai man walked toward me and quietly said: "Welcome Mr. Kahn." He took my one bag and asked. "Any other luggage?" I smiled "no," wondering how he knew who I was, as I followed him outside.

Once outside the bustling terminal we walked to a black stretched lim-ousine. The driver bowed and said, "Welcome Mr. Kahn" and opened the door. Were they all clairvoyant? I wondered. Did I have a secret sign on my forehead that the flight attendants put there while I was sleeping? I entered the limo as he explained that we were waiting for three other passengers. That further piqued my interest. How did they know I was Mr. Kahn if there were four of us they were picking up? I never found out, but it was the beginning of a very pampered trip which centered around the Mandarin and spilled into the restaurants as well as the shops that lined the streets of this very cluttered and busy city of Bangkok in Southeast Asia.

The ride was not too long and we arrived at the front of this magnifi-cent looking hotel. The bellman opened the car door and quickly greeted each of us by name. I was the second to step out and the bellman became the third person to say, "Welcome Mr. Kahn" without possibly knowing for sure who I was. He directed us into the lobby and took our luggage in sepa-rately. There was a large wooden front desk with several hotel staff standing there all smiling. But we were each met before we got to the front desk by a different well-dressed young man who, of course, greeted us individually and correctly by our names and escorted us directly to our rooms.

Once in the room he offered me a leather-bound portfolio and asked me to sign the papers at my leisure and drop them off at the front desk. My luggage was delivered immediately and my room escort offered to unpack my bag. I watched as he placed everything in the draws of a very large wooden dresser; bigger than the one I had at home. I was a little embarrassed as he only needed a small part of two draws because I did not have a lot of clothes as I always traveled light with only a single carryon bag for all the clothes I would need for the trip.

Carryon luggage was my choice over the years of business (and leisure) trips because it facilitated two things—safe transport of my personal belongings which stayed with me at all times and quick egress from the airport. Packing for a week in Southeast Asia, or anywhere in the world, is not that difficult, especially for men. Women need more shoes and cosmetics than men do and often find the need to check their oversized baggage. I understand their requirement for extra things and sympathize with them.

All that a man should need, even on a business trip, is two pair of slacks (one brown, one black), four to five dress shirts and ties, depending on the length of the trip, enough underwear and socks for each day, two pair of shoes, one packed, one to wear on the flight (the airlines don't allow people onboard barefooted), a swimsuit, a couple of polo shirts, some casual, but elegant shirts for relaxed evening dinners, and toiletries, all of which fit into a roller bag suitable for the airline overhead compartments. I wear a black sport coat and beige slacks on the flight which also goes with everything inside my bag. I'm set for every occasion that might arise.

Meanwhile, with my clothes neatly packed away, and maybe lost inside the huge cavernous dresser, my room escort then offered to make me some tea. And when all was done and I went to tip him, he politely refused to take my money and bowed out of the room. That was the very best hotel service I had ever experienced. And it was no different anywhere I went in the hotel.

Bangkok, Thailand is a destination that defies a simple description. It is laden with golden temples and lavish gardens. It is also dominated by a crowded, polluted river that serves as the nerve center of the city. Its people are what make it very special. They are smart, warm and welcoming. Not just those at the Mandarin Oriental, but all the people I encountered throughout my travels in Bangkok and across the countryside.

Of course, Bangkok at night is special on its own and all too well known around the world as the Sex Capital of Asia. There is no way to minimize this. Tourists from Europe, Australia, New Zealand and Asia purchase sex tours which include stops at nightclubs where vacationers watch sex shows or visit sex parlors where they have legal sex at costs that are probably lower than anywhere else in the world.

That would have to wait as we were scheduled to visit a number of Thailand's historic sites on our first day in this very special Southeast Asian country. And yes, before we complete this chapter, I took part in all that Thailand had to offer.

Religion is a central part of Thai culture and we could see Buddhist monks dressed in their traditional yellow drapery walking down the streets of Bangkok throughout the day. Most of these monks lived in the temples, called Wats and there were thousands of Wats across the countryside of Thailand. This is the land of the King of Siam made famous by the Broadway musical *"The King and I"* and movie of the same name. Religion is taken seriously here and you could see it and feel it in the temples that are everywhere.

We drove out of Bangkok in a private car. Once out of the city everywhere we stopped there was a temple or palace that was part of Thai history and religion. We stopped at the Grand Palace a sprawling majestic home of the former Kings of Siam with its famous Wat Phra Kaew, the Temple of the Emerald Buddha. A trip up the long steps leading up to Wat Pho, the temple of the Reclining Buddha, unveiled the largest Buddha in Thailand. This is also rumored to be the birthplace of Thai medicine including Thai massage.

We were amazed by Wat Traimit, the temple of the Golden Buddha, made of solid gold, standing more than nine feet tall and weighing more than five tons. No one is concerned about anyone attempting to steal this gold shrine which is both priceless and immoveable. Then we visited Wat Benchamobophit, the Marble Temple made completely of Italian marble with an assortment of religious marble carvings. Wat Chai Mongkol was another temple, this one housing a large bronze statue of the Reclining Buddha.

Walking up the steep steps to the temples offered many moments of reflection. Seeing Buddha in his many designs of gold, emerald, bronze and marble generated thoughts about how we honor our gods. Having the guide explain the significance of each of the temples and each respective

Buddha provided insight that resulted in inner reflection and made me feel closer to God, the God of all people, no matter what form he or she takes. It made me appreciate the Thai people for all their reverence toward Buddha. I also appreciated that fact that they appeared to be among the most tolerant people I had ever met. It made me reflect on intolerance of others and resulted in another promise I made to God to be more accepting of others.

Upon returning that evening I went with some colleagues (both men and women), who were also in Bangkok for the upcoming conference, to see one of the more popular sex shows in which pairs of men and women, men and men and women and women performed sex acts on stage. You are probably waiting for me to describe what was going on. But suffice it to say that the young man and woman began with foreplay, undressed each other and after an appropriate time in which they performed oral sex to each other, they fornicated on a platform in front of an audience of men and women tourists from around the world. There were a lot of Asians in the audience which I thought to be mostly Japanese.

Two men were next to perform and they both came on stage in only a pair of briefs in which they hid what were extraordinarily large penises. They played with each other and gave each other oral sex and finally sat facing front masturbating each other, somehow managing to come simultaneously with both verbal and bodily explosions which resulted in the audience giving them a standing ovation.

The two women were actually an anti-climax to the men who performed before them as they fondled each other and gave each other oral sex and then used extra large dildos on each other.

From there we split up and I went with Alan Fleschner, my friend and colleague from *Travel Weekly*, to one of the sex parlors. We each paid US$30 to enter. This bought us one hour with a woman of our choice. We were taken into a large theater-style room in which we stood in the center where we viewed four rows of women, at least ten across in each row, all sitting in scanty lingerie outfits facing us. Most of the women smiled, some waved, and some made gestures letting us know in advance what they would do to us. Choosing one from more than forty women was a daunting task, but I managed to make a decision on one. Alan also chose one and we walked off holding hands with our respective choices to private rooms. As we separated with our chosen girls, Alan called back to me, "Wait for me in the lounge, I may take awhile."

An important side note: There were quite a few women patrons there paying to have sex with these Thai women as well. And there were Thai men available for them if they wished. There were also some sex parlors that just catered to gays.

Inside the private room, my tiny Thai girl smiled as she immediately undressed me and neatly put my clothes on a table beside the low platform bed that sat on the floor. There was nothing else in the room. The table sat on one side of the platform bed and had only a pitcher of water and two empty glasses. The large platform bed sat in the middle of the room. The white sheets looked clean and starched. There was a dark red blanket folded neatly at the bottom of the bed and two large white encased pillows at the top of the bed.

The room was actually very bright. I had expected a more dimly lit atmosphere. The platform bed was harder than I would have liked.

Once she had me undressed, she led me to the bed and motioned for me to lie down. She proceeded to take off what little clothes she had on which was a feeble attempt to cover her forbidden parts and then hopped up on the bed like a little child would do. She then crawled over to where I was stationed on the bed in anticipation of what was about to happen. Upon reaching me, she immediately began to. . . . .

I'm sorry, I have to stop there. This book is not Fifty Shades of anything. I just wanted to show the juxtaposition of the fact that Thailand, is a very religious country, and, at the same time, the very openly legal sex capital of Southeast Asia.

It was truly a happy massage with a very happy ending. I tipped her US$20 which made her so happy that she wanted to do it all over again. But I had to meet Alan so I hugged her, got dressed and left.

The conference began the next day and it was a full day of meetings. That night I skipped a formal dinner with some advertisers because I didn't like formal dinners, didn't like kissing ass with advertisers, and I really wanted to get back to the sex parlor from the night before to have another massage from the same young lady with which I had enjoyed such a great experience.

I bid farewell to my colleagues and took a taxi to the massage parlor. I paid my US$30 to get in and went into the theater room to look for the girl I had the night before. I could not find her. Not wanting to try and duplicate the experience and be disappointed, I left without a massage while a dozen, somewhat attractive young ladies pawed me lovingly as they tried to get me to choose them. A few days later, I left Bangkok with a very special memory of their religion and sex.

And the convention was good too, I think.

The Ultimate Religious Experience

As a travel editor, I continued to travel around the world enjoying many different places, people and experiences. And while the aforementioned religious experiences brought me closer to God, one trip stands out from all others. It was a trip to Rome for another one of the American Society of Travel Agents (ASTA) World Travel Conferences.

ASTA was so important to the entire world; and bringing a conference with 10,000 delegates to Rome would provide a momentous boost to both Rome and the rest of Italy as thousands of agents would convene in Rome and then scatter before and after the conference to see Milan, Florence, Venice, Sicily and the Amalfi Coast.

Thanks to ASTA's influence, thousands of delegates were granted an audience with Pope John Paul II. We were ushered into the Vatican in a caravan of buses and walked into St. Peter's Basilica where we were directed into one of the pews that filled the big hall. Years later, I visited St. Peter's once again, but this time the pews had been put away and I marveled at the immense empty hall remembering how this vast church was filled with pews and thousands of hopeful people waiting to see and hear Pope John Paul II.

He spoke in multiple languages. His English was slow but precise. He addressed the travel industry representatives that filled St. Peter's that day and thanked all of us for helping to bring peace to the world by connecting people through travel. He then blessed the entire audience and came down from the magnificent pulpit to walk among his followers. He slowly walked down the center aisle reaching out to touch some people on their shoulder or pause to touch others on their bowed head. He stopped briefly to say a few words to some and hold their hand.

I was one of the lucky people who after being ushered into one of the hundreds of rows of pews ended up on the aisle. I was seated next to some of my travel agent friends approximately in the middle of this vast hall. We all watched, held our breath and hoped that Pope John Paul II would reach us and touch us in some way as he moved slowly down the center of St. Peter's Basilica.

It was a magical moment when he moved in the direction of my aisle. Everyone was standing. Some people were praying. I stood silent on the aisle, in awe.

Pope John Paul II was standing directly in front of me. He smiled, took my hand and said something to me. Not sure what he said, I answered "I am a travel writer." He then blessed me, let go of my hand and moved on to the next row.

I stood motionless. I am not Catholic, was clearly not following any religion with strict adherence, but I believe that day, that moment, I had a direct connection to God. Chills ran through my body, tears rolled down my cheeks. I turned to whoever was standing next to me and said "Wow" as I embraced them and embraced the moment. It remains one of the most powerful moments in my life.

I was one of the few fortunate, lucky people that day to be touched and blessed by Pope John Paul II. I knew I was truly blessed, in more ways than one, and thanked God. I really believed that my good deeds, my concern for other people and giving to others was rewarded in many ways and being touched by Pope John Paul II reaffirmed that belief.

CHAPTER SIXTEEN

TRANSITION TIME AT MURRAY STATE

I'm not the man they think I am at home
Oh no no no I'm a rocket man
Rocket man burning out his fuse up here alone

• • • • • • •

"Rocket Man" by Elton John

Murray State University, as mentioned, was where I grew up, matured and developed into the person I was to eventually become. There were good influences all around me. Murray, Kentucky was securely locked into the Bible Belt of the Southern Baptist theology. And while I did not buy into this sometimes closed minded, often hypocritical view of real life, this religious philosophy did produce an atmosphere that surrounded the good people of this small town with a generally honest reverence for "doing to others what you would want others to do to you."

Most of the people I would meet, both on and off campus were good people. Yes, there were exceptions in this college town where nearly 10,000 people including a little more than 3,000 students (there are 10,000 students there now) of diverse backgrounds comingled.

On campus, I was finding my way with my own diversity. First and foremost were my friends from back East. Steve Tucker, who convinced me to go there, was long gone. He moved on after my freshman year transferring to SIU. That's when I got closer to Jerry and Ebbie. Jerry was my roommate and part time conscience. I should have listened to him more. I would have stayed out of trouble. He was smart and focused on his goal of becoming a physical education teacher. He played football in high school in Brooklyn and in college in Connecticut until he got hurt and lost his scholarship. He transferred to Murray and was steadily on his way to his goal of becoming a teacher and coach. He was a like a rock, both in his build and his clear thinking.

He eventually became that award-winning football coach—at John Adams High School in Queens, NY—that he dreamed of when we were in college.

Ebbie (Henry Paul Woolley) was my poet laureate. We shared our words, our thoughts and our feelings. He was brilliant in the way a genius philosopher shines. His insightful musings captured the essence of everyday life painting a picture that always evoked the words: "I wish I thought of that." We both grew to be better writers as we shared and critiqued each other's poetry. His poetry often turned into songs. And while his guitar playing was very basic, and his voice sweet and soft, he could interpret the emotions that were on the paper and create songs that pleased.

A lifetime had drifted by after college until a few years ago when Henry and I reunited and once again began to share our writings. He had published a number of successful songs over the years and had written many short stories. I had two successful careers; one as a journalist, travel writer and editor and a second one as a public relations and marketing executive. I was finally, in my senior years, getting back to where I started—writing my thoughts, emotions and musings. Henry, once again became my trusted colleague and soundstage for my words. This book, for what's it's worth, is in part a result of Henry's helpful friendship.

Other friends at Murray were a result of my involvement in Alpha Phi Omega, the service fraternity that I joined instead of one of the social fraternities. Fraternities and sororities were the antithesis of what I believed college to be all about. They stood for drinking and sex, both of which were important to me, but not when hidden in a group of pretentious adolescents who banned together for group support and then created the false image that they were above everyone else, both socially and economically. Alpha Phi Omega membership resulted in a number of good friends including the two Johns from Binghamton (which could have been a good movie title).

Studying journalism also produced several good friends on campus, a couple of which joined with me in producing both the official College News written and edited by students under the direction of professor Edmundson, as well as the Underground News, written and edited by several of the same students. The Underground News was produced solely by the students for the students. It was uncensored and covered subjects that we couldn't write about in the College News. We produced this ourselves, ran off copies on a mimeograph machine and distributed them around the campus. We created quite a stir and kept our identities secret for fear of being expelled from the University. I keep their secret even today to protect them from ridicule they might encounter in their now successful careers. But a special shout out to Jay Divine for all his shoulder to shoulder support.

We were the voice that the university administration did not want to hear or be heard. We spoke at a time of widespread protest during the mid-sixties when the Viet Nam war was being escalated and our friends were being drafted to fight and possibly die in a battle that no one believed in. But we also covered local issues that angered the students because the tightlipped administration turned a blind eye and deaf ear to any changes on campus that might improve life for students.

As noted, this was the Bible Belt and students were treated as children under guard rather than as the young adults we were in reality. It was often the little things that angered us most. But rather than change, we were just shut up and shut down. Our only outlets were the Underground News and the opportunities to be heard via poetry and song at Nowhere Coffee House. Even though the coffee house was sponsored by the United Campus Ministry, the religious organizations that gave birth to the coffee house respected our freedom of speech as long as we didn't drink alcohol or smoke anything other than cigarettes. This was years before it was accepted that cigarettes killed people. I wonder how these ministers would have dealt with that fact had they known what we know now about cigarettes.

My theater friends, Suzzane Carlton and Gary Bell, were another group that I hung out with and worked with through my speech and drama classes. This led to a number of gay friends, both male and female, that were involved in the arts. I got close to one of them, a guy named Bob as well as my Speech Professor Bill Bonham. I even emulated them for their coolness and one semester I dyed my hair blond and wore tight white jeans.

But I couldn't keep the white jeans clean and soon returned to my dark, long-hair, mountain-man beard and baggy blue jeans.

I was leading a busy life on campus with a diverse group of friends, most of who never mixed with one another. I was also attending classes and getting decent grades as I headed for graduation and a degree in. . . . . Ah, that was a big question. I started out as a dual major in Physical Education and English. The English professor who was assigned as my curriculum advisor told me that I had to drop the Physical Education major because it did not go well with an English major. I changed advisors instead of changing majors.

My second semester, I did drop Phys Ed and replaced it with History as a major. My sophomore year I added Psychology as a third major while trying to figure out just what I wanted to do and who I wanted to be. I then added Education as a major thinking I would teach. Meanwhile, I also started taking journalism courses and working on the College News. Later, when I added speech courses and drama to my curriculum, I discovered that I could expand my English lit major into an English Area covering English Literature, Speech, Drama and Journalism. I dropped Psychology and Education, but kept moving along with History as a second major. I graduated with 170 credits (fifty more than needed), many of which were in discarded majors.

I'm not sure how I accomplished all of this as I spent a lot of time socializing and dating.

In my freshman year I dated a local girl who was a very cute blond cheerleader. (I am not making this up.) We went to the movies and afterwards sat in her car and talked. She actually asked me a question that, to this day, I still wonder was it really possible that she asked: "I know you are a Jewish person from New York and I have no issues with that, but I am just wondering if you really do have horns, and if so, can I touch them." I told her that it was against my religion to allow anyone to touch them and we never dated again.

Another girl I dated was from Long Island, New York. We went out for several months and I even visited her over the Christmas when we were both back in New York. We never consummated our relationship because we were either in Murray where we were restricted to handholding or when I stayed with her on Long Island, where we slept in different rooms separated by her parent's bedroom. After dating for about four months, she told me that she couldn't see me anymore because she had discovered that she was falling in love with her roommate. Her roommate was another young lady from New Jersey.

Picking up a Date at the Dorm that Bombed

One of the most embarrassing moments in my life took place in one of the women's dorms at Murray State during my sophomore year. I was standing at the front desk in the lobby of the dorm waiting for my date to come down. The desk was at the far end of a large lobby filled with couches, easy chairs, coffee tables and desks where students gathered to spend time together. It was around six o'clock in the evening and the lobby was filled with coeds sitting around and talking with suitors.

I was facing the front desk watching the dorm matrons at work. Their job was to make sure that the women in their dorm remained chaste. There was to be no physical contact other than hand shaking between the visiting men and the women who lived under their austere supervision. And they were very good at their jobs. I stood there watching them intently to distract myself from the pain in my stomach. The pain was from a build-up of gas in my gut that made me feel like a human balloon.

I was trying to get the courage to release some of this gas, slowly, and without the normal audible sounds that accompany farts. While the lobby of the dorm was crowded with students, the atmosphere was more like a library as everyone spoke very softly to avoid the wrath of the matrons. I wasn't concerned if there was an odor released if I passed gas, I only cared that any associated sound be muffled. I wanted to release it with a whimper, not a bang.

Suddenly there was a tap on my shoulder and I swung around to face one of the girls I was friendly with. She immediately, with a big smile and a friendly gesture, thrust her hand into my vulnerable stomach with a playful punch. The result was nature. She inadvertently pushed out all the gas that had built up inside of my gut over the past fifteen minutes. The gas was released with such a force that resulted in a magnificent fart that any six-year-old boy would have found to be wonderfully hilarious. The fart was loud and long. It was a true explosion that reverberated from the desk to the front doors and across every couch and chair in this large, crowded dorm lobby.

All dialogue ceased immediately. All attention was turned in my direction. Every head was focused in silent awe towards what had just happened. My cute young friend, who had accidently caused this explosion stood paralyzed with her hand still extended into my stomach and her smile erased by a jaw-hanging stare. About twenty feet away stood my date, also paralyzed by the sound of the fart that had just exploded from her intended escort. I turned bright red with embarrassment. Then there was laughter, lots of laughter from every corner and crevice of the dormitory lobby.

My friend removed her hand from my stomach and took a step back whispering, "I'm sorry. I am so, so sorry." She continued to stand there, not knowing what to do or where to turn. My date, however, did not remain standing there. She quickly turned and removed herself from any connection to this ultimate embarrassing scene and disappeared, never to be seen again. For all I know she may have even left school after this incident. I never did see her on campus after that.

The matrons quickly threw a verbal net over the room and quieted the laughter with their booming voices. I finally found my own voice loud enough to say: "You shouldn't have done that; I was saving that gas for my date." Several people laughed and my friend stepped forward to embrace me. And those nearest us also began to laugh again. The tension was eased and I did my best to get out of there as I went straight for the doors never looking back. Once outside, I released whatever gas was left inside as I quickly walked away. It was another loud fart. I no longer cared. I just kept walking. I couldn't be any more embarrassed. I continued down the campus walkway with my crimson colored face. I don't think I ever returned to that dorm again.

CHAPTER SEVENTEEN

JO AND FRIENDS IMAGINING OUR WAY TO MEXICO

Workin' on our night moves, trying to lose the awkward teenage blues
Workin' on our night moves, in the summertime
And oh the wonder, felt the lightning
And we waited on the thunder
••••••
"Night Moves" by Bob Seger & The Silver Bullet Band

Fall quickly turned cold in Kentucky and a group of friends including Pete the Bug, Joe the Fish, Claude the Canadian, Al the Guitar, Danny (the real guitar player), John J and John B, Pam and Joanne (girls never had nick-names) all went to a cabin off campus that Peter Z had rented near Aurora overlooking Kentucky Lake. Someone lit a fire in the fireplace (a logical spot which was not always the case) and everyone sat around smoking dope and listening to guitars and occasional songs as the night got colder.

As the fire waned everyone huddled together to keep warm and slowly fell asleep together. I got to spend some much-desired time next to Jo, even if she didn't know it. Morning came and the frost covered everything. It was beautiful, but cold. Over breakfast served up by Pam and Claude, there was talk about escaping for the holidays. Thanksgiving was approaching and I planned to spend the holiday in St. Louis visiting relatives. However, hearing an opportunity to spend some lengthy quality time with Jo was a strong enticement to abandon family.

Peter Z said he would drive if the others chipped in for gas. Claude was not going back to Canada for a holiday that his country didn't even celebrate and was the first to jump on the bandwagon. Pam was secretly interested in developing a relationship with either Peter or Claude so she said she would love to go along, but she didn't really have any extra funds for gas. The guys were quick to say, almost in synchronized harmony, "Don't worry about it, we'll cover you." Jo was next, with, "I'd love to go, but I can' afford anything either, I can hardly pay for my next meal." Claude put his hand on Jo's shoulder (I think he was interested in Jo too) and said, "We'll cover you too."

Danny sat brooding in the corner, a common sight for this very talented musician, and offered: "If you want some music along for the ride, I'm there. I've got some stash, but not much cash." Everyone laughed and Peter said, "Of course, no problem Danny." That numbered five people set to go with three unable to chip in for gas. I did not want to miss the opportunity to be with Jo for an extended period of time. This could be my chance to make a move and let her know how I felt about her. But I too had very little cash. I already had set up a free ride to St. Louis courtesy of one of my fraternity brothers. But I did have my job at Nowhere Coffee House so I could count on some future funds coming in to contribute to this worthy cause.

Peter, meanwhile, had a Ford station wagon that sat six. Back in the 60s most cars had bench seats for both front and back which meant that it could easily accommodate six. Bucket seats were rare and also costly at that time and seen mostly in the sports cars. Five had committed to go on this trip including Peter, Claude, Danny, Pam and Jo already declaring. John B was heading home for the holidays to see his wife. He was the only married one in this particular group.

John J, also interested in both Pam and Joanne, knew of my interest in Jo and had voluntarily backed off, but said, "You better make a move soon or I will," adding, "I think she likes me anyway." That morning I debated things in my head too much and waited just a fraction too long when John J said: "I have some money to contribute and I'm not going home for Thanksgiving, so count me in." That was six and I was left out and feeling sick. My stomach began to develop that empty mixture of dread and fear culminating in nausea. This could mean the loss of any chance with Joanne.

On the ride back to campus later that morning, I told Peter of my interest in going if anyone should back out: "Let me know if anyone decides not to go. I will find some money and I would really like to go." Money didn't come easy in those days, it never did. When I first got to Murray State, I was working two jobs for the school just to pay tuition. One job was as a dishwasher in the school cafeteria where I stood behind the waste counter and took trays full of dirty dishes and cleaned them. The other job was with the school maintenance department where I carried a huge window-washing pole with a large brush on one end and a water hose that ran through it. Balancing this pole and gingerly cleaning windows on the school buildings that were three and four stories high was not always easy. Once I was attacked by a family of blue jays protecting their territory in the trees when I hit the branches with my wavering pole. By my junior year, my work on weekends at Nowhere Coffee House gave me living money for room and board and entertainment.

There was also some money saved from a summer job. That job was interesting too. My grandfather Papa Joe got me the job with a trucking company that distributed cigarettes and candy to stores, supermarkets and other retail outlets. My job was to go over the orders, pack the cartons of cigarettes and candy into larger cardboard boxes, seal and mark the boxes and then load them on the trucks for delivery. Every once in a while, I would get to go with one of the drivers on their deliveries.

Even with these jobs there was rarely any extra money for entertainment, but friends were great in never hesitating to bring me along, often covering costs for meals, movies and concerts. I promised God that I would return the good deeds for others whenever I could. Over subsequent years, many of my good deeds would be accomplished by giving of my time rather than money because there was rarely anything extra. People really appreciated time given freely as a valuable commodity. There was time spent in hospitals at the bedsides of acquaintances that were dying. Others, like my friend Sy, who just needed someone to listen to him while he was in a hospital bed recuperating. And over the years there were many that needed the networking connections so they could get jobs, especially during economic downturns. Later in life I even hired a few downtrodden to help them along, but time was always much more plentiful and often used to help others.

John J was a very similar sort of person. He had developed into a close friend and he went to me a couple of days after first discussing the trip to Mexico and offered to back out if I really wanted to go. "That would be great, John, but I don't have the money right now anyway." "I do," he offered, and with that, that handed me $60 and told me "you can repay me whenever."

A week later, on a cool, almost cold, fall morning in Kentucky, when the leaves had mostly left their trees and were collected by the wind in the corners of the streets and high upon the lawns in front of old wooden homes that housed the citizens of Murray, Peter packed up his car and began his rounds of picking everyone up for the trip to Mexico.

I was probably the most excited person that morning, not because of the trip to Mexico for Thanksgiving, but because of the potential to get some quality time with Jo and maybe take the friendship to the next level, or any other level than just friends. As a group we were all friends and hung out together after classes and on the weekends. As noted, all the guys had interest in developing a closer relationship to both Pam and Joanne. There were times that we relaxed in front of a fire where Jo and I fell comfortably asleep beside each other. Other times, it was John or Al or Pam in which I found next to me. We were just a close group friends hanging together. It was very comfortable, but I wanted more with Jo.

She looked like she was part Indian with rumors that her mother came straight out of the Narragansett tribe in the Northeast. Her father was a Portuguese fisherman who may have found his Pocahontas and married her. Jo was tall with very dark black hair, often kept in the traditional long pigtails of an Indian princess. She had a dark complexion with a few light freckles sprinkled across her face. Her large, dark brown eyes set in white almond shaped orbs along with her wide white tooth smile contrasted well with her mocha complexion. She was pretty by any standards, but more exotic looking which is what usually made people take a second look. She herself, was unsure of her good looks and displayed a lack of confidence which probably was a result of growing up with four or five brothers and no sisters. This also accounted for her frequent displays of tomboy behavior and competitiveness with the guys in our group.

Her good friend Pam was also a tomboy, but had a more girlish look and manner. Pam was average height and fair skinned with bright blue eyes. Her brown hair was straight and kept no longer than shoulder length with a little flip at the ends. Her complexion was very white and smooth and she was very pretty. But she too, avoided the typical girlish look and dressed in jeans and male style denim shirts most of the time. I was also very comfortable with Pam and often engaged in lengthy talks with her as well.

Peter was a quiet guy most of the time. He was ruggedly handsome and well educated. He also had more money than the rest of us. And it was his car that would be the ride off campus most of the time. He was from some very small town upstate New York. The small-town upbringing may have had something to do with his shyness, especially around those from the big city, any big city. But he fit in well with the intellectual atmosphere of this group in the early 1960s counter-culture.

Claude was from Canada. He had jet black hair and dark eyes. He did not have that rugged look that you might expect from someone from the outer reaches of Canada. He also had a great singing voice and had often combined his talents with one or more of the experienced guitarists such as Al or Danny. He even sounded a little like his countryman the popular folk singer Gordon Lightfoot.

Danny was our resident Bob Dylan. Only he played a guitar more masterful than Dylan ever would. Danny had real talent. I always believed that he would eventually go on to recording with some Nashville greats, but he didn't seem to have the confidence to push himself and make it on his own as a performer. Danny was a slight young man. His long brown hair was never combed. There was no reason to comb it. His deep-set eyes told stories as he sang; always directly to you. His voice was perfect for folk singing and his guitar playing was mesmerizing. He said very little outside of singing and playing his guitar. He said it all with his music. And said it beautifully.

At that time in history, I was six foot, three inches tall and weighed about 200 pounds. My hair was near-shoulder length brown and very curly. I sported a full dark brown beard set off by equally dark brown eyes and a perennial smile. I joked a lot and laughed at my own jokes (I still do). It was a way of getting attention and being part of the group.

Like so many others, I had very little money and was struggling to get an education and eventually a job with a newspaper as a reporter. Friends back home thought I was crazy to go to college in Kentucky, but few of them went to college at all, so they didn't understand. One school advisor told me: "You are not meant for college. You are a lousy student. Just go and get a job and get out of your parent's hair."

Two days before leaving on this trip that we had dreamed up several times before (was this another dream or did it really happen?), we were all sitting having coffee at the Student Union Building, a common gathering place during the day. They decided that going to Mexico was going to take longer than allowed for the four-day Thanksgiving holiday. This was not the first trip we planned as a group. There were at least four or five other planned trips that were never completed.

We would sit and dream up plans for wonderful escapes from reality, most often just planned just several days before we would have to leave; and then we would never depart from the campus. One time, plans were made to go to Chicago for a long weekend. Everybody was in agreement on what they would be doing and when we would leave. No one showed up on that morning and no one ever spoke of that planned trip again. It was if it never happened. It was probably just a weak idea that no one wanted to admit to. Other times we would take off for somewhere, but return before getting there.

Meanwhile, we had decided that since none of us had classes on Mondays (scheduled that way in order to take long weekends) and Wednesday before Thanksgiving was a getaway day for both teachers and students, with most teachers being lenient about missing classes the day before a holiday, we now had more time than normal for the perennial dream escape plan.

We decided to also skip classes on the Tuesday before Thanksgiving and therefore, with no Monday classes, and a full weekend prior to the holiday we now had ten full days to get to Mexico, get some weed, and return to Kentucky. Plenty of time.

Peter picked us up one after the other. We were off on another trip dreamed about, planned and rarely accomplished. This dream began on a Friday evening. Peter, Pam and Jo were in the front seat of the car and Claude, Danny and I were in the back seat. The rear of the Ford station wagon was filled with backpacks, pillows and blankets. We intended to sleep in the car when necessary and wanted to make sure that there was as much comfort as possible.

I said goodbye to Jerry and Steve, my two roommates who were staying in the rooms rented upstairs in the Workman's house. Mr. and Mrs.

Workman were two local people that rented out three rooms that their grown kids used to live in. These rooms at the top of the stairs had one bathroom. Renters had to come and exit through the Workman's living room, often with them sitting there watching television or reading. It was not the most comfortable situation since college students come and go at all hours, but it was very cheap and only two blocks from campus. The key to this arrangement was agreeing to never entertain guests in the rooms. Ultimately, it was a place to sleep and that was fine.

I leaned up against the window of Peter's car cushioned by the pillow taken from the Workman's house and went to sleep. I could sleep anywhere, and expecting to be driving one of the early legs of the trip, needed to get some sleep first.

We started out going straight down Highway 641, the North-South road that dissected Murray and brought a lot of truck traffic, but little else to our small town. Highway 641 was a major road connecting Western Kentucky farmland to Western Tennessee farmland. For Murray State students at that time, it was the fastest way to Paris, Tennessee and 3.2% beer. The first stop on this trip to Mexico was Paris where we could load up on beer.

From there we would continue a short distance further south to Camden, Tennessee where we pickup State Route 70 west heading towards Memphis to pick up what was the new Highway 40 which would take us nearly all the way to San Diego, California and Highway 5 for the short drive south to Tijuana, Mexico, cheap pot, beer, food, and live sex entertainment for people of all ages.

Peter stopped at one of the several local bars in Paris and Claude and I got out to buy the beer. There we encountered the first of several not-so-fun experiences on this trip. The bartender sold us two cases of beer (24 cold bottles in all), took the money and told us to go out back to pick up the two cases. Out behind the bar we looked around and couldn't find any cases. Just as we were about to go back into the bar, there emerged from the back door four ugly looking locals, all dressed in dirty, oversized jeans and brown or green plaid shirts.

"Can we help y'all?" one asked. "Lisn to em, how we gonna help them college grads, maybe them kin help us, eh?" said another one.

"We're just here to buy some beer," said Claude. "You did, now git," said the first local. "I'll just check with the bartender," I offered. "He's off duty" one of the other locals said as they continued to approach and surround us. It didn't take Claude and I long to realize that we had two choices, get beat up or run. We ran.

We both immediately took off around the side of the bar and yelled for Peter to start the car as we jumped in breathing heavy and already sweating despite the cold outside. Danny looked back as the car peeled away from the parking lot, but no one was following. "I don't even think they cared about you, they got what they wanted, our money and our pride," Danny said to no one in particular.

College students and townies (as the local kids were called) had a history of difficult relations. Local townies in many small cities across the country did not want the college students to enjoy their local bars, restaurants, movie theaters, etc. We were considered outsiders and interlopers.

It was at a gas station with a convenience store in Milan, Tennessee that we were first able to purchase the beer that would carry through a good portion of the trip. We continued south on 70A looking for a diner to have some light dinner. The first one we stopped in, we sat at a table for four, pulled up two additional chairs and waited for nearly fifteen minutes before realizing we were being ignored.

Seeing a number of locals sitting in booths and at the counter, Pam suggested, "We might not be welcome here, let's leave." We did. On the way out we heard a gruff male voice ask "What, no tip for the waitress?" Peter reached into his pocket and pulled out a dollar and some change and turned to leave it on a table near the door. Quickly getting into the car we took off again empty handed.

This was not a good sign. We all knew the hostility housed by locals. We experienced this in Murray where many of the local residents expressed anger and resentment at the college students, even at their own locals that went to the university. It was us against them, even though we never did anything to them other than move into their town where we spent money and helped boost their economy.

We all just joked about it, laughed and continued to look for a more hospitable diner. The next one was just a few minutes down the road. It was now after eight o'clock and we were all very hungry. This diner looked very much like the previous one, very traditional like an old silver metal trailer set on the side of the road. Part of the red lit sign on the top was out so it read "DI_E_ _PEN." That was not a good omen. We stopped, Peter backed into a parking spot preparing for a quick getaway if needed and we went in with high hopes of something to eat. We all crammed into a booth just to make it easy. A waitress came over almost immediately, but she did not bring menus, nor did she have her trademark pad and pencil in hand. She smiled and simply said, "Sorry, we're closed," and stood there smiling.

Looking around one could see half the booths were taken, apparently with locals looking straight at the group of college kids. The two men at the counter also had turned on their stools and looked straight at us. Danny apologized in his best local accent (he was born and raised in Kentucky) and asked if she knew of another diner that was open. She said, "Sorry, don't think so." We all began to get up, thanking her one after another as she moved backwards, continuing to smile. We did our best to avoid looking at any of the locals sitting there and exited as quickly as possible. Back in the car and on the road again, passing two more diners before coming into Brownsville north of Memphis and just before getting onto Route 40.

Coming into Brownsville meant another tiny town along State Route 70. It was late and the used car dealers that lined the highway were all closed, but we passed an old house that now served as a local restaurant followed by a diner almost hidden by view. Peter had to step on the brakes and make a sharp right turn so as to not pass the small parking lot. Everyone took a deep breath and got out and walked into what was a mostly empty diner with only six booths and a counter.

Two booths were taken by locals, with three men in one and two in another. There was no one at the counter and Danny asked the lone waitress who greeted us, "Hi there, where would y'all like us to set?" She offered, "Y'all can set at the counter f ya like." We did and she gave ever other person a menu to share. Everyone ordered simple things, ate fast, bought some candy and potato chips, paid, left a tip — all within 40 minutes and with no incidents.

A short while later a car full of satiated college students were heading west. There was a lot of construction because the road was being upgraded and widened in parts, but I had just taken over the wheel and took the bypass around the center of Memphis and headed into Arkansas without any delays despite the work crews and lane closures. Fortunately, there were few other cars heading in the same direction. We made good time that first night despite the unproductive multiple food stops and a number of driver changes and sailed through Little Rock and into Oklahoma by early morning.

Somewhere along the way, in the middle of Arkansas, the highway reverted to a dark, empty country road. It was the middle of the night and there were no other cars on the road. I was driving. Jo had moved into the middle seat and had her head on my shoulder. Even though this was a slight interference with my driving mobility as my right arm was somewhat restricted, I didn't want to disturb her and wake her up. I was really thrilled to have her so close and actually touching. It was close moments like these that gave me the feeling that there was some chemistry between us and that something could, indeed, happen.

Pam was in the right front passenger seat and also asleep. Peter was right behind me and sleeping on a pillow leaning up against the window. Danny was curled up asleep on the other side in the rear. Claude was in the middle of the back seat and staring out at the road. Occasionally he would softly say something. I was sure that this was Claude's way of seeing if I was still awake and could drive. I sort of appreciated the thoughtfulness, but was also slightly offended.

Around three o'clock in the morning while driving smoothly along a dark country road, Jo woke up, stretched her long arms and in her strong, deep and loud enough voice to wake everyone up, said, "I've got to pee. Can we stop somewhere, anywhere?"

Yawning came from everywhere, even Danny, who yawned "Good mornin' y'all," and went right back to sleep.

Talk ensued about finding a place to stop, Claude offered "I'm concerned that we may not find a hospitable place to stop in these parts." Recent experiences in the diners could possibly be played out again looking for a place with restrooms.

Jo was quick to offer, "Just stop here, I'm sure we can all find a tree." They laughed, but realized that she was serious and that if she was okay with it, why not the guys. It would be easier for the guys then the girls. Pam did not look pleased, but said, "Okay, I'll try." With that, I pulled over to the side of the road. It was a very dark stretch of road and there were no other cars.

When I turned the car off and shut the lights, we all sat there in silence. The blackness of our surroundings swallowed up the car and all of us inside. No one moved. No one said anything. We just sat there and starred out into the blank, black night. You could not see more than a foot or two in front of your nose. I put my arm around Jo and gave her a hug. "I've got to pee, Rich," she said as she pulled away annoyed.

"I've got flashlights in the back," said Peter as he stepped out of the car. There was no moonlight and no lights on the road or anywhere that could be seen. He fumbled for a moment in the back, opened the rear gate of the station wagon and quickly found two flashlights in the pitch blackness of the night. He did it solely by memory and feeling around. Soon Peter came back around the other side of the car with two flashlights and Pam and Jo got out. I got out of the driver's seat and Claude got out from the back on the driver's side holding out his hand offering, "I'll take over and drive for awhile." I went to hand him the keys in the complete darkness and they just dropped to the pavement. Danny stayed curled up asleep.

Jo took one of the flashlights and surveyed the landscape along the side of the road. "I'm not going in there," she declared. Pam concurred. I was not anxious to step off the side of the road myself, but I also now had to pee. Just talking about peeing generated the urge. However, my first concern was finding the car keys as Claude crawled around searching in the relentless blackness of the moonless night.

Jo turned to Pam and said, "Come with me, you guys stay here." With that she and Pam walked to the rear of the car and Jo handed Pam the flashlight. "Hold this for me and I will then hold it for you." Then Jo unzipped her jeans, pulled them and her underwear down to her ankles and squatted. Peter watched from the side of the car. She didn't care. She started peeing while holding on to the rear of the car for balance. When she finished, she used some tissue to wipe herself, stood up and pulled her underpants and jeans back up. She then took the flashlight from Pam and said, "I feel a lot better, your turn. And why don't yoose guys go do what you need to do. We have no desire to watch you hang out there anyway." With emphasis on "hang."

Pam stood there staring at the guys and said "Well, what are you waiting for, I'm not peeing until y'all disappear." Peter, Claude and I took one of the flashlights to find the car keys and then went to the front of the car and separated to pee while Peter held the flashlight under his arm so we didn't step off into some hole. We all came back to the car at the same time and had a new, heightened appreciation for both Jo and Pam. They did what they needed to do without any embarrassment. They were not shy about peeing outside in the middle of nowhere and were comfortable doing it in front of the guys—to a certain degree.

As they got back into the car Danny welcomed them with, "So Pam, you don't wear undies, do you?" "How do you know, Danny?" Pam retorted. "I watched you take you jeans down and there were no panties in sight," he countered. Everyone laughed and nothing further was said. But you know that the guys were now visualizing Pam putting on jeans without panties.

We switched seating around for the first time without changing drivers. Claude had offered to drive, but then I decided to continue because I liked driving at night with fewer cars on the road. Everyone wanted to sleep so that was fine with all others. Pam moved into the back and alternated between snuggling up on Peter's or Danny's shoulders. A new competition may have been forming there.

It was always complicated as we were such a cohesive group and worked so well as a group, but there was always an undercurrent of feelings moving about, almost like electric currents that connect one of more people to each other, making for a crisscross of wires that represent feelings not expressed but present all the time. Each one had feelings for one or more of the others and none of us had yet to make the outward visible connection that was required to light up their lives. Multiple combinations of two were possible in this connected group of kids. All it would take would be one bold move. I so much wanted to be the one to make that move, but I was still too shy, especially when it counted.

Claude moved into the center seat up front and Jo moved over to the window. Another opportunity to get closer and touch was lost for the moment. I would just concentrate on driving and Claude would keep me awake and alert. Everyone else slept all the way through Little Rock. There was only an occasional other car on the road and that was good because it had begun to rain lightly and it made the windows blurry. I turned the windshield wipers on to slow speed, but they were not as effective as I would have liked.

Another Time, Another Place, Same Rain

The rain continued to build slowly at first, and heavier at times, more in waves then a steady flow. I turned the windshield wipers to fast speed. It was enough to keep the windows clear and also to hypnotize me as well. My mind drifted back in time remembering another girl, Susan Hopkins, and feeble attempts at getting close to her. It was just the beginning of teenage life, I was eleven-years-old, but already failing pitifully as an amorous suitor.

The place was Lake Paradise, a small dot on some New York State maps, usually listed as Paradise Lake. But everyone knew it as Lake Paradise. There were actually two lakes. One a fishing lake and the other a swimming lake. They were connected by a small culvert that went under the road that separated the two lakes.

Vacationers got there by driving from New York City up Old Route 17 to Woodbourne, New York, one of the old Catskill region towns that was already dying back in the 1950s. The few thriving towns included Monticello with its race track, Liberty with its commerce and the neighboring towns of South Fallsburg and Loch Sheldrake with its famous Catskill Borscht Belt hotels Grossingers and The Concorde. These hotels and several others such as the Neville, drew some the top entertainment during the 1940s and 50s including Frank Sinatra, Dean Martin, Sammy Davis Junior and every comedian that had ever thought they could make people laugh. And laugh they did all summer long throughout the Catskills as time stood still for families escaping the steam heat of the New York City summer pavement.

Lake Paradise was one of many "bungalow colonies" where some people owned and others rented small basic houses for the summer season beginning July and ending with Labor Day weekend. The drive from New York City to Woodbourne took about two hours. Continuing from Woodbourne to Lake Paradise went along winding roads through the forest, past open farmlands and finally to the Country Store and Great House at the top of the hill. Down the hill, over the short piece of road separating the long fishing lake from the short round swimming lake and a right turn into the bungalow colony, most of which were privately owned summer homes.

My family rented for the summer and our bungalow was situated straight back alongside a creek with five other small houses. A hundred yards away was one of every kids' favorite spots, a small waterfall which connected the mysterious Catskill Forest that sat above and beyond. Few people ever ventured beyond the top of the waterfall to go deep into the thick, dark forest. The waterfall fed the creek and both lakes with water generated somewhere in the forest.

The waterfall stood about 150 feet and was climbable most of the summer as water just trickled down the center leaving plenty of space and convenient rock platforms to grasp. Kids often climbed as a group and would take excursions into the beginning of the dark green forest to see what was hiding there. Indian artifacts were among the greatest finds. Bear tracks were among the most feared finds. We never went too far into the dark forest.

Sometimes, after a heavy rainfall, one that may have happened fifty miles north of Lake Paradise you could hear the roar of the waterfall and see how furious the water could get.

In order to get to the falls kids would have to trespass on the Issacowitz property which was adjacent to the falls. Anytime they did this, the portly matriarch of the family came out yelling and waving a broom as if she would cast a spell on all of us kids. She didn't like me and my friends, but the main cause for the anger was the fact that we didn't include her son Allan in our group. Kids could be mean and we were no different from any others.

At eleven-years-old, I was a tall, skinny kid standing at five foot, nine inches and weighing about 120 pounds. My hair had turned from platinum blond when I was eight years old to sandy brown over the next three years, but it seemed lighter as the summer sun bleached it once again. It also contrasted nicely with the dark brown eyes and tan body which was largely exposed all day as most of the kids at the lake wore nothing but a bathing suit and sandals from breakfast to dinner.

In the summer of 1955 New York had a lot of rain. It culminated in the second week of August with Hurricane Connie which dropped nearly fourteen inches of rain on Southeastern New York killing about a dozen people in New York State. It had been raining for days. Everyone was holed up in their respective houses and bungalows. The bungalows were particularly small. There was little room to play and I had a brother and sister sharing the space. I was especially devastated by the rain because I hadn't been able to see Susan for days. I was just making progress in getting closer. I had even held her hand one night while hanging out as a group in the pavilion by the lake. She responded by holding tight. But that was it. I was hoping to take this relationship to the next level. Susan was exceptionally pretty in a very exotic way. She had a very dark complexion and her dark hair and almond shaped black eyes made her look Spanish. She lived in a large house above the road by the fishing lake and not close enough for me to visit because of the torrential rain storm we had been experiencing for days.

Fears were growing among the kids that movie night at the Community House would be cancelled. I didn't care so much about the movie, but Susan had agreed to go to the movie with me. It would be our first date. If the movie was canceled then losing that opportunity of the first date would be a supreme tragedy to an eleven-year-old boy. I feared that Susan might forget about how good the hand holding was and someone else might be courting her.

Fortunately, the heavy rain subsided and the parents agreed that it would be good, actually great, to get the kids out of the house for the evening, especially a Saturday evening, so they could play cards and drink as they usually did. The plans to show the movie was back on and everyone showed up at the Community House before seven o'clock. I found Susan after a few moments and said, "Where are you sitting." She smiled, "Wherever you want." I took her warm hand and we found seats together in the center of the third row. I never let her hand go as I led her into the row of hard wooden seats, the kind that fold and can be stacked for easy storing.

No one remembers the movie because just a few minutes after it started, one of the parents came in to take her kids out because the storm had picked up again and thunder and lightning were drowning out the movie anyway. Soon another mother came in and put fear into the air as she warned everyone at the movies that the waterfalls was going to overflow and flood the entire area.

The movie was turned off, the lights went on and everyone began to gather at the doors. I could even hear the roar of the water from where we were which was quite a distance from the falls. The combination of the waterfalls roaring into the creek and the rising water of the creek rushing higher and higher behind the row of houses plus the heavy rain was getting everyone concerned. I too was concerned, but had other priorities. I had been sitting next to Susan and needed time to make the next move to show her how much I cared for her. (Sound familiar?)

It wasn't long after the first two mothers had come to take her kids home that someone was leaning over and whispering to Susan and her sister Eileen. It was their grandfather. He was there to take them back to the house. The creek was threatening to overflow and he was taking them back because they were on the other side of the creek and he did not want them stranded. I was stunned. I said good night and wished them well reluctantly letting go of my grip on Susan's hand. And they were gone. A few minutes later we were informed that the rain was too heavy and that pathways and roads were beginning to get flooded. Everyone now needed to go back home. Those without an escort were to wait for parents or someone else to come. I walked back to our bungalow by myself.

Back at the bungalow, I tried to look out the back bedroom window which stood only a hundred yards from the roaring waterfall. I could hear it, but in the darkness could not see anything. The roar was like a never-ending roll of thunder. I shared the bedroom with my younger brother Ed and sister Barbara and remembered comforting them so they would fall asleep. I lay awake with flashes of lightening and distant rumbling of thunder to keep me reminded of what was happening out there. I waited patiently for the next flash of lightening to light up the sky and illuminate the waterfall. The flashes were frequent, but not long enough to really see what was happening out back of the house.

It was shortly after midnight when I heard the fire engines coming down the road with sirens blaring. At first, I thought, how could there be a fire with all this rain? The sirens got louder and louder as if they were coming straight to my house. Then, there was silence, followed by a lot of talk from a lot of voices. They were all outside our bungalow. I ventured from the bedroom and could see the flashing red lights illuminating everything. Even the thick trees that surrounded the group of five closely arranged bungalows were now flashing brilliant red in the dark, wet night.

The rain continued its steady flow. It was more than just a light rain, but not heavy enough to soak you unless you stood outside for a while. My Mom and a bunch of her friends were outside talking with the firemen who had come all the way from Woodbourne, more than seven miles in the rain that night. (Most of the Dads had returned to New York City already because of the storm.) Discussion turned into action plans that resulted in everyone moving in multiple directions. Mom came in the house, told me to wake up Ed and Barbara and get warm clothes on. Everyone was going to the Big House on the hill to get away from the waterfalls and creek that were about to overflow and flood our area.

Excitement of seeing the huge red fire truck in the yard with the bright flashing lights had now turned to fear. This was now an evacuation. There had been talk of evacuations earlier in the day, but no one thought it would really happen. It had never happened before. Even old man Fink, who had lived there forever, said that it "never happened, never would." But it was real and I began to shake with fear as I shook the shoulders of a peacefully sleeping brother and sister.

We got dressed very quickly, putting shirts and pants on top of pajamas and socks and sneakers on bare feet. We went to the porch to watch and wait for instructions. It was beginning to rain harder and we were told to wait inside until the firefighters were ready. I watched them loading the fire truck with children and mothers, each being helped as they climbed to the top where the firemen normally sat alongside ladders and hoses. Finally, it was my family's turn. Fear had turned back to excitement as we were getting to ride on top of this enormous truck in the middle of the night with these heroic firemen. This was going to be some excursion for both the moment and the memory.

I also conjured meeting up with Susan once we got to the Big House and talking about the experience riding the fire truck. I was sure that they would be rescued too. We would now turn this first date for two eleven-year-olds into an all-night slumber party. This was turning out to be better than I could ever imagine. I no longer shook with fear. I was standing there feeling stronger and calmer by the moment, and getting very wet as the rain splashed my face. I climbed up the side of the fire truck with very little assistance from the firemen and positioned myself so I could continue to see what was happening.

Once everyone was on board, with the exception of the Issacowitz family, as they refused to go even though their house was closest to the waterfalls, the truck began to back up through the mud and onto the road. It turned towards the exit and the main road, but when it got near the road that separates the fishing lake from the swimming lake, I could not see the road. It was gone. It was underwater.

The driver stopped the fire truck and one of the firemen on the side jumped off and waded over to the road to see how deep it was. "Not too deep, only two foot or less, but soft," he said. "Not sure it will hold our weight," he added. The chief, who was sitting in the front of the truck with the driver got out and walked over with two other firemen and poked at the ground under the water with long metal poles. They talked among themselves, one pointed to the far end of the swimming lake where a small paved, but very steep path led up the hill to the Big House and they nodded to each other.

When they came back to the truck, they got in without saying anything to any of us or even the other firemen. The driver began to back up again and then turned towards the swimming lake, driving past the lake and around to the far side where the diving board stood. The lights of the truck were shinning on the steep path up the hill to the Big House. The steady rain had created a steam of water that flowed over the path and down the hill into the swimming lake. The chief got out of the truck with a megaphone in his hand and told us: "We can't take the truck over the road because we fear it will collapse. We are going to carry each one of you up the hill to the road so you can get to the Big House. Stay on the fire truck until one of my men get you. Don't anyone get off the truck until one of my men get you. It is not safe out here."

I was one of the last to get on the truck by the bungalows, but did not want to be one of the first up the hill. I wanted to watch and experience everything, so I told one of the firemen, "I can help you get the small kids off the top of the truck." It gave me extra time and a purpose in this growing crisis that we were experiencing. I became so busy that I really did not watch everyone being carried up the hill by the firemen. My time to get carried came soon enough and I realized that this was not an easy task for the firemen, especially going up the steep hill as water came cascading down around their feet. They all wore knee high rubber boots and that must have given them the traction they needed. They unloaded the truck and carried all women and children to safety, walking hand in hand with some of the bigger men and women, carrying other women and children, all up the steep path to the top of the road. Everyone then scampered across the road to the Big House where it was dry and warm.

The fire truck then made two other trips around the back roads that housed more than fifty bungalows. And carried countless other children and mothers up the hillside. Once inside, we were given towels to dry off and the children were directed into various rooms where blankets and pillows had been placed on the floor for expanded sleeping accommodations. The Big House was operated by the owner of Lake Paradise and the vast property that housed all the homes and bungalows. It also served as a guest house that provided rooms for visitors during the summer. There were even a couple of rooms occupied that night. The rest of us from around the bungalow colony found space wherever we could.

After being directed to a room with several friends, I went searching other rooms for Susan. I found Bobby Rome, a close friend of mine (and also Susan's cousin) and asked, "Where's Susan?" His answer both shocked and saddened me. "They refused to evacuate when the fire truck got there and decided to stay in their house because it sits high off the road," he told me. As I was trying to digest the disastrous turn of events, knowing that one moment I was envisioning spending the night with Susan and now that treasured opportunity had faded away because her parents decided not to evacuate, suddenly the lights went out and we were immersed in darkness. A couple of screams later, there were candles and flashlights coming to the rescue. Someone's mother came in to remind the kids to "go to sleep, once you close your eyes it won't matter whether the lights are on or not."

I sat there devastated by the thought of having one of the most exciting nights of my life without Susan. I was not worried about her, knowing that her parents were probably correct in that their house sat high above the road and lake and the worst thing that would happen is that they would be stranded by the flood below them. The Issacowitz family were foolish because their house sat so close to the roaring waterfall and overflowing creek and they could be flooded with no way to escape. My thoughts were all over the place. I was also upset that the lights went out because that resulted in being forced to stay put. Just before the lights failed, we were planning to go room to room searching for other friends such as Audrey and Marla, two sisters, who were somewhere else in the Big House. My cousin Steve liked Audrey. But the lack of lights killed that plan.

It had been a rollercoaster night with emotions skyrocketing as Susan held my hand and dropping as she was taken away from me at the movies. Then I rose again with the thought of a night in the Big House together, disappearing into what would be a dark night alone. Somewhere in the middle of the night frustration migrated to sleep.

The creek did overflow that night. Some houses were flooded, but no significant damage that I recall, and no one was injured. Our bungalow was untouched by the floods. The Issacowitz house was surrounded by water, but they were safe. Susan and her family were cut off from the rest of the world for a couple of days until the water receded. The sun did eventually shine again.

OKLAHOMA OKAY, KANSAS BETTER

The rain had subsided. It was daybreak and I remained at the wheel while Claude had long ago drifted off to sleep leaning to his right on Jo's shoulder. During the night we crossed over into Oklahoma and I felt safe again. There was a certain feeling that Arkansas did not provide enough comfort for a bunch of scruffy looking college kids, but Oklahoma was a more sophisticated state and we would all be safe. This strange prejudicial outlook was, of course, outrageous in itself. Borders were nothing more than street markers. People living in Van Buren, Arkansas had relatives living across the border thirty miles away in Sallisaw, Oklahoma. They were no different because they lived in two different states.

They went back and forth to work along Interstate 40 and shopped in the same strip malls along the way. If you'd lined them up next to each other, looked carefully at them and listened to them speak, you might think they all came from Arkansas because of the Southern style and sound. But that too was a subjective view and Oklahoma, a cowboy state, was a combination of southern and western culture especially near the borders—borders that existed only on the small maps and in the small minds of some people.

The sun was just coming up over the Oklahoma plains and everyone was waking up after a good night sleep. At one point I had pulled into an all-night gas station to fill up and no one moved. They were all in a dead sleep. I was in a zone and driving straight along the interstate. Daybreak brought bright light into the car and one-by-one everyone began to wake up; and, as might be expected, they were hungry and began talking about breakfast. Peter suddenly said there's a diner on the left and seeing that I was about to pass it, I quickly turned left across oncoming traffic cutting off several cars and trucks that were going east. All I heard was a bunch of horns blasting, not sure of why or for who they were meant.

"That's it for you," said Peter. "I'm really awake now," said Claude, adding, "Please don't do that again." Everyone had something to say. I just said, "You wanted to stop here for breakfast and I didn't want to miss the turn. We didn't get hit, did we?"

We stopped for breakfast and to change drivers in Checotah, Oklahoma at a large diner called The Truck Stop on Route 40. The parking lot was filled with trucks, some of which contained sleeping drivers. It was early in the morning and I was both hungry and tired. I put my arm around Jo as we walked to the diner and asked, "Did you sleep well?" She nodded affirmatively and smiled, "You must be tired. Your turn to sleep after breakfast." She also reached her arm around my waist and gave me a hug. We walked across the parking lot with my arm around her shoulder and her arm around my waist. A good sign I thought. A great feeling came over me. I was no longer tired.

Breakfast was great. Even the smell was great. I loved country diners and while this was a large truck stop diner, the cooking was still country. All the guys had eggs and bacon with biscuits and gravy. The country gravy was a milk gravy using the grease from the bacon and sausage grill put in a skillet with a little milk and some flour for thickening. A little salt and pepper and it's done and ready for dipping your biscuit. It's not the healthiest breakfast, but sure is the tastiest.

Following breakfast, I moved to the back of the car and went right into a deep, much needed sleep. Jo and Pam also took their turns sitting in the back but I was oblivious and did not get to experience this or enjoy the moment with them as I was out cold up against the window. Sleep was not to be fully enjoyed anyway as Claude had only driven about two hours when Peter noticed the oil indicator on the dashboard had moved into the danger zone. He asked Claude to pull into one of the many gas stations in Midwest City right on Interstate 40, just outside of Oklahoma City. Everyone got out except me. I was still fast asleep.

I was awakened when the mechanic surveyed the engine under the hood and loudly said "pears y'all pump won't pump no mo."

Peter asked if he could fix it, and got a simple "Yup."

Peter then said, "Okay then, how much will it cost?"

"Dunno," was the mechanic's answer.

Peter countered with, "Can you find out so we can get it done? We're heading to Mexico for a short vacation and need to get back to school."

"Yup," he said and went inside the small office and thumbed through a big book, found what he was looking for and then picked up the telephone. A few minutes later, he came out and told Peter that the new oil pump would be "$90 installed."

"Great, let's get it done," said Peter, adding, "When will it be ready?"

"Dunno," was the mechanic's answer as he stared at Peter waiting for Peter's next move.

Peter stared at him, waiting and then said, "What do you mean you don't know when it will be ready? How long will it take to put in the new oil pump?"

The mechanic offered, "Not lung win I git da pump."

The reality of this small service station in this small town so close to the big city was becoming very clear. This could end up being a major delay "or we could drive on a find another service station to fix this" mused Claude out loud.

"Thet' wone happen," the mechanic advised us, "Ya kin drive off wit that pump not pumpin and ya freeze ya pistins fa gud. I be picking ya up fir trash after that."

There didn't seem to be much choice. We were just outside of Oklahoma City, a vibrant city with lots to do. We were also a few hours south of Emporia, Kansas, home of Emporia State College where my cousins Bobby and Harriett were attending. Bobby was my first cousin on my mother's side from New York. Harriett was my first cousin on my father's side from St. Louis. They knew each other before they discovered that they were in a small world and were both related to me on different sides of the family. Meanwhile, I was supposed to be in St. Louis for Thanksgiving where I would be having dinner with Harriett and her family. But Bobby would be staying on campus for the holiday and we decided to see if we could rent a car and go there while waiting for Peter's car to be repaired.

Emporia, Kansas in the 1960s was very much like Murray, Kentucky, a small town with a college that dominated the scenery and atmosphere. We would fit right in; that is, as much as a bunch of misfits fit in anywhere. I called Bobby who offered to come and pick us up. However, the mechanic offered to loan us one of his pick-up trucks for just $20 and the cost of a full tank of gas while he fixed Peter's car. We agreed.

While waiting for the mechanic to get the truck cleaned out, we did the natural thing and went next door to a diner to drink coffee. We all sat there watching Peter pour sugar in his coffee cup as if it were the coffee itself. He could literally stand a spoon up in the sugar that was piled thick in the bottom of the coffee cup. He liked his coffee sweet which elicited "Oh, you are so sweet already," from Pam.

As soon as the pick-up truck was ready, Jo and Pam hopped in the cab with Peter and the rest of us climbed into the back bed of the truck and got positioned for the windy ride up to Emporia, Kansas. I sat in one corner with back to the cab, Claude sat in the other corner, and Danny in the middle huddled beneath the rear window. The wind whipped around to the back and my long hair and beard created a wild-man look. "You look more scary than normal," Jo smiled when we arrived in Emporia about three hours later.

We crashed at Bobby's place with five or six bedrooms which accommodated other students who were all away for the holidays. Over the next three days, as we waited for Peter's car to be fixed, we met a number of students from Emporia State, some of which crashed with us at Bobby's just for the hell of it since we brought the party to them. Harriett, as mentioned, was not around because she was back in St. Louis where I was supposed to be. It was a convivial bunch of students including some recent graduates that just hung out together, very much like we did at Murray. Everyone fit right in.

My only problem was that several of the Kansas guys were interested in talking with Joanne and this cut into my time with her. I didn't fear anyone taking my place as this was just a moment in time away from reality and we were all having a great time together. But it prevented me from making my move and caused a pause in our relationship as she related to our new friends in a nonstop party for three days in Emporia.

Sleeping arrangements were relaxed and we moved from one room to the next, sometimes sleeping all together on this giant pillow bed on the floor in one of the bedrooms. With everyone around I was getting no closer to Jo and desperately needed to let her know how I felt.

One evening walking down the street in Emporia as we headed to a diner for dinner, I somehow gained the courage and slowly began to make a move to take Jo's hand. I stared straight ahead as I reached for her hand, fearing even to look her in the face, waiting for an answer to this finally "bold move." The answer came fast as she squeezed my hand with a reassuring and affectionate pressure and put her head on my shoulder for three seconds. Finally, real contact with acceptance. And the world was a better place for it.

As we walked down the street, jokes began to fly around from Peter, Claude and even Pam. Later Danny even chimed in with a few lyrics about "the cute lovers holding hands on the street, as they got tangled up by their big ugly feet." It signaled that it was accepted that Jo and I had finally become a thing. All it took was for me to take her hand and we were finally a couple. It happened without any fanfare (other than the friendly jokes thrown at us). Everyone said it was "about time."

When we got seated in the diner, Pam was the first to say something sweet, "What took the two of you so long to connect?"

Peter chimed in with "Now that Jo and Rich are finally together, I need to find my own true love." But he avoided looking at Pam. She quickly added, "I'm available." Everyone laughed, but we also knew that it was only time before those two might also get together. Pam was hoping it wouldn't take Peter as long as it took me to make a move.

I was inherently shy, especially when it mattered. I had no problem approaching a girl for a casual fling, but it was different with Jo. I had real feelings for her and that made the quest more complex. I had to watch my words to make sure that I did not say the wrong thing. This resulted in saying very little. But the few times I put my arm around her and now finally taking her hand had said it all in a nice quiet, shy and simple way. This couldn't have been more perfect because Jo was often hit on by guys and detested an aggressive approach. She was comforted by a shy, cautious courtship. And so my courtship of Jo continued to move very, very slowly. Holding hands and occasionally snuggling together at night was as far as we would get on this trip.

We hadn't even kissed yet. There were two reasons for this gaff. First, we were never alone and I was not about to launch the first kiss with a very attentive audience always around. I could just imagine the song that Danny would have written about that. And second, the trip to Mexico was aborted because of the delay in getting Peter's car fixed. Several days later, we were back on the road again, but too much time was lost so we left Kansas, stopped in Oklahoma to pick up Peter's car and headed back to Murray and school.

It was a somewhat depressing trip back and we tried to find a way to make it more interesting by searching maps for alternative routes. Also, we did not want to return through the redneck countryside that seemed to have a propensity to hate college students even though we were relatively innocuous looking college kids out for a harmless excursion. Maybe it was the long hair and beards that Danny and I sported or maybe it was just the fact that we were obviously college students and the rednecks were hard knocks blue collar workers. We never found out why so many of them reacted to us kids just walking into their diners. We never had the chance to ask them for fear that we would end up with their shoes on our faces.

Even back in Murray we had experienced an uncomfortable relationship with locals that was avoided whenever possible. I later found out it was no different in any of the other college towns across the country from Binghamton, New York to Tucson, Arizona.

Meanwhile, we found highway 60 north of Oklahoma City and took it east across Missouri, stopping just south of Springfield in Aurora and once again in Poplar Bluff, having absolutely no problems. We crossed into Kentucky near Cairo, Missouri and continued on 60 into Paducah. We were then back on familiar ground and took route 45 south through Mayfield and into Murray.

[*Full disclosure: The accounts of this aforementioned trip to Mexico were in reality a compilation of several unrelated excursions combined to provide a perspective of multiple experiences that resulted in a single outcome.*]

BACK ON CAMPUS

Back on campus, hand-holding turned to hugs and kisses. And yes, I do remember the first kiss. Women often think that men are so obtuse that they have no romantic inclinations outside of their sex drives. It is not so. Many men may not be as romantic as women, but there is no doubt that some men can match even the most romantic ladies who cry at those tear-jerking television ads. You know the ones in which a family is welcoming their grandfather as he gets off a long airplane flight at the airport and sees his grandkids, or any of those heartwarming dog commercials. (Excuse me a moment, I need to get a tissue.)

Jo and I were spending a lot of time together, even when not with the others. One night I was walking Jo back to her dorm—all the women on campus were required by local law to live in one of the dormitories. It was interesting that men attending Murray State had the choice to live in a dorm or off-campus, unless they got in trouble. And, of course, I got into trouble.

Trouble found me during my first year at Murray. It was when I was living in the trailer park just a fifteen-minute walk off campus. My first infraction with the school administration and the first of two "jail sentences" in the men's dorm (I was sentenced to confinement in the men's dorm for a week under supervision) was because of my dogs.

Yes dogs. Seven of them to be exact. It all started when I said that I missed not having a dog. It's not that I always had dogs, but just before going away to college my mother had allowed a dog, a cute cocker spaniel, into our apartment in Brooklyn. The dog died after a few months due to distemper and I had been bitten by the desire to have another dog to nurture. One of our friends on campus, Joe the Fish, complied by knocking on the trailer door early one morning and dropping this cute mutt on my chest as I slept.

Awakened by the dog's kisses, I said "He's really cute, like Benton," which had become a standing joke among the guys. Benton was a small, very cute town north of Murray that was the first small town I observed when driving into Kentucky on the way to school that first year. "So, this is Benton," I said as Steve drove down Main Street, "Benton is cute, Benton is good," I said. From that point on, anything that was either cute or good was "That's good, like Benton." So, Benton became the dog's name.

I could not keep Benton in the trailer because he smelled like a dog and in the close quarters of a trailer that would have been a disaster for everyone. Benton would sleep outside, under the trailer at night and I would feed him in the morning and Benton would then take the short walk with me to the campus and wait outside the buildings while I was in classes. Benton would mostly sleep in a corner under the bushes until I came out and went to the next class. At the end of the day we would walk back to the trailer park together and I would feed him again.

What happened next was an interesting phenomenon. Benton brought a beagle home to the trailer one day and after feeding them both, I found that the beagle went everywhere that Benton went. I eventually named the beagle Angel. A few days later, there was another dog, it was a small mutt. After a few days of regular visits, the mutt became a part of the family as well and he was named Tiny. Next was a three-legged collie that was appropriately named Lassie. She was followed by a big white and black-spotted Dalmatian which we called Firetruck. A week later there were two other dogs, both mutts, but both big dogs, one a Sheppard mix and the last a short-haired dog that could have been some sort of terrier.

Seven dogs in all. And all of them hanging around the trailer park. I suspected that two of the dogs were actually owned by two different families at the trailer park but they didn't care that my friends and I were feeding them. They all appeared to sleep under the trailer at night which provided the dogs with a certain amount of warmth.

One night I found out why Eskimos in Alaska refer to the cold nights as a "three-dog night" or a "four-dog night." On those really brutal Alaskan nights, they bring in their huskies and have them sleep on top of their blankets for the added warmth that they provide. On one very cold night, with the temperature down into the teens, I felt bad for the dogs huddled together under the trailer. With the outside temperature dropping and even the dishwater in the trailer sink beginning to freeze, I brought the dogs in, fearing that they would freeze to death. There were only four of them under the trailer at that time. And when three of them climbed on top of me I found that they provided the extra warmth that was needed that night. Hence, I had my own Three Dog Night.

The next morning, after feeding the dogs and chasing them out of the trailer, I got ready to leave for classes. This time, however, along with Benton beside me, I found that all seven dogs had gathered outside the trailer and were escorting me to school. They walked together down the road to Five Points, across 641 to the beginning of campus and across the campus to where my first class was about to begin. I waved the dogs away and they just hovered at the door. A few minutes later, while sitting in English Lit class, I could hear a bunch of dogs barking and howling outside the classroom window. The noise let up after a while, but occasionally picked up again with some intensity.

An hour later, upon leaving the building on my way to the next class,

I was greeted and surrounded by seven loving dogs. After petting all of them we walked across campus to the next class where the dogs continued to hang out until I appeared before them once again. This went on until I was ready to walk home in which seven dogs joined the parade back to the trailer park. Back at the trailer I gave them all a treat and left them outside to play. This scenario repeated itself daily for the next week or so until one day, when exiting class, I found the dogs surrounding one of the campus police, who had his gun draw and was shouting profanities at the dogs.

"Don't shoot, they're mine," I screamed. "Yes, I know, but they better back off or I'll kill em all," the officer cried. "Over here, c'mere, NOW," I called to the dogs. Benton led the way, as usual, and they all followed. Now surrounding and jumping up on me, I greeting them, petted them and asked the officer, "What's wrong, what happened?" The campus police officer returned his gun to his holster and told me, "You need to come wit me to the Dean's office. Now."

I had no idea what I had done, but immediately told the dogs to stay in which several of them lay down while I went with the officer towards the Administration Building to see the Dean. The dogs followed quietly, maybe sensing that something was wrong.

Once there, we were immediately greeted by the Dean who pointed out the window towards the sound of dogs barking asking, "Are those dogs yours?" I nodded and softly said, "Yes sir." The Dean then barked "One, git them off campus NOW. And two, you are hereby detained for the next week in the dormitory. Not git." I turned to leave, but turning back said, "Sir," then hesitated for a moment before saying, "I don't live in the dorm." This time it was the Dean's turn to hesitate. "Well, well, now," he said, "Then we will make arrangements. See me in my office tomorrow at two o'clock and we will have a dorm room for your confinement for the next week."

I did stay in the dorm in a room that connected by an adjoining bathroom to another room with a student that was supposed to monitor me. I slept there for two nights and left on Friday because there was no one else around to see that I stayed. It made no sense to monitor myself.

Meanwhile, it was now a cold December night when walking Jo back to the dorm after dinner at the College Grille which was across the street from her dorm. I walked her up the steep steps leading to the big doors that kept hundreds of coeds hidden behind the thick gray walls of Wells Hall.

We stopped at the top plateau and stepped aside to stand behind one of the tall, thick columns that stood on either side of the doors. The columns were so wide that they hid the two of us from view inside where matronly monitors watched every move that the coeds made to ensure that they did nothing to betray the archaic traditions of chastity. This was still a time of separation of boy and girl until they wed. It may have been the 1960s, but just as Calloway County was a dry region, it too was a chaste county.

Both Jo and I knew what was about to happen and there was no hesitation by either of us. We had both waited a long time for this to happen. The moon was bright and lit up the area surrounding the front of the dorm. The air was cold and crisp. We were holding hands as we walked up the steps. We turned towards each other simultaneously. I took Jo's other hand for a brief moment. Then let go of her left hand and reached up to her cheek and slightly behind her neck, bringing her face close to mine. Our eyes were locked on each other. Our faces moved closer, lips touched for just a moment and parted then came together for a long, hard emotional kiss.

Several other students standing near the doors applauded. It was well known that we two young lovebirds had only just united. Jo smiled. I smiled. We kissed again. And then one of the matrons tapped me on the shoulder with, "That's quite enough young man. You will not devour this young girl on my watch." We were stunned. We were caught. The matron then said, "You, Miss Gomes, go inside this instant and wait for me at the front desk. You sir, will wait right here for the campus police who will take good care of you." It was only moments before one of the campus police cars pulled up. The matron actually took my ear in her hand and led me down the stairs never letting go of my ear until I was in custody by the waiting police. "In the car fella," said the policeman. I quietly obeyed.

Jo received a week's detention in the dormitory. She was allowed out only to attend classes. Over the weekend she wasn't allowed out at all. It could have been worse, but this was her first offense and they were lenient. My punishment was another week in the men's dorm in which I too was restricted to the dorm after classes. However, again I stayed only two nights. This time I was paroled because as photo editor and assistant news editor on the College News, I was needed to cover some major campus activities over the weekend.

"Was it worth the kiss?" Jerry asked me on my return home after my brief incarceration in the dormitory. "I'll never forget that moment," I said.

CHAPTER EIGHTEEN

SUCCESS SOURS AS I UNDERMINE MYSELF

He said I wanna see you again, but I'm stuck in colder weather
Maybe tomorrow will be better, can I call you then?
She said you're ramblin' man, and You ain't ever gonna change
You got a gypsy soul to blame, and you were born for leavin'
• • • • • • •

"Colder Weather" by Zac Brown Band

By my junior year I was one of the editors on the College News, had started an underground newsletter to enable students to talk about issues that the College News wouldn't touch, was an officer in Alpha Phi Omega, the service fraternity, ran the very successful Nowhere Coffee House for the United Campus Ministry and was now in love with Joanne. But the moral code in Kentucky at that time would not allow even hand-holding on campus, let alone kissing. And we wanted to live together. So naturally we decided to get married. Yes, it was a very impulsive move, but we decided that our families needed to know and they talked us into waiting until the summer, and if we still felt that way, they would hold a wedding for us.

Waiting was hard. We couldn't really get together for fear of getting caught and being expelled. The forced waiting made our forbidden love seem larger than life. In retrospect, if we had been allowed to cohabitate, we probably would never have gotten married. But we had this unresolved desire and when summer came, our families met in Rhode Island and we were married overlooking a quiet lake with a small reception for family and friends in her parent's home.

Back on campus in Murray we rented and moved into a small two-family house just off campus and easy walking distance to classes. We also celebrated back on campus and our friends welcomed opportunities to party at our house all year long, including a surprise celebration for our first anniversary a year later. But the real surprise was when we announced on that same first anniversary evening, a year to the day after we were married, that we were splitting up and going separate ways.

Our friends were shocked. There were no outward signs that there were problems and many of our friends thought we were the ideal couple on campus. Jo and I were friends, but the marriage went astray and living together was not working, most likely because of my insecurities and immaturity. I was not ready to be married. I loved her dearly, respected her immensely, but I was not mature enough for a committed relationship, for any relationship. I failed to hold the marriage together, but no one knew there was trouble in Camelot.

Joanne and I split on our first anniversary, but remained friends for years after until she disappeared on tour with the "Maharajah something or other."

I had graduated soon after we separated and was working several jobs in addition to the Nowhere Coffee House. I did a weekly radio show at WNBS, worked part time as a reporter on the Murray Democrat, the local newspaper and I was caretaker at a swimming pool at the local country club where I also coached young kids for their swim team. Among these kids were two very talented girls from the Boone Laundry family, one of the most prominent families in town. This had helped me with connections to both the radio station and the newspaper. All these jobs together provided me with a comfortable living in Murray. I was doing a number of things that I loved such as MC at the coffee house, telling stories on the radio while playing Top 40 music, being a reporter for the newspaper and coaching the kids in swimming.

But just as I self destructed my Camelot marriage with Jo, I allowed my absurd mind to undermine everything else with one ego-crazed act. It began when my friend Tony asked me to do him a favor. Tony worked as the Top 40 DJ on WNBS Radio and I enjoyed riding shotgun with him as navigator in his British racing green Triumph TR-4 as we traveled the country roads of Calloway County on rally road races that we never won but had great fun piecing together a puzzle with clues provided along the route.

Tony needed to visit a friend out of town and asked me to fill in for him on a particular Saturday morning Top 40 show. The catch was that I had to handle a scheduled visit and planned live radio interview with the six young contestants for Miss Kentucky that would be competing for the opportunity to go to the Miss America contest. Interviewing them was not something I wanted to do. It was contrary to all that I believed in. And in those college days, beliefs were crucial to existence. I had no respect for beauty pageants and all that they stood for, especially the surface beauty that resulted in the crowning of some young girl that may have had a beautiful face and body, but no brains.

Sorry if I just offended millions of people. I know that many of today's beauty pageants are populated by talented and intelligent young ladies. But how important is it to win a "beauty" contest and what does it really mean. How can we, as an intelligent population place so much credence and importance on the beauty that is only skin deep. With this in mind, I still had to interview those six young ladies on Saturday morning. My mind began to whirl with ideas on how to do this effectively.

All that week I told my listeners that I would be uncovering and revealing the real winner of the Miss Kentucky contest on air Saturday morning ahead of the judges and audience which wouldn't be seeing them until Saturday night at the University auditorium. Word spread and a lot of people were talking about the fact that the six finalists would be on radio with me Saturday morning.

Saturday morning finally came and so did the six young girls vying for Miss Kentucky. I was already on air and publicly welcomed the girls as they entered the radio studio and took their seats at a long table opposite me. We had positioned microphones at each seat so each of them could answer questions posed to them. Here's how the live, on air interview went.

"Well folks, here they are, the six finalists for Miss Kentucky. You will be able to see them tonight live on stage at the MSU auditorium where a group of honorable judges will vote and choose one of these wonderful young ladies as Miss Kentucky 1968. But first, here and now I will reveal the real Miss Kentucky here in our WNBS studios. Welcome girls."

A chorus of "hello", "good morning sir" and "howdy" followed from the girls.

"Now girls, I have been promising my listeners all week long that I, and I alone, will reveal, and I mean really reveal, the true Miss Kentucky here this morning. So I first need y'all to disrobe."

Giggles from a couple of the girls could be heard on the radio.

"That's right girls, I need y'all to take your clothes off so I can reveal the real beauty of the next Miss Kentucky here."

More giggles. Nothing more than some shy giggles as the girls began to fidget not knowing what the hell was going on other than some radio jock was making some absurd statements.

"Come on girls, I promised my listeners that I would reveal your true beauty and I can't reveal anything until you undress and let me see what you have underneath those cute dresses." This time there were less giggles from the girls.

Then I said, "Okay, Mary Beth is now taking her blouse off revealing a very cute bra." For the record, Mary Beth was sitting there giggling until I singled her out and now she was sitting there blushing.

"Great, now we have Betty Sue taking her sweater off and wow, she is not wearing a bra." For the record, Betty Sue sat there staring back at me with arms crossed and face turning a crimson red.

"Now let's see if we can get the rest of the girls to undress. Wow, I wish you could see what I. . . . ."

With that, the studio "On Air" light went out and music was being piped over the airwaves. I was cut off. The assistant manager came into the studio and told everyone that the interview session was over. The girls got up to leave. One of them even reached out to shake my hand and say thank you. They mumbled to each other as they left the studio.

A stern-faced young assistant manager said: "You went over the cliff this time, Kahn. Mr. [the station owner] called. You have been fired effective immediately. Please leave."

I left the studio and when I got back to my house, the phone was ringing. It was a call from the publisher of the Murray Democrat, the local newspaper at which I worked part time. He was calling to tell me that I was fired for what I had done on the radio that morning. It was less than an hour since I was on air doing my mock interview imaginarily exposing the six Miss Kentucky contestants and I had been fired from both of my main jobs.

A short while later I got a call from Mrs. Boone asking me to stop by her house to discuss what I had done. News travels very, very fast in a small town. I hopped on my motorcycle, a 650 cc Jawa (Czechoslovakian bike) and rode out to the Boone home.

Mrs. Boone opened the door and at first smiled at me. Then she gave me one of those mother-like head shakes slowly side to side, back and forth, pursing her lips. She had an envelope in her hand. She handed it to me and said: "I am so sorry, but we can't have you coaching our swim team any longer. You were wonderful and we will miss you. My girls will miss you. They have learned so much from you. But your childish act on the radio this morning has reverberated across town and I have no choice but to fire you."

I tried to explain that it was just a silly stupid joke. She said: "You're a good person, but you crossed the line and angered too many important people. My husband and I can't save you from this."

I took the envelope, thanked her, got on my bike and rode back home. That evening at the Nowhere Coffee House, one of the Ministers came by in a rare appearance and took me aside to talk. "You probably should take a leave and let the others manage things for a while. Everything is running well anyway and you probably need a break to straighten things out. Any references that you need you can count on our United Campus Ministry to provide. For now, let the others manage Nowhere." Suddenly, I was nowhere.

I had now lost all four jobs and was most likely *persona non grata* around Murray. The ultimate message came one day later when, on Sunday morning, I was returning from town on my Jawa when a police car pulled me over with flashing lights and loud speaker blaring "Pull over." I immediately did.

The officer walked over to me and said. "Your motorcycle is too loud. I can give you a ticket for that you know." I apologized, knowing that nothing was wrong with the muffler, and said that I would take it to a local mechanic to have it checked out.

He then said: "I strongly suggest that you take it back to where you came from, you are no longer wanted here in Murray. I suggest you leave town as soon as possible." With that he turned and got back in his car.

I stood there beside my bike on Main Street in Murray, Kentucky—frozen in place. I had come to love Murray. I had worked hard to become accepted. I had lived there more than six years. I felt at home. Murray, Kentucky had become my home. My driver's license said so. My friends said so. My heart said so.

As I stood there frozen in place on a hot August afternoon in Murray, Kentucky in 1968, a rush of thoughts cascaded through my mind: Did one impetuous act of rebelliousness destroy everything I had built over the past few years? Where would I go now? I had split with Jo. I couldn't go live with my parents because they had moved and there was no longer any room or bed for me in their house. Anytime I visited I had to sleep on a tiny hard-surface couch in the foyer right by the front door.

The only thing I had was a new found confidence in myself gained over the many years of growth and learning at Murray State. However, this confidence had a false bottom that, in time, would eventually give way. For now, I was determined to use that confidence to return to New York and find a job as a journalist.

I had no choice.

CHAPTER NINETEEN

AUSTRALIA: LONG WAY TO GO FOR A FAVORITE STOP

"Your living is determined not so much by what life brings to you
as by the attitude you bring to life;
not so much by what happens to you as by the way
your mind looks at what happens."
•••••••
Khalil Gibran

Thanks to my lucky break in getting a reporting job at *Aviation Week &*
Space Technology, followed by my move to *The Travel Agent* magazine, I
was off on some of the most sought-after trips to destinations I had only
dreamed about. Australia, the land down under that was closest in kinship
to America, was one of those destinations. Once again, it was a planned
press trip in which I chose to attend.

We boarded our Qantas 747 in Los Angeles headed for Sydney, Australia
and I relaxed the moment I got onboard and received my first glass of wine
from the flight attendant. We were on a press trip, seated in Business Class
and I was in the front row with plenty of leg room to stretch out my six-
foot, three-inch frame without tripping anyone. Robin, a public relations
consultant for Australia tourism, was seated across the aisle from me and we
were good business friends often meeting for drinks after work at the Pig

& Whistle in Manhattan and chatting late into the night. I loved flying in those days. It was the 1970s and I was a happy editor at *The Travel Agent* magazine traveling around the world.

We took our shoes off, put on the Qantas-supplied slippers from the seat pocket and sat back to enjoy good food, wine and conversation. We would get up and walk around the spacious lounge area on the 747s in those days and enjoy a long, but relaxed flight "down under" to what would become one of my favorite destinations in the world.

We landed, checked into our hotel and headed over to the tourist office to meet with the Australian officials. We spent the afternoon there at one meeting after another. It was all business. We learned everything that they could cram into an afternoon session and at five o'clock the staff were shutting down and leaving.

We quickly discovered that nearly everyone was heading for one pub or another to have a quick drink or two before heading home, out to dinner or whatever. The head of the tourist office asked us to join them at dinner, and a few of us also agreed to accompany them for their happy-hour drinking before going to the restaurant.

Observation #1 about Australia:

The Aussies, as they called themselves, worked hard all day and played just as hard all night. I liked that about them. They were very honest, serious people who were very conscientious about work. But when they left the office, they took their leisure time just as serious and enjoyed every waking moment.

I admired them and wanted to emulate them. We drank and talked and met more people at the first pub we visited. Then we went to a second pub where we were supposed to meet some other officials for dinner. We drank there for longer than I expected and some of the journalists on the trip with us decided to return the hotel without dinner. Those of us that were left, continued to drink, finally had dinner, and then went to a third pub for a nightcap or two. I got back to my hotel in the early morning hours and fell into bed.

I awoke later that morning for a free day to do whatever we wished. I planned on visiting one of the local beaches near Sydney. I knew several others that were also planning to go to the beach as it was mid-January and we New Yorkers were sun-deprived, while Australia was experiencing its wonderful early summer weather. I had a leisurely breakfast by myself and headed out to find the right bus to take to the beach.

Once there I walked along a crowded beach filled with Europeans, Asians. New Zealanders and some Australians. There were quite a few women sunbathing topless. I wasn't sure where they were from, but assumed they were Europeans. Few people were swimming because earlier that day there were shark sightings just beyond the swimming area off the beach. Some brave children were in the water and a few bold men and women were swimming not too far from the shore. I stood with my feet in the waves at the shore, but did not go for a swim. There were no further shark sightings, no one was hurt or even threatened and everything was back to normal the next day as if there never was a shark in the area. It was commonplace in Australia and the reaction of the Aussies was simply "no worries."

The sun was strong and I needed to get back to my hotel to rest, shower and get ready for our press dinner that night. I didn't get enough sleep the night before and the sun was beginning to get to me. I left the beach and went to the bus stop where I had gotten off to find the bus back to my hotel. Only the bus route was not as simple as that. The bus that I took to get there did not go directly back to my hotel. I had to take a different bus which would take me on a much more direct return route to where I began my day. I was suitably and justifiably confused.

I turned to question two older women (this reference may need some clarification—I was 34 at this time and they were probably in their mid-50s). I asked them which was the bus that would get me back to my hotel. The bus stop area was crowded and I had noticed different destinations listed on each of the signs where buses were stopping, but none of them matched where I was hoping to go. These two women, who were waiting there at the bus stop in the queue right behind me, looked at each other and one turned to me and said: "Just follow us. We'll get you there."

One of them took my hand and led me to the next bus stop where we joined yet another queue. When the first bus came along they explained that it was not the right bus for me, "You can get there on that bus, but it will end up being a long walk for you when you get back into Sydney." Two more buses came along and both times they said, "No, not yours. We will wait for yours to come."

While we were waiting, we began to talk as they asked questions about who I was and what I was doing there and I asked similar questions of them. We had been waiting nearly fifteen minutes and it was still hot. When the correct bus did come, they told me to follow them onto the bus and they even paid for my ticket because I did not have the right change.

On the bus I sat next to one of them who gave me a sightseeing review along the route explaining the significance of some of the local parks we were passing and the difference between the local residences and the business districts. "You have to find a place to live outside of the business district so you can separate work from play," one of them told me. Finally, twenty long minutes later they said, "it's time to get off and we will show you which way it is to your hotel."

We exited together at the foot of a bridge with a large walkway. Not sure what the bridge crossed, but they pointed out my hotel to me. It was over the bridge and just a few blocks past. I could see it over the smaller buildings that faced us. I thanked them and asked them if they would like to have a drink with me before they continue on home. They declined, explaining "We would have loved to, but we need to catch the next bus back to the beach where we started so that we can get our bus home."

It took me a moment to realize what had just happened and that they went completely out of their way including a twenty-minute bus ride to get me back to my hotel. I asked them why, "You could have just put me on the correct bus and I would have been fine." They both smiled, almost in stereo saying, "We just wanted to make sure that you didn't get lost on your first day in Sydney."

We hugged and kissed and suddenly their bus was there and they got on before I could get phone numbers or addresses so I could properly thank them. It didn't matter to them. They were just happy to have been able to help a stranger. It was indicative of what I found in Australia.

Observation #2 about Australia:

People will help anyone and everyone and often go out of their way, especially for strangers and they will never expect anything in return. They know that they are doing for others as they would like others to do for them and it will happen over and over again. It was a way of life; the Golden Rule lives on in Australia.

The next day the eight reporters on the trip, six from the US and two from Canada, were taken on a morning sightseeing trip on a small bus ending up for lunch at the far end of Sydney Harbour at Doyle's Restaurant, hosted by Peter Doyle himself. Peter Doyle was a famous entrepreneur in Australia. He typified the Australian personality of working hard and playing harder. His great-grandfather supposedly was a Brit who was sent to prison in Australia at a time when Great Britain used Australia as a penal colony. The Doyle family evolved into an influential wealthy family and Doyle's Restaurant was one of the best in the area.

Following a lengthy lunch of multiple appetizers, plenty of shrimp, a great plate of fish and then multiple deserts, we were supposed to get back on the bus and head back to our hotel to change for our VIP performance at the famous Sydney Opera House which sits prominently in Sydney Harbour. The tourist office had secured VIP seating for us in the 4th row center with other VIPs from the Australian entertainment industry for this, the opening event of the season. However, Peter Doyle had sent the bus back to Sydney telling the tourist office that he would either put us in taxis or take us back to Sydney by boat.

At three o'clock, two hours after we had arrived at Doyle's, we were just getting served our lunch. You see, Peter Doyle liked to entertain—and drink—and we had many drinks, and many appetizers. Also, Peter Doyle was enjoying telling us stories about the history of Australia as a penal colony and how his family evolved from crooks to credible business people. And we reporters were soaking up the stories as well as the drinks. It was a great lunch, enjoying the outdoor fresh air setting on the patio facing the Sydney Harbour with the Sydney skyline in the distance.

It was a perfect afternoon. The breeze off of the water cooled us enough. The food was more than abundant and the conversation was exhilarating with Peter Doyle leading the way with his stories and also enticing us to share our stories with him. Everyone told stories that day. We all got to learn things about each other as well.

Suddenly it was 5:30 p.m. We were supposed to be back at the hotel changing for our transport and seven o'clock VIP entrance to the Sydney

Opera House. The restaurant manager came out to our group and told Peter that the tourist office wanted to know "Where are our journalists?" Peter's answer was: "I have kidnapped them and I am holding them for ransom, but I have not yet decided what I want in return for giving them back."

Several frantic calls from the tourist office including one from the director of tourism himself, Peter Doyle assured him that we would be leaving the restaurant shortly and he would be personally escorting us back to Sydney on his boat. The boat trip across the Harbour would take about thirty-five minutes so Peter decided he could leave at six o'clock and get us to the Sydney Opera House on time for our VIP entrance.

He did not think we needed to change since we were all dressed well enough, the men in nice slacks and shirts and the women in nice dresses or pants with nice blouses. He told us everyone else would be dressed in tuxedos or other stuffy suits, but we would be more comfortable. We were young journalists so we were indeed more comfortable in our relaxed out-fits. Naturally, we all agreed with him.

Assurances made to the tourist office, we continued to share stories, eat and drink. I was having one of the best afternoons of my life. Peter Doyle was the center of it and he was having as much fun as we were. He didn't want it to end and neither did we.

Finally, after a six-hour lunch at Doyle's Restaurant, we did board his boat, a forty-foot cabin cruiser, and began sailing across the Sydney Harbour. Our destination, the famous Sydney Opera House sitting on the Sydney Harbour with its futuristic modern design welcoming all to Sydney, Australia. There would be no problem arriving by boat since the Opera House faced the Harbour and had a huge pier adjacent to its entrance. Guests sometimes reached the Opera House by boat. But our entrance was to become historic.

Our now drunken and raucous group of journalists sang and continued to party our way across the Harbour. Our thirty-five-minute trip took lon-ger than usual as Peter insisted that Maggie, one of our group of journalists, take the controls and steer the boat. Maggie had never steered anything on the water before, but she was game.

It began innocently enough. Marvin Perton (another reporter) and I sat on the front bow and hung our feet over the edge enjoying the up and down movement of the boat as we navigated the undulating waves of the Harbour. Suddenly Maggie turned the boat into the waves. We laughed as the boat splashed forward and we got a little wet. She, however, thought she did something wrong, which she didn't, but she tried to correct this by making a sharp left turn.

Marvin and I were sitting on the right side of the boat and when the boat lurched left, we kept going right—right off the front of the boat. I caught the railing and held on. Marvin caught my leg and held on. We could hear Peter laughing above us as we screamed, Maggie screamed, everybody screamed. Peter grabbed the controls, righted the boat and brought it to a quick stop resulting in the waves rising up over the bow drenching everyone including those sitting on the bow along with Marvin and I who were hanging off the bow.

Peter's crew members rushed to help us back on the boat and while we were a little in shock, we were too drunk to realize what really had just happened, and what had nearly happened, so we just laughed along with everyone else who were laughing at us. Peter Doyle laughed the loudest. "This is the best press group ever," he declared. We were proud of that. We then continued on to the Sydney Opera House where the tourist office along with the opera house officials were now waiting for our arrival.

Peter had radioed ahead to let them know we were running late and told us that they were angry at him, but he took all the blame so we had nothing to be concerned about. Nothing to worry about other than we were all soaking wet and we were going to the opera. Actually, Maggie was still dry. Most of the group were just wet. Marvin and I were dripping. Our shoes were wet and when we walked, they made that squish squish sound that you would expect from wet shoes.

We arrived at the opera house and slowly walked off the boat to the shocked faces of the tourist office executives and the opera house officials. They never asked what happened. They just quickly conferred and decided that there was no time for us to go back to the hotel and change. We stood there on the pier and waited for instruction. They simply said "follow us" and we did. "squish, squish, squish" as we walked along the pier to the entrance of the opera house. It was a magnificent sight. Not us, the Sydney Opera House. There is no other building like it in the world. I felt like I was entering a very special place with steel and glass welcoming you inside to the magnificent chandeliers, red carpeted stairways and an auditorium like nowhere else.

As we walked down the red carpeted isles to our VIP seats you could see all the heads and eyes of the dignitaries turning to face our group of VIP journalists. All you could hear was the "squish, squish, squish" of our shoes. We took our seats and sat there wet and watched the performance as if nothing had happened and this was perfectly normal.

Observation #3

Everything is normal in Australia. Nothing is considered out of line or extraordinary. Everyone accepted you for what you were with no exceptions. Maybe it comes from the history of the Continent being a penal colony at its beginnings or just from the accepting and welcoming culture of the people, but it works for all.

Observation #4:

Peter Doyle and his irreverent attitude towards authority is indicative of the attitude of the people, but there also is the feeling of respect for other people and ideas. It makes for a personality and culture that always welcomes others no matter who they are or where they come from as long as they don't try and dictate what you need to do or who you need to be.

I loved Australia so much that several years later, when I had an opportunity to take another brief trip to Sydney for the release of a White Paper on World Aviation, I jumped at the chance to spend more time with the Aussies.

This time, however, we left New York on a Friday night, arriving twenty-seven hours later on Sunday morning in a different time zone that was fourteen hours ahead of New York. I had a great time getting together with my friends and associates in Sydney that day and a fantastic dinner and party that night. I was severely hung over Monday morning when I showed up for the press conference where they were releasing this important White Paper that would change the way aviation regulations were negotiated by nations around the world. I took notes, interviewed a couple of officials from a variety of countries, and taped all the interviews.

I remembered the time when I was granted an exclusive interview with Joel Nadel, president of Nationwide Leisure Company, a major travel agency chain, which had gone bust leaving thousands of clients stranded and allegedly responsible for millions of dollars missing. Hundreds of travel agents were now out of work and thousands of people had lost vacations and money. It was, at that time, the largest "bust-out" of a travel company ever, impacting thousands of people and leaving them with un-booked or false vacation vouchers and no way to get their money back. The president, of the company wanted to tell his side of the story before possibly going to jail and chose me to hear it exclusively, complete with details of how, why, and who else was involved.

We sat down in his hotel room at the Grand Hyatt on 42nd Street above Grand Central Station in New York City. With a glass of water in front of him, he began to unfold this amazing story with lots of anecdotes. I had both my note pad and my trusty tape recorder. I put in a fresh tape which would last 45 minutes. I checked my pen, flipped open my note pad and sat back.

He began his detailed and lengthy story and asked me not to interrupt him. I could ask questions at the end, but he did not want to be interrupted while he unfolded a tale of deceit which would incriminate several other prominent travel industry people. I took only a few notes at the beginning and then sat back as I was so enthralled by his story. At the end, he stood up, asked if I had any questions. He was sweating profusely. He excused himself and left the room for the bathroom. I picked up my tape recorder, mostly unused notepad and left the room.

I got back to my office and now I was sweating as I was about to replay this amazing tale and write my story for my magazine. Only there was nothing on the tape. I had forgotten to press "record."

So, there I was, hung over in Australia, which was not unusual, but I did remember to press record on my tape recorder as I interviewed airline executives from Qantas, Singapore Airlines, Lufthansa and American Airlines. Following the press conference I was quickly escorted to a taxi and back to the airport and my return flight to New York. It was twenty-four hours later and I touched down at Kennedy Airport. It was Monday night.

I had been gone technically three days from Friday night to Monday night with associated time zone changes. I had spent fifty-one hours in the air and only twenty-eight hours in Sydney, Australia. But I would gladly do it again just to be there. Australia remains one of my all-time favorite destinations to visit outside the US, and it is the Australian people that make it so attractive.

CHAPTER TWENTY

FROM BROOKLYN TO JAMAICA AND BACK

Get along while we can
Always give love the upper hand
Paint a wall, learn to dance
Call your mom, buy a boat
Drink a beer, sing a song
Make a friend, can't we all get along
•••••••

"Get Along" sung by Kenny Chesney

While Australia and Greece are two of my three favorite destinations (I've saved the best for last in Chapter 34), the country that I have visited the most over the years is Jamaica, an island in the Caribbean that holds a very special place in my heart and provides many vivid and fond memories. One year, around 1985, I traveled to Jamaica a total of seven times for a variety of reasons including a hotel industry convention and a travel agent education seminar. But let me get back to the beginning where my love of Jamaica and the Jamaican people first began.

Growing up in the 1950s in Brooklyn we lived in a very mixed, but totally white neighborhood. My neighborhood was dominated by Italians, Irish and Jews. It was the small Kensington section of the vast area called Flatbush. Most of the Jewish families lived in the apartment buildings that lined the main avenues. Most of the Italian and Irish families lived in the private homes that lined the side streets. We played in the streets in those days and hung out mostly on the side streets to avoid the car and bus traffic on the main avenues. Stickball, touch football and stoopball were the games we played in the streets.

Stickball was a simple form of street baseball in which a thin stick bat was used to hit a pink rubber ball about the same size of a baseball, but very soft. The game could be played by as few as two people, one pitching and one hitting with designated spots that the batter could hit for singles, doubles, triples and home runs. If there were enough players, we would actually run bases, often using parked cars as first and third base and manhole covers as second base and home plate. It was not easy to hit the ball with the thin stick bat. Although my neighbor Michael seemed to have the eye and ability to smack the ball every time he got up. I, on the other hand, could handle the outfield and catch, but was terrible at bat.

Stoop ball may have been a Brooklyn invention. It is another variation on a baseball theme, but this time played mostly with just two persons, although additional players can play as both batters and in the field. The soft pink ball is also used here and the batter throws the ball against the stoop (the stairs leading up to the apartment building or house) and the fielder tries to catch the ball as it bounces and flies off the stoop. Positions for single, double, triple and home run as well as out of bounds are predetermined. Ground balls are fielded and thrown against the stoop by the fielder to get an out. It was also possible to play a solitary game of stoop ball throwing and catching by oneself. I played a lot by myself and was very good at stoop ball.

Touch football was another game played in the narrow side streets, but one in which at least four players were required; on one team, a passer and a receiver and on the other team one to prevent the run and one to defend the receiver. Additional receivers and defenders were added if there were enough kids to play. What made this interesting was the use of parked cars as blockers of sorts. Depending on local rules, if a passed ball hit a parked car and was then caught, it remained in play until it touched the ground. And, of course, tackling was replaced by the two-hand tag, which sometimes became a hard two-hand push as tempers flared. I was never the quarterback. I couldn't throw the ball well, but I could run and catch and I was very good on defense.

When, at age fifteen I had grown to six-foot, three-inches and 225 pounds, I went out for the Erasmus Hall High School football team. Erasmus Hall was a huge school drawing students from all over the large Flatbush section of Brooklyn. It was the oldest high school in the US, dating back to 1786. There were 8,000 students attending Erasmus in the 1950s and 60s and 2,000 kids in my graduating class of 1961. Erasmus was famous for its basketball teams. I grew up with Billy Cunningham, an NBA Hall of Famer, who played for Erasmus, went on to North Carolina and then to become a star for the Philadelphia 76ers. He and Charlie "Sparky" Donovan, a five-foot, eight-inch guard, lead Erasmus to several New York City championships.

While the basketball team was winning the City championships, the football team was going 0-7 year after year. I, therefore, joined the football team as soon as I got there. Erasmus Hall was one of the most equally-integrated high schools in Brooklyn representing diversity of the Flatbush section of the Borough. It was half white and half black. The football team, however, was mostly black and many of these black kids came from families that had roots in Jamaica and other Caribbean nations. I practiced with them, sweated with them and struggled with them as we lost game after game. I played a number of positions including right guard, back-up fullback to my friend Steve Colletti and defensive end. It was at defensive end that I had my one and only shining moment in my entire football career.

We were playing against Midwood High School, a mostly white school in a predominantly Jewish neighborhood. It was late in a losing battle, but we kept fighting on. Midwood had the ball and was going down the field to score another touchdown. The call was for a screen pass to the tight end. I stepped in front of the passing lane and the Midwood quarterback passed the ball directly at me. I intercepted the ball and ran down the field for a touchdown which brought the score close. I was a hero despite us losing the game.

When the season was over. Clarence, one of my teammates from the football team asked me if I wanted to join him and a number of other teammates for a game of pick-up football in their neighborhood on Sunday morning. He explained that they had their own off-season team that played other made-up teams each Sunday on Eastern Parkway in the East New

York section of Brooklyn. East New York was, in the 50s and 60s, (and I think still today), a predominantly black neighborhood, made up largely of Caribbean nationals who relocated to the US. I told Clarence I was in.

I arrived around eleven o'clock on a cold, snowy Sunday morning in December. We had to wait for a few of the players to get there because they had gone to church with their families. When everyone finally showed up, I noticed that I was the only white person on the team—either team. At first, I kept this to myself, hoping that they didn't notice. We were playing a regular tackle game and we wore full gear with shoulder pads and helmets. I kept my helmet on at all times hoping to hide my very white face. It was a cold December morning and the heavy gear helped keep me warm. Despite this, I was shivering. Not sure whether the shivering was from the cold or the concern for being the lone white kid in a ghetto neighborhood playing pick-up football on a Sunday morning.

I quickly found out that others on my team noticed I was white when someone in the huddle said, "Let's give it to the white guy on the next play, they won't suspect that." We broke huddle and several of the guys slapped me on the rear as we lined up. I was in the backfield at the fullback position. The quarterback took the ball and handed it off to me. I started through the line and was quickly tackled for no gain. When I got back to the huddle, Clarence said, "Well that didn't work, the white guy stands out too much." They then agreed to ignore me for a while until the opposing team forgot about me. Late in the second half it worked as I carried the ball for a long gain.

This became my weekly Sunday morning routine. I traveled an hour by bus to get to Eastern Parkway to play football. After a few weeks, I was invited to one of my teammate's home for lunch after the game. I had become an accepted member of the group. I met his Jamaican family and enjoyed family time with his brothers and sisters. They either forgot that I was white or didn't care. I forgot that I was the lone white in a black world and enjoyed my growing friendships with Jamaicans, Trinidadians, Bajans and others. It was 20 years later, in 1978, that I first went to Jamaica and began what was to become a very special relationship with many more Jamaicans.

My first trip to Jamaica, as the editor of *The Travel Agent* magazine, was as a guest of the Jamaica Tourist Board to see some new hotels that were being built. The new prime minister was trying to restore confidence in Jamaica tourism that hadn't existed for a number of years. I arrived late afternoon and was met at the airport by a very attractive light-skinned Jamaican girl. Andrea (name changed for privacy) looked like she was in her early 20s. She identified herself as my escort and guide for my stay in Jamaica. She advised me that I would be having dinner with the director of tourism that evening and she drove me to my hotel.

At the scheduled time for dinner, Andrea met me in the lobby and escorted me to the table where the director of tourism along with the public relations director were waiting to greet me. The four of us had a great dinner and the tourism director excused himself after dinner leaving me with the two women. The PR director suggested we have a drink in the bar where we could listen to music and watch people dance. They were playing reggae music and the two of them took me onto the dance floor to show me how to move like a Jamaican. I tried, but if you believe my wife, I never learned the subtle moves of a Jamaican and I move my hips too much.

The PR director then gave me the schedule for the next day, excused herself and left. Andrea offered to have another drink with me, but I was tired. She then escorted me back to my room (which I thought was odd) and stood there asking if there was anything else I needed. I thanked her, shook her hand, as she pulled my head close, kissed me on either cheek (as is customary in the Caribbean) and handed me her card telling me, "Please call me if you need anything, anything at all." She then smiled and left.

The next morning Andrea was not there to meet me for breakfast as planned. The PR director showed up while I was having breakfast and when I was finished directed me to a car with a driver and tour guide. Off we went to visit the new hotels, some just under construction and others just breaking ground. After touring I was dropped off at the tourist office for a scheduled formal interview with the tourism director. Before I got a chance to begin questioning him, he opened the interview with a very awkward question for me. "Did you not like Andrea, the girl we provided for you last night?"

I was dumbfounded. I was not sure how to reply. Crazy thoughts were rushing through my mind. Andrea worked for the tourist office. Were they pimping her out? How was I supposed to reply? I stammered. I choked on my own words. I had no idea what to say. I finally said: "She was very pretty and smart. I enjoyed talking with her. I liked her very much. I was sorry not to see her at breakfast this morning." He just smiled and said, she would pick me up for the scheduled tour later that day and have a gift for me.

I thanked him explaining: "I'm not used to getting gifts. I'm not allowed to accept gifts. The magazine frowns upon that. Even at Christmas, they don't want us to get more than a bottle of wine or something like that as a gift." He laughed and then laughed harder; "Okay, Okay, very good mon, let's hear what you need from me." And we moved into the actual interview process. I later learned that sometimes governments provide escorts for their VIP guests to ensure they are kept happy, very happy.

Andrea was waiting for me after the interview. She held her warm hand out and smiled, directing me to our car and driver that would take us on the two-day tour that was ahead of me. Andrea and I spent a lot of time together, laughed a lot and I learned a lot about Jamaica. We had a lot of fun together. I did not sleep with her.

A few years later, in 1980, I got a visit in my office at *The Travel Agent* magazine from an exuberant man with a thick Jamaican accent. He was a white Jamaican. While color is generally not an issue, there are whites, blacks and light-skinned mocha colored people all across Jamaica. Jamaicans are descendants of Europeans that settled Jamaica in the 1600s. Generations of whites and blacks grew together to make Jamaica one of the most productive and respected islands in the Caribbean. I often wonder why we can't do that in the US?

Meanwhile, back in my office, this heavy-set man with a generous smile sat before me excitedly telling me about his new hotel and how it will revolutionize resorts in the Caribbean. He was very wealthy, having earned millions of dollars through his Appliance Trading Company in which he supplied heavy duty appliances and air conditioning to residents and commercial companies. Now he was buying the defunct Bay Roc Hotel that sat adjacent to the airport in Montego Bay. His name—Gordon "Butch" Stewart and he was converting the closed Bay Roc Hotel into Sandals Montego Bay. He was a visionary.

"I will turn the airport proximity into a blessing," he told me, adding quickly: "We will stop everything when a plane is landing or taking off and have everyone wave at the plane. We will give everyone miniature sandals for doing this. We will give them drinks, all the drinks for free, all the food for free, all the activities for free. We will give them rooms filled with amenities. I am putting in Italian tile, French toiletries. The best of everything. I have traveled around the world and stayed at the best hotels in the world and I want my guests at my hotel to experience what I have experienced. Sandals Montego Bay will offer luxury not seen before in Jamaica."

When he came up for a breath, I began to ask questions and put together a feature article about this new "all-inclusive" concept that Butch Stewart was launching with Sandals Montego Bay. There was actually another hotel called Couples on the road between Montego Bay and Ocho Rios where another entrepreneur named John Issa had already begun to offer an all-inclusive package for guests, but Butch Stewart took the concept and polished it as only he could have done. At last count, Butch Stewart, along with his son Adam, oversee sixteen Sandals resorts on six Caribbean islands.

When he was opening his third resort in Jamaica he called me up from his home in Kingston, Jamaica and said: "Richie ma boy, I'm sending you a ticket to come down and see the next star in our family. You were so good to me to profile our Sandals resorts; I want to reward you with an exclusive look at the next bright star." I flew down to Kingston, had dinner with him and breakfast with the family the next morning. His daughter Jaime was 4 and his son Adam was 2. I had them both sitting on my lap for breakfast. Jaime seemed fascinated by my beard. I fed Adam breakfast. We formed a bond that morning that was special. I think they remembered years later when I sat with them when their dad was being honored with a lifetime achievement award by the Caribbean Hotel Association for his dedication to promoting the region.

After breakfast, Butch and I then flew over to Montego Bay to see the new Sandals Royal Caribbean. We traveled in his private plane. Butch was at the controls. When he sat down in the pilot's seat, he took out his gun and placed it on the console. There was another pilot along with us and he sat beside Butch and had the same controls. Normally I would have been frightened by flying with someone other than a professional pilot, but this was Butch Stewart. Nothing frightened him and nothing associated with him would ever undermine my confidence in him. I was relaxed—except for the gun that sat on the console.

Butch Stewart went on to become one of the most honored hoteliers in the world and his Sandals chain, now run by son Adam, continues to be the trendsetter in the Caribbean as the luxury all-inclusive chain. Much of this comes from a rigorous training and education program established early on for the employees. This training has resulted in an attitude that good service is an experience to be treasured. Over the years I have stayed at nearly all the Sandals in Jamaica as well as those in St. Lucia, Antigua and the Bahamas. Service is consistent with Butch Stewart's vision. To this day, every time I see Butch Stewart, he greets me with "Richie ma boy, how is my favorite travel writer?" It feels good to hear that Jamaican accent.

My love affair with Jamaica continued in the 1980s when I headed up a team that produced a series of Caribbean Sales Seminars for the Caribbean Tourism Organization (CTO). I was a volunteer president of the Greater New York Chapter of CTO, a regional organization that promoted the entire Caribbean. Along with colleagues and close friends Jim and Barbara Furey and Barbara Raskin we created, promoted and orchestrated a series of fun educational seminars to teach travel agents about the Caribbean and how to sell the region to consumers. We went from island to island doing a few of these each year. Jamaica asked us to come and do a long weekend program for them.

We did an initial scouting trip followed by a second planning trip and several other meetings all leading up to the seminar trip with more than 300 travel agents in tow. We were working closely with the director of tourism at that time, a wonderful, committed lady named Carrole Guntley who had been working in tourism for more than thirty years. I had gotten close to Carrole who was close friends with the minister of tourism who affectionately called her Bubbles (she'll kill me for that), a nickname from their childhood days together. She wanted to show the travel agents that Jamaica was more than just Montego Bay and Ocho Rios and asked that we bring the agents across the island to Kingston.

This was not my first encounter with Kingston. The city was not known for tourism for a number of years. It was the capital of Jamaica, one of the largest cities in the Caribbean and far from the calm beaches of Ocho Rios, Montego Bay and Negril. Kingston was a bustling city as compared to these resort destinations. It had an interesting pirate history, high-rise hotels and a thriving commercial center. It also had poverty and occasional demonstrations, such as the tire burning riots in the early 80s when demonstrators, raging against rising prices, blocked all access to the city with fires in the streets. Coincidentally, I was in Kingston at that time. (You can't be shocked after my track record of being in the wrong place at the wrong time as previously noted in earlier Chapters.)

We were attending a Caribbean Hotel Association Marketplace in which more than 1,500 delegates gathered from across the Caribbean and around the world to meet with each other and plan promotions to attract vacationers to the region for the following year. I was on the board of directors of the association and involved in the Caribbean Hospitality Training Institute teaching hoteliers how to better promote their individual resorts. Tony Mack, a former hotelier born in Britain and living in the Caribbean, headed up the training for the association. I worked closely with him as a volunteer. On the first day of the four-day conference, Tony took sick and was taken to the local Kingston hospital. The next day I took a taxi to visit Tony. We had to pass several spots where demonstrators were blocking the streets with tire burnings. Each time, the taxi driver spoke to the demonstrators in a clipped Jamaican lilt that I did not understand. But each time, they allowed us to pass.

We arrived at the hospital; a sprawling one-story wood building that looked very old. I was concerned, but Tony was in good spirits despite his yellow jaundice color and pain in his side. They said it was his liver and they were treating him for an assortment of potential ailments. I went to visit Tony every day. I also got the same taxi driver every day because I wanted to make sure that I got through the roadblocks. There weren't a lot of taxis stationed at our Pegasus Hotel anyway, and I made sure that Jacob, the driver I had the first day, knew I would need him at a specific time the next day.

This worked out well for me. I stayed an extra day to clear up things and see Tony once more. Jacob the taxi driver became my personal driver. On the morning I was leaving Jamaica, the protestors around Kingston had increased their demonstrations. It was now making national news in the US. American Airlines was planning on cancelling flights to Kingston. I needed to get out on the last flight. Jacob did his job. We got stopped at one barricade leading to the only road to the airport. He explained to them that I was a Jamaican and that I had a relative in the hospital that I had been caring for. A young Jamaican with a large machete in hand, looked in at me, tapped my shoulder and wished me well. They then allowed us to drive up on the sidewalk to bypass the barricade and get to the airport.

Tony Mack, died that week in Jamaica of an erupted gallbladder. Unfortunately, the missed diagnosis resulted in his death. Jim Furey spread his ashes out across the Caribbean Sea a few weeks later.

On another trip to Jamaica I was almost arrested for smuggling drugs—which I wasn't doing. It began with a late arrival on American Airlines. As soon as we got off the airplane I looked at my watch and realized that I needed to call my son Josh to read him the nightly chapter of the children's story I had been reading to him over the telephone whether I was home or away. It was now 7:15 p.m. and I wouldn't get to the hotel until 8:45 at the earliest and needed to call him before he went to sleep. I needed this nightly connection to him to provide him with consistency.

I had copied pages out of the book I was currently reading him so that I could easily read him a chapter from anywhere. The story was about a turtle and a frog. The turtle was bringing presents to the frog in hope of building a friendship. This particular chapter talked about those presents and how the turtle had to hide the presents from the other animals or they would get jealous. Someone standing nearby overheard my telephone conversation with my son and when I hung up the phone, two Jamaican policemen surrounded me and escorted me into a private room to discuss my drug deals.

They told me that they overheard the conversation with the code words I was using and knew that I was the turtle, but wanted to know who was the frog and where the drugs were hidden. It took me a while to explain everything to them, but they didn't believe me until they contacted Carrole Guntley who vouched for me and explained who I was. I think the police still thought I was dealing drugs, but they let me go on Carrole's insistence.

Back in Montego Bay with Carrole Guntley and the travel agent seminar several years later, everything went well until Sunday when I was scheduled to return to New York. Early in the day we heard that there were issues with flights and that my flight home from Montego Bay might be cancelled. I spoke to Carrole explaining that I needed to get home that night because I was scheduled to appear at my six-year-old son's class on Monday morning to do a magic show for the class to celebrate Josh's birthday.

Carrole immediately made some calls. She didn't designate this to someone else. She made the calls herself to make sure that Air Jamaica re-routed me and got me on another flight to get me home Sunday night. When I got to the airport, I was told I would be on a flight from Montego

Bay to Miami where I would connect to an Air Jamaica flight coming from Kingston to Miami and then on to New York.

There was chaos in Montego Bay as several flights were cancelled that day including the Miami flight I was supposed to be on. I managed to get to the gate attendant. I told him what was supposed to happen. He looked at the record and said he could do nothing. I called Carrole, who was now at a dinner party. This was before cell phones, so it was not easy to reach anyone. But Carrole somehow got the message and worked her magic as I was given the last seat on a flight from Montego Bay to Kingston where I was then given one of the last seats on a flight to Philadelphia.

When I arrived in Philly, I had no idea what I would then do, but figured I could take the next train out to Penn Station in New York City and then get home. But when I arrived and exited the plane there was a Jamaican man standing with a sign with my name on it. He said, "I'm here mon to take you home to Brooklyn. Where da ya live?" Carrole had arranged to have someone from the Jamaica tourist board Philly office have a car ready for me.

I got home at six o'clock in the morning, showered, changed, got my bag of magic tricks and did some magic of my own, but nothing compared to the magic that Air Jamaica and my Jamaican friends had done to get me home.

Jamaica always seems to do something to ease the mind. On one trip to Grand Lido resort in the fall of 1990, I was relaxing in a hammock with Linda. We were only dating for a little more than three months at that time and I took her away for the first of what would eventually be many weekend escapes to Jamaica. As we relaxed in the hammock and enjoyed the cool Caribbean breeze, I couldn't help myself and blurted out, "I think I am falling in love with you." With that, she leaped up and screamed: "No you don't. Don't say that. I'm not ready." As she suddenly leaped off the hammock, causing it to spin quickly—with me in it—I became wrapped in a net hanging innocently between two tall trees. I hung there suspended in both the air and in time. I said nothing further and eventually Linda helped unravel me. That was just the beginning.

Linda continued to unravel and steady me and in 1993, she finally agreed to marry me. At first, we were not going to have a big wedding, but I like parties and she agreed to a Sunday afternoon wedding at Thatched

Cottage on the water in Centerport, New York. It was late January when we began planning the wedding for May and we forgot to plan a honeymoon. Sooooo, we turned once again to Butch Stewart and ended up at Sandals St. Lucia where we enjoyed a five-day escape, including playing golf with the cows. But that's another story.

Over the years I have grown to love the Caribbean. I often joke that I was born in the Caribbean; the Brooklyn suburb of the Caribbean. Today, there must be more than a million Caribbean nationals living in Brooklyn. I played football with some of those Caribbean nationals a long time ago. They were my friends long before I ever traveled to the Caribbean. They helped me see the vast variety of colors in a black and white world.

CHAPTER TWENTY-ONE

SPAIN: I SHOULD HAVE LEARNED THE LANGUAGE

"Would you please speak Spanish when you are in my class. I will tolerate your buffoonery if you say it in Spanish…and you just might pass this class."
•••••••
Miss Yagerman, my 9th grade homeroom and Spanish teacher

I failed Spanish in school. I had no propensity to learn any language. Some people say I never really learned to speak English well. That goes along with my inability to carry a tune or learn to play a musical instrument. While I worked with Aury for the better part of five years and dated her for some of that time, I never took the time to learn her language. It would have helped me many times in my travels over the years.

Madrid is one of the most cosmopolitan and comfortable cities I have ever visited. I arrived there for a two-city media tour, which would include Barcelona, to write about the diverse tourism products that Spain offers. After arriving and having a meeting with the tourism director at her office, she escorted me to the Hotel Villa Real overlooking the bustling city center. The view from my hotel window was of wide streets with a never-ending stream of cars, buses and bicyclists moving in almost symphonic sway as they twisted along the winding avenues of Madrid.

As she turned me over to the hotel concierge, she added an invitation to a dinner party she was having for some friends at her apartment. I hesitated, but having nothing specific planned for that first evening in Madrid, I said, "Yes, that would be really great." She gave me the address and told me to come any time after seven o'clock, adding: "It is not a table dinner, just a buffet and you can arrive at any time you are convenient." I liked her English with a twist of Spanish placement for certain words. She had just a hint of an accent when she spoke English and her vocabulary was excellent.

I arrived at 7:30 so as not to be first and found a crowded apartment filled with local Spaniards all engaged in conversation—of course in Spanish. My gracious host took me around and one-by-one introduced me to each and every one of her guests including a brief explanation of who they were. There were a couple of lawyers, a judge, two or three doctors (both male and female), a thoroughbred horse trainer and an assortment of businessmen and businesswomen. I was exhausted by the time I got through all the introductions.

Somewhere along the way, one attractive lady handed me a glass of Chardonnay to quench my thirst. And once the introductions were completed, I was led to the buffet table where the spread of food was as diverse as the gathering of people.

I filled a plate and then stood in the corner and balanced the plate and glass of wine in one hand while digging in with a fork and eating with the other hand. This was a procedure I had mastered as a result of far too many standup cocktail parties in which you either learned to hold your wine and eat at the same time or forsake one of these crucial pleasures. I simply slip the wine glass stem in between my pinky and ring fingers of my left hand and hold the plate with my thumb and forefinger of the same hand. That frees up my other hand to use a fork to eat, shake hands with strangers and fix the seat of my pants.

I walked around the room, eating as I went, stopping to have my wine glass filled a second time and smiling whenever I thought I caught someone looking at me. I listened intently and earnestly to their banter, not understanding a single word. But I thought that by listening earnestly, I would appear to understand and therefore not look like I was a lost soul in the city of Babel.

One of the men was dominating the dialogue and telling stories which resulted in everyone laughing multiple times during the story telling. I smiled, even chuckled politely once or twice, but I didn't laugh. They continued speaking Spanish which was perfectly natural since we were in Spain and they were all Spanish. I did understand a word here and there such as *por favor* and *gracias.* I just kept smiling. I even began to join the laughing at one time when all the guests were rocking and rolling in hysterical laughter after something that must have been really funny. Everyone was either bent over laughing through their knees or wiping tears away from their eyes in between convulsions.

Laughter is infectious and I suddenly found myself laughing too, but caught myself before I got too carried away as I didn't understand what I was laughing at and didn't want someone to say something to me in Spanish such as *"porque mi amigo, que hora es tu laughing at?"*

My host, the tourist office lady came over to me at one point as I stood in the corner having just filled my wine glass a third time. She looked straight at me and said: *"Habla Espanol?"* I understood that and said *"No"* (which is Spanish for No) with a big smile, "but I am enjoying myself, the food is really, really great and I like your friends, thanks for inviting me." With that, she turned towards the couch where four people had crowded together along with a half a dozen others on chairs that circled out from the couch past the coffee table and back to the other side of the couch. There were also several people standing or sitting on the floor all centered and focused on the couch as the man telling the funny stories was holding court and making everyone laugh.

My gracious host took back the attention of everyone in the room and, in perfect English said: "We've been poor hosts to our guest from America as we sat here enjoying ourselves in our own language when we should be entertaining him in English." I immediately objected and apologized for not being able to speak Spanish.

At that point, the man who had commanded everyone's attention stood up and said, in perfect English, "If I may speak for all of us—it is we who must apologize to you. For you see, we felt more comfortable speaking in Spanish as we are embarrassed that our English is not of the quality and clarity that you are used to hearing and speaking." My jaw dropped two inches as I listened to his deep, resonant voice explaining how he and the others were too embarrassed to speak English in front of me. "Sir, your English is far better than I normally hear in my native Brooklyn, New York. So please, no need to apologize."

With that, everyone stood up and suddenly I was surrounded by people, all speaking English and all wanting to converse with me and ask me questions about my work and my travels in Spain and elsewhere. I also had moments in which I could ask many of them questions and enjoyed learning some interesting tidbits about several of them. For the rest of the long evening, I was the center of attention and it was in English so I was able to understand.

At one point I even asked the man who had everyone laughing what the joke was about that resulted in all that laughter. He explained that it was not a joke, but a story about a lost whale off the coast of Spain and how the whale searched for the Moors to help him find his way home, but couldn't find any because they were all walking around in circles. I knew that the Moors were nomadic people, but still did not understand the humor, especially the raucous laughter that resulted from this story. I guess you had to hear it in Spanish in its entirety and had to be there for the whole story and know that the Moors were often the butt of jokes from some Spaniards. I smiled as I had smiled before and thanked him.

The next day I returned to my scheduled plans for seeing Madrid and spent a lot of time that first full day at the Prada Museum. Two days later I was off to Barcelona for more sightseeing in an equally interesting city, but one with a clear undercurrent of rebellion as many of the people in this ancient city would rather not be part of Spain and made no attempt to hide that. I did my best not to offend and kept my conversions simple.

I was given a gift on my last day in Barcelona. The local tourist office handed me a set of eight skewers modeled after swords from the Middle Ages. "You will have wonderful barbecues filled with meats on these authentic skewers from Barcelona's glorious past." was written on the note in the box that was presented to me over breakfast that morning.

Soon after breakfast, I left for the airport. Upon entering the line for clearance at the security checkpoint I placed the box of skewers on the conveyor belt along with my carryon bag and walked through the metal detector.

Bells went off and one of the security guards came over and began to look into the box of skewers. Something was said in Spanish and I assumed that they were talking about the skewers since they were pointing to them. I tried to explain to him what they were. He kept shaking his head and saying things in Spanish. I kept trying to explain and then there were three security guards standing around me all speaking loudly in Spanish. One of them picked up the box of skewers and went to throw them in the trash. I went for them and was grabbed by the other two guards.

I tried again to explain to the first one who I was and what the skewers meant to me. "You can't take these on the plane," he said—sort of. What he actually said was something in Spanish, but after nearly ten minutes of arguing, I was whisked away by two security guards and locked in a small, very small room with no windows and just two chairs facing each other. A young man came into the room and told me that I can't take those skewers on the plane. He then left the room leaving me with these two security guards.

No one understood that this was a gift from the tourist office. Nor did they understand that these were special skewers with a Middle Ages design. All they understood was that there were eight sword-like pointed weapons that could possibly be used by someone to hijack an airplane.

I was getting more anxious. I kept speaking English, which was the only language that I knew and these security guards kept yelling at me in Spanish and shaking their heads back and forth. I didn't know what the head shaking meant either. One of the guards left the room and then came back to get the other guard. He left with the first guard and I was alone in the room. I waited a moment and went to the door and opened it. Standing outside was the second guard. He turned to look at me and I fully understood the scowl on his face. He pushed me back into the room and slammed the door. I sat down to contemplate my latest travel predicament.

I didn't have to wait too long before a new young man in a suit came in and smiled at me. He was the first person to smile during this entire episode. I calmly tried to explain to this person who, at least understood English, who I was and where I got the skewers from. He listened, said little, and then went out to make a telephone call to verify what I told him.

He must have reached someone in the tourist office who verified who I was because he came back a short while later telling me that he was arranging to have the skewers packaged in a container that would be put through as luggage and could be picked up when I arrived in New York at the end of my trip. I was skeptical, but after nearly a half hour in this predicament, most of it which was spent in this tiny room with no windows, I just hung my head and smiled "okay."

I was released from the room, escorted back to security where I was given back my carryon bag and a claim check for the package which contained the skewers. I was the last person to board the Iberia Airlines aircraft (this was getting to be standard procedure for me) headed for London where I had a two-hour layover before boarding a TWA flight to New York. After departing the plane in New York, I went to the luggage carousel assigned to our flight. I waited for the luggage to come out, something I rarely did because I hated having to wait—sometimes as long as a half hour—for baggage to arrive.

As often is the case, all passengers were deplaned and standing around a silent baggage carousel, while the luggage remained somewhere unknown to either passengers or baggage handlers. And, there will always be some of those passengers that never get their luggage or end up getting luggage that was half destroyed. I preferred to travel light with one carryon and all my possessions with me at all times.

But there I was waiting for my skewers to come along with the luggage and I was pleasantly surprised when I saw a large circular tube coming at me on the carousel. I surely thought it would never make it to New York, especially since we had to change planes and airlines in London. I leaned over, lifted the package and compared the claim check that I had with the one attached to the tube. They matched and I was on my way home with my skewers.

Once at home I opened the tube to find only four of the eight skewers. I stood silent for a moment as the anger began to build, but then sat down, looked at my four skewers and was thankful that I had four special skewers forged in the Middle Ages in Spain. I didn't entertain much anyway and couldn't think of eight people that I liked well enough to share my skewers with over dinner.

CHAPTER TWENTY-TWO

JAZZ AND REINDEER IN FINLAND

No matter what the trouble we carry round inside
We're never safe from the truth but in the truth we can survive
. . . .

"Wall of Denial" by Stevie Ray Vaughan

One of the greatest trips of my life was an off-the-beaten-path visit to the Pori Jazz Festival in the northern regions of Finland, which is already in the northern regions of Europe, which also are in the northern regions of the world just south of the North Pole. Despite this ultimately northern location, it was a warm scene in Finland. It was actually a very hot night in July 1985 in New York when I boarded the Finnair flight for Helsinki with a connection to Pori.

I was fortunate to have been upgraded to first class and enjoyed the comfort and service provided to those that paid the much higher prices to sit in the much wider seats as well as enjoy the much better dinner than most people experienced with airline food. And while no one really likes airline food, a few cold glasses of chardonnay, some warm nuts as an appetizer and I am ready for dinner at 30,000 feet above the earth. It's not gourmet and often not even good, but sometimes, especially in first class, it is satisfying.

In addition, sitting in first class affords me the opportunity to meet and talk with other interesting first-class passengers which adds to the overall travel experience and sometimes becomes the focus of the experience.

On this trip it turned out that I was traveling the same route with the same ultimate destination as the renown guitarist Stevie Ray Vaughan and his band Double Trouble. They were among the famous headliners that would be performing at the Pori Jazz Festival and I had the opportunity and privilege to meet them on the flight, get to know a little more about them then I previously knew and actually help them navigate the transfer from Helsinki to the domestic Finish airline and small aircraft that would take us to Pori.

Stevie Ray Vaughan was considered one of the best jazz and rock guitarist on the music scene, but he was a humble and friendly guy who didn't enjoy traveling as much as he loved performing. He and his band mates couldn't wait to get there and perform. Guitars came out at any interval in our travels and you could tell they loved what they were doing. And they were all, each and every one of the band, really great. It reiterated to me that if you love what you do, you can make it great, no matter if it was playing music, painting, dancing or writing.

I told them I was a travel writer on this trip to cover the Pori festival. They opened up to me and we talked about the difficulties of traveling around the world to perform. But they were quick to note that going to destinations such as Pori brought them closer to their fans that couldn't be reached outside of the radio, television or record player. They loved performing in front of a live audience and said that many of the European audiences were more exuberant than those in the US. Maybe because they didn't have as much opportunity to see superstar performances as in the US. They were excited about this trip and also looked forward to meeting and jamming with other performers that would be featured at the Pori festival.

But first we had to get from our Helsinki flight with all their luggage, instruments, and sound equipment to this much smaller aircraft that would ferry us up to Pori. By this time in my career, I was a seasoned traveler and while I had not previously been to Helsinki or Finland, I used my instincts to find our connecting gate and once they had their luggage and we had cleared customs and immigration, I lead them to our connecting flight to Pori.

They were not happy with the size of this new transportation. And I must note that the airline crew were not happy with the size and number of pieces of luggage that the band needed to bring with them. There was a major discussion going on by both sides that jeopardized this flight continuing on to Pori as planned. A couple of members of the band had an aversion to small planes. So did I. And while I knew that these small aircraft were the safest form of air travel from my initial airline industry education when I was a reporter at *Aviation Week* magazine, I still hesitated to book small craft if at all avoidable.

Several of the band members took their instruments and all the sound equipment and moved over to bus transportation for their trip up to Pori. Stevie Ray Vaughan and a couple of the band and I took the flight and arrived safely in Pori a short while later. The rest of the band arrived the next day. That was not a problem since it was two days before they were scheduled to perform and everyone would be ready for their first concert.

This gave me more time to get to know Stevie and find him a most likeable, unassuming star. And later that week when I watched and listened to him perform, both with his band and in jam sessions with other performers, I realized that I was experiencing true genius at work. And all he did was smile. He smiled a lot because he was happy in his role as a guitarist performing for appreciative fans. He was a true artist.

Pori was located pretty far north so that summer days were twenty-two hours long. That meant there would be only two hours of real nighttime for normal sleeping in the dark. This presented unique opportunities for late night concerts in daylight settings and sleepless nights even with dark shades drawn. Walking around Pori at dinner time in complete daylight, going back to the park for a midnight concert in complete daylight and returning to my hotel at two o'clock in the morning in complete daylight was a unique experience. I didn't sleep much on that trip.

I had missed seeing Fats Domino who, along with the Dirty Dozen Brass Band opened the week-long festival on Saturday while we were first traveling to Pori. I had idolized Fats Domino as a child growing up in Brooklyn and had traveled into New York City with a couple of friends to attend the Dick Clark Saturday Night show in which Fats Domino was the featured performer. I had all his records in the old style 45-rpm singles. My favorites were *Blue Monday, My Blue Heaven, I Hear You Knocking, Blueberry Hill* and especially *I'm Walking.* I was sorry I missed him, but caught him later that week in one of the many late-night jam sessions that brought together The Fat Man, the Dirty Dozen and Stevie Ray Vaughan.

These jam sessions were mostly in small venues enabling fans to get up close and personal.

I had separated myself from the band as I moved around the many venues that performers were appearing in and around Pori. Some of these venues were in hotels, bars and other intimate indoor locations. Others were in open air parks where thousands of fans gathered.

While Finnair had provided me with a Press Pass to attend all events at the Pori Festival, thanks to my new connection to Stevie Ray Vaughan, I was given a backstage pass to be able to hang out on the edge of the stage before and during their performance. They were appearing in the Kirjurinluoto Park, an island park in Pori with a huge open-air concert theater. I almost didn't make it to their opening as it took me quite a while to navigate through the park filled with thousands upon thousands of fans from all over the world. This was a major concert and one of a string of music festivals in Europe that drew hundreds of thousands of ardent fans.

Mombasa was on stage as I cut my way through the crowds of people that covered the lawns of Kirjurinluoto Park and finally arrived at the side of the stage. I didn't get a chance to meet up with the band before they went on stage as we had planned, but I stood beside the MC on the sideline as he proudly and loudly announced to a screaming crowd: "Ladies and Gentlemen, I ask you to welcome to Pori Jazz Festival the renown genius of Stevie Ray Vaughan and the Double Trouble." He hardly got the words out as the sea of people that lay out across the park rose with cheers and applauds that overwhelmed me. I stood there with tears welling up in my eyes knowing that the band would appreciate this welcome. I felt great for them. I can't imagine how they felt, but I could tell it was special because they played with a lot of emotion and went on and on beyond the planned set.

A couple of days later I left Pori for Helsinki, a great walking city. I was staying at one of the local boutique hotels in the city center just off Mannerheiminte, the main avenue that runs through central Helsinki. From there I visited a number of sites including the National Museum and Parliament building. But it was three churches that spoke volumes about Helsinki and the Finish people. First there was the red brick Uspenski Cathedral with its ornate interior dating back hundreds of years. Then the white brick Cathedral built in the 19th century and finally, the unique Temppeliaukio Church built in the late 1960s into the side of a huge rock wall with the natural rock interior exposed. Each of these churches provide a magnificent interior view of their own and a look into the history, culture and progression of the Finish people.

I spent one day walking just a few of the many trails that line Suomenlinna, an island fortress that sits just off the coast of Helsinki, a short trip away from this bustling city and easily accessible by ferry. One of my best remembered moments in Helsinki, however, was spent in Sibelius Park sitting near the modern monument dedicated to the famous composer. I got lost in thought and could almost hear his music as I sat there thinking about how fortunate I was to have these opportunities in my life to enjoy these travels.

One night in Helsinki it was suggested that I go to a particular night-club to enjoy some local folk music. Finding the club was not easy. The average street name is 16 or more letters long and difficult for me to discern from one to the other. I was told it was walking distance from my hotel and given verbal directions which I quickly forgot. A few friendly directions on the street from the very friendly Finns got me where I was going. I was not sure I was in the right place, but there was music playing and a guy and girl were singing Bob Dylan's "Positively Fourth Street."

I found a place to sit at a table with other people which is common in clubs and even some restaurants. I was quickly welcomed with nods from the four others sitting around this table with seats for eight. The performers moved into Finish folk songs which sounded great, but of course, I did not understand a word. I pictured long words with eighteen letters strung out in melodic tunes and sat, drank local beer and watched the people around me. These two singers ended their set that night with Bruce Springsteen's *"Born in the USA."* Half the audience joined in singing along with them.

During the break as we waited for the next performer, my tablemates asked me where I was from—in perfect English. They must have heard me ordering my beer and realized I was not local. They were from Sweden and had also been up to the Pori Jazz Festival. We talked about that and other music and then refocused on the next performer. Soon two others joined us. They were from Holland and also spoke perfect English. I enjoyed a great night in Finland with these friendly people from Sweden, Holland and Helsinki. This is common in Europe.

The next morning I walked around Helsinki again, found a great outdoor cafe to enjoy some coffee and Danish and watched people come and go. I sat for a long time before returning to my hotel to pack and depart for the airport and my return to New York.

I returned with a mind full of memorable experiences capped by a perfect flight where I watched the sunset from above the clouds. I knew how blessed I was.

CHAPTER TWENTY-THREE

TRADING A PAIR OF JEANS IN RUSSIA

Why do we never get an answer when we're knocking at the door
With a thousand million questions about hate and death and war?
'Cause when we stop and look around us there is nothing that we need
In a world of persecution that is burning in its greed

•••••••

"Question" sung by The Moody Blues

By this time in my life and travels (1989), I had enjoyed excursions and experiences throughout the Caribbean, South America, Europe, Asia, and Africa. For some reason, I had never visited Russia. Moscow was never on my "to do" list because it was too cold and political. St. Petersburg, while full of intriguing sites, also never made it on the itinerary chart. And I was not about to venture off into the less important and even colder cities.

Then along came the Cruise Lines International Association (CLIA), an organization made up of all the major world cruise lines with its primary interest of promoting cruising through travel agents. I had just stepped down from my lofty role as editor and publisher of *The Travel Agent* magazine and CLIA was running an educational cruise for travel agents in the Baltic Sea. They asked me to go with them and provide a motivational seminar to the hundreds of travel agents that would be sailing on one of Royal Caribbean's ships. And I loved speaking engagements.

It was a free cruise that would enable me to visit some of my favorite northern capitals of Europe. It would also stop in St. Petersburg, Russia, so I would be able to check off another country on my climb to reach more than 100 nations and become a member of the exclusive Century Club for those that had visited 100 or more sovereign destinations.

Before getting to St. Petersburg we stopped in Copenhagen, Denmark, Oslo, Norway, Stockholm, Sweden and Helsinki, Finland. Each of them had unique sites, but all are great walking cities much like New York where you can easily find your way around. The only problem I found was in reading and pronouncing street signs, some of which may have 20 or more letters in the name.

Copenhagen has an ancient rococo city center that serves as a gathering place for locals and visitors, often presenting music and art festivities that draw thousands. Oslo has some of the best maritime museums including one dedicated to Viking history. Stockholm with its old town has some wonderful 13th century churches and museums. Helsinki has a bunch of islands and parks great for walking. While all these countries and capital cities were great to visit, St. Petersburg became the most memorable of the Baltic stops.

When we arrived in St. Petersburg we were scheduled to stay there for two days which enabled us to walk around downtown and explore the local shops and cafes. However, this was 1989, and buying anything presented an issue because most shops could not change dollars and offered only rubles in exchange which were worthless because they could not be used or converted back to dollars by Americans. The "cold war" between the US and Russia was still ongoing at that time.

I was exploring the streets along with three of the travel agents that were on the cruise with me when we were approached by a young couple. The girl, a sweet looking teenager, asked if I would sell them my jeans. We all laughed. I answered: "I don't have another pair with me. Just these that I am wearing. So I'm sorry, but I cannot sell them to you."

The boy, who looked maybe twenty-years-old, and did not speak as fluently as his companion said, "My sister and me, we give you lacquer boxes for jeans." She then suggested that, "We go back to your hotel and change your clothes and we give you two lacquer boxes for your jeans." She noted that lacquer boxes were worth hundreds of dollars in the US. In reality at that time the average size box was said to be worth more than $100 each if they were genuine.

I explained that we were not staying at a hotel, but were here for just a short stay on a cruise ship which was a taxi ride away. We were not going back to the ship just so I could change and trade them my jeans for lacquer boxes. But they didn't give up. "What are you doing tonight?" she asked. "We are going to the theater," I offered. She said that they could meet us on the escalator going up to the entranceway of the theater. "You come up the escalator with your jeans in a paper bag, and we will go down the escalator with two lacquer boxes in a paper bag. We hand off midway on the escalator. It's very safe."

I hesitated, but then said okay and we set a time to meet. My travel agent companions began to warn me that I was crazy to do this. They reminded me that this was Russia and the communist regime strongly frowns on these sorts of exchanges. I could get arrested and thrown in a Russian jail.

I kept going back and forth in my mind. Lacquer boxes had recently risen in value on the world market. A good hand-painted lacquer box could possibly cost hundreds of dollars or more, depending on size and weight. Even cheap lacquer boxes at that time were valued at $100 each. That meant I could potentially trade a pair of old jeans that were well worn for $200 worth of lacquer boxes. Seemed like a good deal for me.

Back on the ship I was getting dressed to go to the theater and packed my jeans in a plastic bag I found in the cabin. On my way out of the room I picked up the bag, stood there for a moment thinking about the potential of getting caught, and the additional potential of being scammed by these two young Russians. They could hand me a paper bag with nothing more than bricks and I would have no recourse. But then I would only be losing a pair of old, very worn jeans. I thought, what the heck, why not do this and left the cabin.

Once in the hallway, I had another thought about being arrested because some police officer sees this strange exchange in the middle of an escalator with people passing bags while one goes up and another goes down. I pictured something right out of a spy movie. I was in Russia in 1989 when spies were still prevalent. I stood in the hallway motionless for a long time trying to decide what to do.

Soon after, I was on my way. Once off the ship we took buses to the theater which was in the city center and sat on the second level of a shopping mall. There were hundreds of people roaming around the mall and when we reached the escalator that went up to the theater I looked up and saw the young couple with whom I had agreed to trade my jeans and saw them holding their large brown paper bag. When they saw me getting onto the "up" side of the long escalator, they got on the other side heading down. As we passed each other they reached out to exchange their package for mine. I turned away, fearing even to look at them.

When I got to the top of the escalator, I was stopped by a man in a worn brown suit that was too large for his slight frame. He asked me to step aside for a moment. His English was good, but laced with a strong Russian accent. "Do you know those two being questioned at the floor below," he asked as he pointed to the two kids with whom I was supposed to have traded my jeans. I looked down to the bottom of the escalator to see two security guards in uniform and one man in a similar brown suit surrounding the two kids. All of them were looking up at me.

I looked at the kids and shook my head telling the man questioning me, "No, I have no idea who they are." (I was so glad I had turned back and left my jeans in my cabin on the ship.) I then added: "I'm here with the US travel agent group from the cruise line and we are being hosted by your tourist office for the theater tonight." He apologized for the inconvenience and wished me a pleasant evening. I was so nervous I had an urgent need to pee so I asked him where the public toilets were located. He pointed to the corner of the hallway in front of the theater and off I went to relieve myself.

While standing at the urinal in this large public toilet, a man at the urinal next to me began talking to me, also in a very respectable English with a Russian accent. "Sir, can you do me a favor?" he asked, all the while standing at the urinal supposedly doing what you do at a urinal.

What the hell was happening now, I said to myself—or maybe even out loud. "This is okay," the man said, "I just need to exchange some rubles for your dollars. I will give you $100 worth of rubles for US$50, a great deal for you."

"No thank you," I offered, still standing and unable to pee even though I really had to go. It is very difficult to pee when being accosted for an illegal transaction in Russia—or anywhere else. "Please sir," he insisted, "I need to take my family to dinner at the American restaurant here in the mall and they only accept US dollars. My rubles are good."

"Please leave me for a moment so I can pee," I pleaded. He moved away, I relaxed a bit and took a long-needed piss. While washing my hands, he came back to me getting much too close to where I feared that he was going to pick my pocket or mug me. There were others in the toilet, but none appeared to care that something illegal may be going down here. It was as if they avoided looking because they didn't want to get involved.

"Wait here," I suddenly said to this man, adding: "I will be right back." I then slipped past him and quickly out the bathroom door and back into the mall. I looked for the plain clothes officer that had stopped me, but he was nowhere in sight. I just decided to move on and walked fast straight to the theater not looking back to the toilets for fear that the man would be coming after me. Once inside the theater I found my seat next to my travel agent friends. These two quick back-to-back experiences left me nervous and I found it difficult to concentrate. I think the performance was good, but I don't remember what it was about.

While these "very special" experiences were memorable, if not sobering, I did have some positive highlights of my visit to St. Petersburg including the Presidential Palace constructed for Peter the Great and the Hermitage, possibly the greatest art museum in the world.

The Palace, often referred to as the Summer Palace was built around 1700. A visit to the Palace always includes a dance recital and some vodka, but it is the famous Gold Room, built for a wedding in the 1800s that stands out. The entire room, vaulted ceiling, archways, walls, windows, mirrors are all gold, either solid or covered, but nevertheless all gold. It is truly a magnificent sight. There is nothing like this room anywhere else in the world. It is worth the trip just outside of St. Petersburg.

The Hermitage is a sight unto itself. Standing on Palace Bridge over the Neva River you can view the buildings that make up the Hermitage. I don't know if this is a fact, but I can't imagine another museum structure that is larger than the Hermitage. It was the former Winter Palace, the main residence for the Tsar of Russia. It goes on and on with one sprawl-ing building connecting to another. It houses one of the largest, if not the largest collections of antiquities and artwork in the world. It also serves as a history lesson for the world with everything from ancient Egypt, Greece and Rome including whole sections of bronze statues, buildings filled with archeological treasures and corridors and rooms filled with some of the most famous art from the Renaissance period to Pablo Picasso and more.

I spent a day there on more than one occasion (including return visits to St. Petersburg years later) and barely touched the surface and depth of what is contained within those walls. I imagine you could vacation for a week in the Hermitage and leave without seeing everything. Some of the highlights on my visit included seeing Leonardo da Vinci's Madonna, Rembrandt's Return of the Prodigal Son, early paintings by Pablo Picasso, and collections from Van Gogh, Paul Gauguin, and Thomas Gainsborough. And while many of these famous paintings are housed in the Hermitage, they are sometimes loaned out to other museums around the world.

Once seeing those famous paintings—all in one magnificent museum—I was able to better appreciate the history of art and its connection to the history of the world, a connected world that my travels allowed me to experience. And I remembered and thought about Pope John Paul II thanking the travel agents and travel writers for helping to promote peace through travel.

If only more people could visit other countries and experience other cultures, we could better understand other people and hopefully abandon our prejudices and live more peacefully. But then, the realist in me returns to thoughts about the vast amount of ignorance across the world and the jealousies that exist between nations and peoples and I realize that traveling can only open those eyes that want to see things clearly. And I fear that most people like to live with blinders on, like race horses going around a never-ending track.

CHAPTER TWENTY-FOUR

AMSTERDAM: SMOKING WEED AND THE RED-LIGHT DISTRICT

I hope you never lose your sense of wonder
You get your fill to eat but always keep that hunger...
May you never take one single breath for granted...
Give the heavens above more than just a passing glance
And when you get the choice to sit it out or dance
I hope you dance
•••••••

"I Hope You Dance" by Tia Sillers & Mark Sanders sung by Lee Ann Womack

The Netherlands, better known as Holland, land of wooden shoes, is one very relaxed destination in Northern Europe. Amsterdam is its largest cosmopolitan city which claims at least two unique attributes—the world's most famous red-light district and a pot smoking culture that allows people to imbibe in public. While both these experiences may offend some people, it's existence in Amsterdam is what makes this city special, even if you never partake in either activity.

Amsterdam is also a great walking city enabling visitors to enjoy so much without having to drive anywhere. Sightseeing while walking around this city is so prevalent and easy, but walker beware, the bicycles are there. Sometimes they fly by so fast you would swear they are motorized. They are just pedals flying from the Dutch population of tall, blond men and women who choose the bike rather than cars or buses. I must warn you that the local residents take their bicycles very seriously and compete very effectively with the automobiles in mowing down innocent pedestrians that often pay little attention to where they walk.

I've been to Amsterdam about a dozen times during my travels, but it's still my first visit that stands out as a vivid picture in my mind. I was being exposed to all that makes Amsterdam unique, beginning with pot smoking residents and visitors alike along the sidewalk cafes that line so many of the streets. I stayed in a hotel on one side of Amsterdam and walked daily across town to the city center near the rail station. As I walked, I passed several sidewalk cafes where patrons were enjoying food and drink along with smokes. Some of those smoking enjoyed cigarettes filled with a strong European tobacco while others emitted the more pungent odor of marijuana.

When in Amsterdam, do as they do. I found an empty table at one of the sidewalk cafes and ordered a coffee and pastry and offered a joke that I would like a "joint" as well. The young waiter smiled. But that was all. I had hoped that someone would hear my request and offer a stick of pot as they called it. No one did. However, the smoke that sailed across the tables provided me with just enough to almost taste the marijuana. I moved on, stopping to enjoy some magnificent old churches and eventually arrived at the famous "red-light district."

The red-light district is quite small, just a few blocks of storefronts with large windows where girls of all sizes and shapes sit or stand and exhibit themselves in an effort to win over men (or women) searching for sex. These girls, both young and old, smile and coax people to come in and buy an hour of sex for prices that I found surprisingly low. If the window is empty, that means she is engaged with a customer.

Selling sex was, and still is legal in Amsterdam. Everything is government regulated. The girls have to be checked regularly for health. Protection has to be used and the rates that they charge are regulated as well. Sex is a business in Amsterdam and that's a good thing. It takes the criminal link out of the business and protects both the women and the patrons.

This was back in the early 1970s. I was single and free to enjoy anything I chose to experience. Without hesitation (and without the benefit of any pot) I walked up and down the streets of the red-light district in Amsterdam and stopped in front of every window that had an unoccupied girl. I talked with a few, thanked them and moved on until I found one young, very young, pretty blond with a pageboy haircut. We talked briefly and she invited me in for the going rate of $30 (at that time - circa 1970) for an hour of pleasure.

I went in, enjoyed some fast (I was excited), safe sex using the condoms that she provided and then sat and talked with her until my hour was up. What I found out was that she was a student attending the local university studying to be a journalist. We talked a lot about that. As a journalist myself, and naturally curious, I wanted to know why she was working as a prostitute and what it meant to her.

She explained that she was doing this to put herself through school. "I tried waitressing, but kept dropping drinks in the laps of diners," she told me, adding with a smile: "I did a better job cleaning off their laps then serving them." She explained that the money was good, it was a very safe job, she only worked days and went to school at night. Her boyfriend, who she lived with, worked as a bartender at night, so they would spend mornings together. She did mention that her parents were not excited about her working in a sex shop, but they didn't talk about it.

I asked how her boyfriend felt about her having sex all day long with other men and she said, they talked about it before she started, and then he asked how she felt after she performed her first full day. She told him that most people were both gentle and generous. They don't talk about it anymore. It's just work and she said that the only thing that means anything was the money, which she gets to keep. She pays a daily fee for use of the room and that's it. It sounded very much like some beauty salons in New York where the haircutters pay rent for the chair they use to the owner of the salon and the haircutters get to keep their clients' fees.

I don't remember much about that encounter, but I can still picture this sweet looking young girl and I do remember a lot about the conversation we enjoyed together. And one other point to ponder; while we never experienced the following, we were told that it happens fairly often that obnoxious men approach some of these women by heckling them, and these generally sweet women in the windows have been known to have a can or jar of urine by their side and they are not against tossing the urine at those that deserve to be pissed upon.

I've been to Amsterdam many times since, always taking the time to walk through the red-light district, but never experiencing any of the merchandise again. I have taken friends there and years later even strolled the streets with my wife, enjoying the sights and an occasional conversation with one of the young ladies sitting in their windows. I also have enjoyed the pot there, especially from the legal shops that sell, what I considered, the cleanest marijuana on the planet.

The food is also great in Amsterdam with croissants or Danish and coffee for breakfast in the sidewalk cafes, light sandwiches and a beer for lunch, also in the sidewalk cafes, and an assortment of cheese dishes for dinner in comfortable old-world restaurants. The sidewalk cafes are for dining, resting, reading, talking with friends, meeting new friends, or just people watching, The Dutch do it and so should everyone.

The Dutch are among the nicest people in the world. They are friendly, welcome Americans, speak English, and help each other enjoy life—mostly with a smile on their classically chiseled faces often draped with long blond hair (men and women alike). One of the things I always cherish when traveling is meeting nice people and when in Holland, it is hard not to find nice people at every turn.

And last, when in Amsterdam a visit to the Anne Frank Museum just outside of the city center of Amsterdam is a must-see experience. Also, a must is reserving tickets in advance. It's a piece of World War II history that gets large crowds year-round.

CHAPTER TWENTY-FIVE

MEXICO OR CANADA: DO WE GO SOUTH OR NORTH?

Yes, 'n' how many times must a man look up before he can see the sky?
Yes, 'n' how many ears must one man have before he can hear people cry?
Yes, 'n' how many deaths will it take 'til he knows
that too many people have died?
The answer, my friend, is blowin' in the wind

• • • • • • •

"Blowin in the Wind" by Bob Dylan

Before I go any further, I need to clarify one thing. I like Mexican people; I don't like Mexico. And while that might be hard to separate because most travel experiences are very much about the interaction with the people of the destination and the culture of the people, Mexico provides a challenge for me in many ways because of the high level of corruption.

Mexico is a beautiful country. The eastern areas from Cancun, along the Riviera Maya, past Playa del Carmen south to Tulum are full of fascinating ancient Aztec history and culture. Cancun and Riviera Maya are known for one luxury resort after another teeming with Mexican employees whose only mission is to provide service to their guests. The western shores of Acapulco, Guadalajara and Puerto Vallarta have wonderful stretches of beaches. Cabo San Lucas draws the rich and famous to its luxury enclaves.

Even chaotic Mexico City has an old-school charm of Latin mystery and history.

Now that all sounds great. But, there is a "but" and it comes with experiences that have left me and many others shaking our heads and avoiding Mexico vacations.

I was attending a convention (like so much of my travel in the 1980s) and we were being treated with lavish care at our hotels and convention center in Acapulco. It was a beautiful day and we were leaving a wonderful luncheon and heading back to our hotel. One of my colleagues offered me a ride in the rental car he was using. Rather than wait for everyone (other convention delegates) to exit the mass luncheon and take one of the convention buses back to the hotel, I jumped at the chance to drive with my friend and return to my room early.

It should have been a quick twenty-minute ride back to the hotel in slow moving traffic. We were not far and it was a straight drive along the shore. It was midday and there was more than enough traffic. We were stopped at a light waiting for traffic to move when a car came out of a parking lot and rammed our car. We were shocked, but not hurt. We got out and found enough damage to necessitate calling the police. The scruffy man that hit us spoke only Spanish. We didn't understand what he was saying.

When the police arrived a few minutes later, the man that hit us took over the conversation and exchanged some lengthy dialogue with the police. We were immediately told to stand aside. The police then approached us and asked us what happened. My friend told them we were waiting for the light to change when this car came out of the parking lot and hit us in the rear as if we weren't there. The policeman said he got a different story from the man who said that we suddenly drove in front of him causing him to hit us. He then asked us both for our driver's licenses. I explained that I was just a passenger and he just repeated "Driver's license please." After we surrendered our driver's licenses, we were instructed to follow the police to the police station. The man who hit us was also instructed to come to the police station. He never showed up. We never saw him again.

Once at the police station we were put into separate interrogation rooms and asked by new policemen about the accident. We were told that we did not have the proper insurance and that we needed to pay $500 for repairs to the other car or we would be held in jail. I explained over and over again that I was just a passenger and that we were hit as we stood still. I was told that, even as a passenger I was responsible for the drunk driving of my colleague. This was ludicrous and I asked for an attorney to help me. The police told me I could call whoever I wished to call, but I would stay in jail until, I either paid the $500 "in cash," or have my attorney show up at the police station to pay $500 to bail me out.

I told him that I did not have $500 on me and was told that I could pay what I have and that an officer would escort me to my hotel room to get the rest. Only then would I get my license back and only then would we get the rental car back.

We were being held for ransom. I did not trust the police to take me back to my room and opened my wallet to find $420. He took the money and then changed his approach, telling me that he felt sorry for me and that he would make up the difference of $80 to cover my charges and that I could go. My friend had a little over $300 and had the same reaction from his police captor.

When I got out to the lobby, my colleague was waiting. We left immediately, drove very carefully back to the hotel and he called the rental car company to report what had happened. Later that day, someone from the rental car company arrived to exchange cars. My friend told him he no longer needed a car and they could take both cars back. He was told he may be responsible for the damages as the insurance may not cover everything. He just shook his head. He was already out $300 to the corrupt police. I was out $420 and I was just a passenger. There was nothing we could do. We were in a foreign country. We thought about calling the US embassy, but talked with others who suggested that would be futile.

When I recounted the story to a couple of my travel writer colleagues later that night, they all had stories about muggings, pick-pocketing and corrupt police. Acapulco has gone through a roller-coaster history of such corruption and crime, but remains one of the main vacation destinations in Mexico because most visitors never have these experiences.

A few years later, on a trip to Cozumel, I took a taxi to the beach for an afternoon with some friends. Upon my return trip to my hotel, I got in the taxi and said: "*Cuanto pesos to Casita de Maya?*" He said something like 850 pesos which was about US$4 in 1985. We got to the hotel and I handed him 850 pesos. He then said: "*No peso, el dolars.*" I told him that I did not have *dineros,* and reminded him he quoted me in pesos. He kept repeating "*dolars*" and tried to give me back my pesos. I finally gave up arguing with him and got out of the taxi. He followed me out and jumped on my back placing a stiff choke hold around my neck with his arm, pulling me down on the ground right in front of the door to the hotel lobby. The doorman jumped to my aid and pulled this crazed taxi driver off of me.

What then happened is bizarre as the taxi driver exchanged words with the doorman who then turned to me and explained that I must either give him $4 in dollars and get back my pesos or just give him another 20 pesos and be done with it. That meant that the taxi driver was demanding what amounted to another 10 cents in pesos to settle the fare. I gave him the 20 pesos and stood there wondering what would have happened if the difference was a full dollar.

And yet, years later, in a different life as a public relations executive, I would end up promoting Mexico as I represented Viva Resorts and tour wholesalers Travel Impressions and Apple Vacations, all of which had serious interests in Mexico tourism. Viva opened a hotel in Riviera Maya, just south of Cancun and I took press there on several occasions where we enjoyed a wonderfully pampered experience in a luxury hotel. At the same time, Mexico was one of the top warm weather vacation spots for both Travel Impressions and Apple Vacations and we promoted that successfully. But I couldn't forget the difficult experiences in Mexico and the fact that Mexico City had the reputation as one of the leading cities where people were kidnapped for ransom.

I've had much better experiences traveling to our neighbor to the north as Canada and Canadians have more in common with us Americans; even those French-speaking residents of Quebec province.

Multiple visits to Canada have produced nothing less than a true feeling of kinship with the northern reaches of North America. From the desolate, almost untouched regions on the east where Nova Scotia reaches out into the cold North Atlantic, to the modern city of Vancouver on the Pacific coast, Canada is one of the most diverse counties in the world—and friendly at every turn.

Quebec Province is French, very French. They speak French, act like French and, if given the opportunity, would remove itself from the rest of English-speaking Canada. But this French style and attitude makes the region and its two main cities very appealing to vacationers.

Montreal is a great city mixing old and new. Quebec City remains mostly an old city built into the mountain side and very much worth a visit. Although I am not a fan of funiculars, it is the way most people travel from the lower town of Old Quebec to the upper, town. I do suggest going up the mountainside to Montmorency Falls for the views and a taste of homemade bread smothered in maple butter (my mouth waters as I remember the taste of their warm bread).

Moving slightly west, just north of Buffalo, New York is Toronto, probably the most cosmopolitan of all Canadian cities with a young-person vibe that is more like New York's Greenwich Village, but with a lot of modern buildings, skyscrapers and congestion. I like Toronto. It is the main business district in Canada.

Moving further west we find Calgary, famous for its country and western flair highlighted by the annual Calgary Stampede in July which combines old and new with a traditional rodeo and a great music festival. It had been going on for more than 50 years and attracts visitors from across the world to this very traditional western town.

Finally, we reach the Pacific West Coast and Vancouver, a very modern city within reach of two major points in the US, one south and one to the north. As a matter of fact, Vancouver serves as a natural connection between Seattle and Alaska and often is the intermediate point for vacationers on their way to Alaska either by sea or air. Many of the cruise ships sailing the waters of Southeast Alaska and Glacier Bay depart from Vancouver on their seven-night voyages.

Vancouver is a great city for relaxed sightseeing with many lush parks and a seaside that offers opportunities for various recreations. The restaurants and nightclubs are great and I have always had a wonderful time there.

Now don't get me wrong, while I prefer Canada to our southern neighbor Mexico, I have had some excellent times in Mexico over the years, particularly in Cancun and the Riviera Maya on the east coast of the country. In the end, it's all your choice to go south or north, of both.

CHAPTER TWENTY-SIX

ALASKA AND THE CASE OF THE DISAPPEARING GLACIER

Hey Shell, you know it's kind of funny
Texas always seemed so big
But you know you're in the largest state in the union
When you're anchored down in Anchorage

• • • • • • •

"Anchorage" by Michelle Shocked

Most people visit Alaska by cruiseline, sailing out of Vancouver or Seattle along the Southeast Alaska shoreline and into famous Glacier Bay. It was no different for me on my first of several trips to Alaska. I chose Holland America Cruises for my first trip to Alaska in the 1980s because at that time Holland America owned, not only most of the cruise ships that sailed in Alaska waters, but the sightseeing buses and many of the hotels. It was Holland America territory. The cruise company was based in Seattle and they had a great reputation.

I was sailing by myself in early June so I could write about the trip and help travel agents be better prepared for their clients looking to visit Alaska. Alaska has a very short season in which vacationers can enjoy decent weather to experience all that the destination has to offer. The prime months for sailing are June through September. The peak months are July and August.

Since I was by myself, Holland America sat me at a table for ten with nine other guests, most of whom were also single sailors. There was one couple celebrating their fiftieth wedding anniversary and their friends who had been married for fifty-three years. These two couples were in their late seventies. Then there was the retired machinist from Detroit who was celebrating his eightieth birthday. There were two women who were rooming together courtesy of Holland America so that they could avoid having to pay the single supplement for a cabin of their own. They were both eighty-three years old. There was one other man who was eighty-eight-years-old and last, but surely not least, a woman ninety-one-years-old who had vacationed on more than 100 Holland America cruises. I was a little out of their class. I was turning forty in September.

This diverse group of mostly octogenarians took good care of me. They all became my substitute parents looking out to find me a mate and make sure that I was having a great time on the cruise, getting enough sleep, eating the right stuff and not drinking too much. However, sailing by myself left me little to do at night other than drink during dinner, have an after-dinner drink while watching the shows, and a couple of nightcaps at the bar after hours.

Several days of this routine produced a startling result. I woke up one morning and while brushing my teeth I noticed that my tongue had turned black. I stood there, tongue hanging out staring at the mirror. My first reaction was to quickly brush my tongue with more toothpaste. That didn't work. I then washed my tongue with soap. That only made me gag and remember when my mother did that to me because I had uttered some curse words when I was eight-years old. I went to breakfast hoping that I would eat something to help my tongue recover.

Now I have to digress for a moment to let you know that on this particular cruise there also was a large group of doctors (about thirty of them) sailing together. They were all from California, mostly from northern California, San Jose, Oakland, San Francisco and a few from Los Angeles. What they all had in common, besides being doctors from California, was that they were all men and all of them were gay.

One of the tables of gay doctors was adjacent to our table of octogenarians and right from the start of our cruise they were kidding me about being a misfit at my table and trying to coax me to move to their table. We had some fun banter back and forth and everyone, including my octogenarians were having a good time kidding me.

So it was only natural that when I found my tongue had turned black, I turned to this table of doctors to analyze, diagnose and prescribe for my ailment. What I did not expect, but should have, was the hilarity I set off when I stuck my tongue out at them. "We knew you were gay all along, but you should really clean that tongue after sex," was the first joke thrown my way. "Surprised that your nose is not brown," was also offered. "You've caught black tongue, a kissing disease that only gays get when they kiss too many other gays," followed. "Let me get a closer look with my tongue," was another offering. "You stuck it in the wrong place," was the final joke.

After the laughter died down, one of the doctors put his hand on my shoulder and smiled: "You've been drinking too much and have a simple bile issue because the liver can't handle all that alcohol. Cut down on the drinking, eat some yogurt for breakfast and again at lunch. Most likely by dinner time your tongue will be pink again." He paused, put his arm fully around my shoulder, hugged me and said: "My cabin number is Panoramic 1014 and I can provide a lot of other treatments, but only once your tongue clears up." Everyone laughed.

I ate yogurt several times that day, only drank ice tea and water, and by dinner time, my tongue was on the way to becoming pink again.

Several years and three kids later, my wife Linda and I flew into Seattle with Josh (15 years old) Erik (14 years old) and Ryan (13 years old) for an Alaskan cruise. We proceeded to have one of our best vacations ever. The kids (now grown) still talk about the Alaska cruise on Holland America Cruises as being the most magnificent trip they ever experienced.

Alaska at that time was still an adventure vacation. Ketchikan, with its totem poles was very much an Eskimo village. Sitka was the Russian city east of the Bering Sea. Skagway was an old fishing village that was still a major seaport for working sailors. Juneau was where we would walk on the Mendenhall Glacier.

We took all the excursions we could fit into the seven-day sailing. We went whale watching and saw whales breach as they playfully waved their tales at us. At the same time, we saw equally playful pippins float on their backs in the warm Alaska sun.

We went whitewater river rafting and I almost lost it as our guide took our rubber raft over the rocks and dove straight into the rapids drenching everyone on board with the ice-cold river water that enveloped the entire

RICHARD S. KAHN

raft. We were all wearing boots that they gave us to protect our feet. When we landed on shore, I emptied the boots of the water that had filled when we were temporarily submerged and watched as a small fish flowed out of my boot back into the river.

We took a canoe ride where an equally adventurous guide had our party row within feet of a waterfalls before ordering us to quickly row backwards to escape what could have been a death-defying experience. Most people, like me realized we were close to the falls and began rowing vigorously. Others thought it was just a joke—until she started yelling for everyone to row, "Row, row hard. keep rowing." It was exhilarating.

But the most exciting and thrilling part of the trip was entering pristine blue-white Glacier Bay on a still and quiet morning. The huge glaciers stood before us and smiled as they glistened in the August sun. The ship paused for a couple of hours and allowed us to wait and watch as the glacier released a piece or two of its own skin.

We could see an ice wall break off a piece along its side (actually quite a large piece of ice that could sink a boat) and begin to slowly slide down the massive wall of the glacier into the bay below. The ice would moan as it cracked and then make an eerie squeal as it slid down. The shrill sound would soon become a roar as the ice would hit the bay below. This was truly a unique experience that we would keep in our minds eye for many years.

Our first Alaska trip was completed with a visit to Seattle so that the kids could enjoy the grunge music that was popular in the 1990s. Some of us rode to the top of the Space Needle to see the views of Seattle and the Pacific Ocean. We also went to the famous Pike's Place Fish Market to literally catch fish that was being thrown across the isles at patrons who were buying fish for dinner.

FAST FORWARD MORE THAN TWENTY YEARS LATER

"Moose, moose, moose," yelled one person followed by other shouts moments later, all taking place just ten minutes after the train pulled out of Anchorage. Everyone applauded. We were all excited. We were on our way to Denali and we'd seen our first moose, a large bull moose just a few feet away from the train tracks. The conductor slowed the train so we could exchange looks. The moose just stood there looking at us as we looked at him. He was very big.

A year before this exciting moment, several of our friends had asked: "Let's take an Alaska cruise." These friends normally hang out together from spring to fall on Cossayuna Lake, a three-and-a-half-mile-long lake near Saratoga Springs in the southern Adirondacks. All summer long we share stories, drinks and food as we hook up our pontoon boats and float around the lake.

Many years ago, our friends (and next-door neighbors on the lake) Charlie and Sheila Rappazzo suggested that we should get together each winter and take a cruise somewhere in the Caribbean to escape the cold north and reunite with other friends who spent so much time together in the summer. For this trip to Alaska, we combined the lake group with some of our close friends from Long Island and suddenly there were thirteen people going to Alaska. But this cruise would be in summer since that's when the cruise ships sail along the Alaskan coast.

Linda and I had been to Alaska twenty-one years earlier with our three boys, so we had one provision: "We will do this again, but we need to begin with a trip into the Denali wilderness." We once again chose Holland America Cruises.

Alaska is often number one on people's bucket-list for vacations, but often left until people reach their 60s or older. We don't quite understand that because it's clearly a destination for families with kids and I can assure you that everyone will remember that vacation as one of the best ever. How can it not be great when you can get up close with grizzly bears, caribou, moose and even whales that leap out of their home in the ocean to playfully splash you.

Anchored down in Anchorage we found ourselves in a very welcoming small city. The downtown area was clean and un-crowded on a Wednesday afternoon. We walked around and slipped into a rooftop bar to sample the Alaska amber which was cold and tasty as were the nachos, shrimp and artichoke dip.

Dinner was more complicated because there were thirteen of us and only the large, noisy tourist restaurants could accommodate such a large group; plus, we were warned about long waits at the larger restaurants. One place told us the wait would be about an hour or so, even for a party of four.

And this was at the early dining hour of six o'clock. We split up and went different ways. One highly recommended restaurant could accommodate six of us, but when we arrived, we found that they did not have air conditioning and the weather was providing us with a rare tropical heat wave that reached 81 degrees that day and was not cool enough to dine indoors. We opted for an open-air restaurant as most people did on this exceptionally warm evening in Anchorage and enjoyed local fish and chips and more Alaska amber beer.

The next day we boarded the train to Denali. Warned that it was an eight-hour train ride did not dissuade us from wanting to go to Denali, a true American frontier and a region consisting of one of the largest national parks in the US. This is a wilderness adventure in our own homeland.

The train ride on the McKinley Observer was half the fun and a whole day long. Just ten minutes out of Anchorage we saw that big bull moose standing alongside the railroad tracks grazing. As we slowly chugged past, he turned and calmly walked off into the woods. The train engineer blew the train whistle to warn any other moose nearby to stay clear of the tracks as he picked up speed. Shortly later we saw another moose on the tracks as the train slowed down to allow him to get out of our way. He (or she) seemed in no rush to move and the train almost came to a full stop to allow the moose time to walk off.

An entertaining and educational tour guide named Ben described the sights along the way detailing the history and culture of each of the local towns we passed, including Wasilla, home to Sarah Palin, once the hopeful vice-presidential candidate. The lovely and creative bartender Griffin served us bloody marys (our choice) to start the day and a coffee-Kailua concoction as the morning wore on. This was the way to travel and see the Alaska countryside as we crossed the mountains on our way to Denali.

Denali is both a wilderness park and a mountain. In native American language, Denali means the big one. It was the original name for the mountain which we have come to know as Mount McKinley. A wealthy conservationist named the mountain for then senator McKinley because McKinley supported the movement to protect the lands from development during the gold rush years. Alaska has returned to calling the mountain by its original name Denali. (No disrespect for President McKinley,)

The next day we boarded a bus to tour the Denali Park and Mike, our guide (a sailor in real life) warned us that we have only a thirty percent chance as visitors to see "the mountain" (Mt. McKinley/Denali/the big one). We found out that President McKinley, by the way, never got to see the mountain named for him. I mention the thirty percent chance of seeing the mountain because we were among the lucky thirty percent to have a clear, and surprisingly warm day to be able to see and photograph Denali in all her magnificence as she stands there peak and shoulders above all its brethren mountains. She is shrouded in snow and glistened in the summer sun.

Speaking of sun, it hardly slept during the long summer nights with sunsets around 10:30 p.m. in August and an absence of total darkness even at two or three o'clock in the morning. But be warned, in winter the typical day is only four-hours-long from sunrise at around 10 a.m. and sunset by two o'clock followed by a deep darkness until the next short day. Alaska in winter is covered with a misty, dreary shadow that never brightens.

RETURNING TO THE SCENE OF THE EXCITEMENT

Over the years I have returned to destinations visited earlier and often found them disappointing. It's not the Thomas Wolfe syndrome "you can't go home again," but rather the changes that have taken place over the years that alter the scenic views, the destinations, the attractions, and sometimes, even the people.

Alaska in the 1990s was magnificent. The brilliant white and blue ice in the natural theater of Glacier Bay was one of the most breathtaking experiences of my life. Standing on the deck of the Holland America ship as we floated silently in the still sea in the midst of this living land of ice. We had listened for and heard the cracking of the glacier and marveled at the brilliance of the blue ice.

Fast forward 21 years later we stood on another Holland America ship in this same Glacier Bay. But, as I stood there looking around, I failed to recognize that we had arrived. "Where are we?" Linda asked one of the helpful Holland America personnel. "We are in Glacier Bay," he smiled back. "No way this is Glacier Bay," she said.

I looked around and around with my mouth wide open, chin hanging down. The white and blue wall of ice had all but disappeared and was severely diminished in size as the glacier had receded over the years. Most of the glacier wall had turned black with dirt from years of pollution. It was not how we remembered. The glacier had lost much of the magnificence we had previously experienced. I suddenly felt blessed that I had the chance to experience this site before. I was sorry for the others on this trip that could not appreciate what Linda and I had seen on our previous trip to Alaska.

Time had not been good to Alaska and particularly to Glacier Bay. Global warming had eroded what was once a magnificent sight. This is not a political statement. It is a visual fact verified by photos from the past against the backdrop of what remains in Glacier Bay today.

It was no different in the villages that we visited along the Alaskan coast. Time and reluctant changes had altered everything. Ketchikan was no longer the quaint Eskimo village, but had turned into a tourist attraction filled with too many souvenir shops. It still had some of its charm, but much of it was lost underneath the growth of tourism.

While it was not the same Alaska, we visited in the 1990s, this truly American wilderness remains a wonderful, peaceful, special place on earth and still is a destination worth visiting to experience all that makes it the last frontier of America. But the landscape has become worn and tired when compared to the vibrant scenes of the past that we were fortunate to have experienced.

Arriving in Ketchikan: It was eight o'clock in the morning and I was sitting on my verandah doing my favorite cruise activity—watching the sea. Enjoying the slow ease of the swells as the ship glided smoothly past mountains on our way to Ketchikan. The warm early morning sun surprises my body. I let the warmth surround me.

We pass a stationary fishing boat and I wave to the local fishermen. No one notices. The sea is calm, but not placid. I could watch the water all day as it calms my senses. There is blue sky and wispy clouds caught in the mountains. This is truly a picture-perfect morning. but I don't dare leave my post on the verandah to get my camera as I don't want to disturb the moment. I will have this moment in my mind's eye and enjoy the peace without taking pictures for a change.

One of our stops on this trip was Haines, a quaint seaside fishing village focused on eagles, ravens, totem poles and hammers. It was the hammers that stood out for me at the only Hammer Museum I am aware of. There are hundreds of hammers and none duplicated. There was even an electric hammer, but you will have to get to Haines to hear the story behind that particular hammer.

Skagway, Sitka and Juneau are some of the other stops on various Alaska Inside Passage cruises and there are a slew of other lines like Celebrity Cruises, one of our favorite cruise lines, that provide a touch of luxury and excellent service while sailing for a week or more in these calm waters.

Our friends all experienced a very special destination and returned with stories to tell their friends and children. For many of them, another bucket-list item was scratched off their charts. We were glad that we included the Denali wilderness and strongly recommend that vacationers include both the Inside Passage and Denali on any Alaska trip. You may be fortunate to see the tip of Denali (Mount McKinley) glistening in the summer sun. If you do, savor the moment and know that you are among the lucky thirty percent.

CHAPTER TWENTY-SEVEN

AROUND THE WORLD IN THE CARIBBEAN

This old man and me,
were at the bar and we
Were having us some beers and ...
We talked about God's grace
and all the hell we raised
Then I heard the ol' man say
"God is great, beer is good
and people are crazy"
. . . .
"People Are Crazy" sung by Billy Currington

When I worked at *The Travel Agent Magazine,* I was often called upon to make speeches or be on panels at industry conferences. So it was not unusual for me to find myself on a flight to the Caribbean in 1978 to attend what was a combined annual conference for the Caribbean Tourism Association and the Caribbean Hotel Association.

This was my first foray into this market and I was excited to be on a panel and meet some of the Caribbean dignitaries. Only this initial foray and my panel were disrupted on the second morning by the discovery of a dead body in the center of the lobby of our hotel in Caracas, Venezuela. The dead person had been murdered, we were told, but had nothing to do with our conference. The chaotic scene that followed with travel agents, tour operators and Caribbean dignitaries all trying to escape Venezuela did put a damper on our meetings.

I did, however, begin to meet and get to know some of the officials of both organizations and decided to follow up on my volunteer work back in New York in the local Chapter of the Caribbean Tourism Association. There I met several people who would become some of my closest business friends throughout the years with some remaining real friends today.

Over the years and hundreds of trips to the Caribbean region enabled me to become somewhat of an expert on this popular warm-weather destination just to our south. Some of my visits was as a reporter experiencing the grand opening of a hotel or a new destination marketing program. At other times, my volunteer position with the Caribbean Hotel Association and the Caribbean Tourism Organization enabled me to work in the region to help grow tourism and improve the product.

When I left *The Travel Agent* in 1989, I launched Kahn Travel Communications and began writing freelance articles for special sections in *The New York Times* specifically on the Caribbean. This was soon followed by a regular freelance opportunity at Newhouse Newspapers' *Star Ledger* and *Trenton Times* where I wrote several special sections each year for a period of more than ten years focusing mostly on the Caribbean. When *USA Today* launched their travel section I began writing two annual special sections on the Caribbean, one in the fall and one in the spring. I also wrote articles for special sections in *Business Week*, *US News & World Report* and other publications. Many of these special sections were linked to advertising sales which were handled by my friend Jim Furey.

I also helped launch the *USA Today* Travel Section with a month-long sweepstakes promotion in 1990. We got both governments and hoteliers to cooperate (a rarity at that time) and featured twenty hotels giving away a trip each day, every weekday for a month, along with two airline tickets for each trip (forty tickets in all) from American Airlines. It generated more than two million participants and a lot of publicity for the new *USA Today* Travel Section.

When I launched my public relations division of Kahn Travel Communications, many of my clients were based in the Caribbean and eventually both the Caribbean Hotel Association and the Caribbean Tourism Organization became clients. I also served on the Board of Directors for the Caribbean Hotel Association for twenty-four years. When I look back on how this all evolved it started with a trip to Dominica as a volunteer to help the island grow its tourism product.

ABOVE THE CLOUDS IN DOMINICA

Three business friends Jim and Barbara Furey and Bill Moore and I met up in Antigua one afternoon. Jim and Barbara and I had gotten to know each other in New York at local events. Bill and I first met when all four of us convened in Antigua for an overnight on our way to Dominica (a small English/French island and not the Dominican Republic which is a Spanish speaking island). We were on our way to provide the local tourism interests with a week-long series of educational seminars on how to build their tourism infrastructure. The year was 1980.

Jim and Barbara were marketing and publishing specialists. We would end up working closely together on special sections for a variety of publications. Bill was a chef and worked for the Caribbean Hotel Association on their education programs for hoteliers across the region. I was an editor who would tell the Dominicans how to build interest in Dominica and how to reach the travel community and the public. Once there, we all worked together helping each other help this fledgling destination.

Getting there, however, was a trip unto itself. After an overnight in Antigua, the four of us climbed into a small plane that sat four, but only had three seats available because of all the educational equipment, camera, films, books, etc. I was directed into the co-pilot seat while the three of them sat behind the cockpit.

We took off easily but as we continued to climb skyward, I asked the pilot when we would be leveling off. You may recall that I had worked for *Aviation Week* magazine and knew a fair amount about how planes flew— at least enough to be concerned. The pilot explained that he was having difficulty leveling off because of all the weight in the back with all the equipment. He said it would not be a problem as we were flying straight. His only concern was landing.

That became my concern too as we approached Dominica and Cane Field came into view. The airport was built along the Caribbean Sea, but parallel to the mountain so that planes had to approach directly at the mountain and make a sharp right turn onto the runway—a very sharp right turn or the plane would fly into the mountainside. This was normally an easy maneuver for these small planes, but not when you can't get the nose down to a level position.

As we approached the small mountainous island we headed straight for the mountain itself. I could see the runway below, but as expected, it was perpendicular to our approach. The pilot kept lowering the plane as we got closer to the runway, but we were still headed straight into the side of the mountain. We were just above the water line as we came close to landing and he made an abrupt, *very abrupt* right turn that threw all of us to the side. The next thing we knew we were on the runway with the mountain still there but to our left. And the nose of the plane had finally come down and we were safely on the ground. It was a scary, but safe landing and we were welcomed by smiling tourism and hotel officials.

The local hoteliers and their staff took the seminars and training sessions very seriously. I too, was learning a lot about how to operate a hotel and even how to better serve as a waiter or waitress. So were the young Dominicans. One evening at a local restaurant Bill Moore and I were seated at a table out on the deck overlooking the sea. Below us was a rock formation that welcomed the waves with furious splashes.

Our table was up against the railing and when the young lady that was serving us came to place my plate of food down, in order to do as she was taught at Bill's training session, she leaned over the railing behind me and tried to reach around the outside of the railing to correctly serve me from the left side. In trying to do this she almost went over the railing to a most certain death. Bill's eyes opened wide, I reacted and grabbed her, pulling her back, saving both her and my food. Bill then thanked her for trying and explained that there are times and situations that allow for exceptions. This was one of them. I'll never forget that or that you serve from the left and take from the right.

The Dominica tourism director, Mr. Dyer, kept asking me to join him on a drive up the mountainside to Trafalgar Falls. The only problem was it kept raining day after day and we kept postponing the trip until the last full day I would be on the island.

On that day, I boarded his Jeep for the trip up the mountain to Trafalgar Falls, a magnificent falls at the peak of this mountainous island. We stopped for lunch at a small four-room resort called Papillote in the rainforest and had a fantastic local lunch including mountain chicken (giant frog's legs). From there we continued, stopping again at the Emerald Pool, a small waterfalls surrounded by lush, tropical vegetation that gave the clear mountain water a brilliant green hue.

Then we were off for the final leg of our journey up the mountainside. Here the dirt road became a narrow path in which several times I had to look away as the drop off outside my window was unimaginable. Several times I felt the wheels of the old Jeep slipping on the wet dirt road. Trying to cover up my nervous tone, I told Mr. Dyer that, "I had seen enough and appreciated the beautiful landscape of Dominica with the rainforest and Emerald Pool and that we did not need to go any further up the mountain to Trafalgar Falls." He said there was no reason not to continue upwards. I tried to convince him that the road was steep and wet and narrow and I was concerned. He then told me, "There is nothing to be concerned about. My constituency is up here in Morne Trois and I come up here every Monday night."

I gasped: "You make this trip at night? In the dark?" He smiled and then said "Look, look, we are rising about the clouds." And sure enough, we began to drive through what first appeared to be fog, but was actually the low hanging clouds that formed a ring around the mountain. Once through the clouds, there was the bright sunlight that had been hidden by the clouds for days. I finally had my first view of the magnificent Trafalgar Falls.

More impressive to me was looking down at the clouds that we now road above. I wondered if this is what those that die get to see as they rise to heaven? Then I wondered if I were still alive as I experienced this rare drive above the clouds and reached the top of one of the tallest falls in the Southern Hemisphere.

I survived that trip and fell in love with Dominica, made some lifelong friends in Jim and Barbara and Bill and returned to help Dominica survive and grow its tourism on several occasions. It is a destination that provides much more than a Caribbean beach. The mountains are a hiker's dream. And there are few other places where rising above the clouds is so accessible.

On to a Party in Barbados

After a week giving seminars and participating in training sessions in Dominica, I took the liberty to rest for the weekend in Barbados. I had never been to Barbados before that trip and my connecting flight home from Dominica stopped there so it was the perfect place for R&R. I called upon Ken, the general manager of the Barbados Hilton, for a room for the weekend. He was a business associate that I knew from the Caribbean Hotel Association. He welcomed me and informed me that he was attending a pre-May Day party on the *Jolly Roger* sailing vessel that evening and I was to join him for the festivities.

I had never been to Barbados and I did not know that May Day was celebrated with such fervor, similar to our Fourth of July or even New Year's Eve. The party began early and the Barbados rum, some of the best rum in the world, was flowing. So was I.

Bajans (what Barbadians call themselves) were welcoming me into their world and I was loving it. The ship returned to dock sometime in the early morning hours, but few people got off. I managed to get an hour or two of sleep (I think I just passed out) on one of the ship's hardwood couches. Breakfast was being served at seven o'clock and I saw Ken with some coffee so I joined him there. After breakfast I returned to the hotel for some real sleep. That night I woke up and there were several messages from Bajans I had met the night before inviting me to dinner. The party continued through a second night and I then called it quits. This was great fun, but it was too much for me after the long week in Dominica.

I would return to Barbados more than 100 times over the subsequent years, opening hotels, advising tourism directors and ministers and managing public relations campaigns for several hotels including working many years with Peter Odle and the Mango Bay resorts group. Linda and the kids would also join me exploring Barbados including Harrison's Caves where a mile down you can enjoy total darkness in the cold silence of the earth. Once, we were at the bottom of the cave when the tour leader could not get the cart that carried our group restarted.

We were with more than a dozen tourists below the earth with limited light from lamps imbedded in the cave walls. The guide kept calling for assistance but we could not hear whether or not his calls were going through.

He said we might have to walk up in the dark if they could not get another one of the trams down to pick us up. I don't like the dark, especially the total dark that one experiences when you are a mile below the earth. However, we were saved by another tram before we had to venture up the steep incline to freedom and sunshine.

The destination is great for snorkeling and scuba diving, but what makes Barbados special is the people—the Bajans themselves. Barbados is probably the most educated and sophisticated of all the Caribbean nations. It was tied to England for many years before independence and continues a link to its British ancestry. The economy is one of the strongest in the Caribbean and the overall friendliness of the local residents may be attributed to their higher education.

Also, if I may digress for a moment. Throughout the Caribbean islands the local residents are just that—local residents or islanders. Please do not call them natives. They may be natives in the true definition of the word "native," but the connotation is that a native is an unsophisticated original resident and most of the Caribbean people are anything but unsophisticated. The original Caribbean native residents, the Arawaks, who had spread across the region, were eaten by the other Caribbean natives, the Caribs for which the Caribbean is now named.

REMEMBERING A DIFFERENT HAITI

On the opposite end of the spectrum from Barbados, we find Haiti, one of the poorest nations in the world. But it wasn't always so. As a matter of fact, Haiti was once the playground of the rich and famous who escaped to the warm weather of the Caribbean back in the 1950s and 60s. At that time there were a number of high-end luxury boutique resorts and vacationers flocked to a variety of beach and mountain retreats.

Papa Doc Duvalier was president of the country from 1957 to 1971 and ran the country with an iron hand. He welcomed tourists because they generated funds for his government. My friend Jim knew Papa Doc well and had worked with him and his tourism officials to help promote the island. On one business trip late in the life of Papa Doc, when the old man had turned blind, but still ran the country, Jim walked into the palace with a large group of officials from around the Caribbean. When Papa Doc heard Jim's voice, he stopped and moved directly towards Jim welcoming him as an old friend. He was always a gracious host.

His son, suitably named Baby Doc, took over for his father and ran the country until a popular rebellion overthrew the government in 1985. The country has not regained its prominence since that rebellion. Ironically, the dictator that ran the country produced more wealth than the supposed democracy that replaced him.

Meanwhile Haiti has long been famous for its Voodoo magic and its very colorful Haitian art characterized by abstract drawings accented with brilliant colors. I experienced a little of both on a trip to Cap Haitian in the early 1970s.

Wanting to acquire a piece of Haitian art, but not being able to afford the high prices being paid to some of the world renown Haitian artists at that time, I purchased a painting from an artist hawking his work on the street. He asked $20 for a black and gray painting of a woman and child. I handed him the $20, and he was shocked that I did not haggle. He then told me to take a second painting. I told him that I valued his work and would not question his price of $20. He thanked me profusely and kept trying to give me a second painting. I asked if I could take his picture, but he was very reluctant because of religious beliefs. Finally, he relented, probably because I had paid more than he expected for this work.

When I returned home after that trip, I unwrapped the Haitian painting and sprayed the frame with insecticide because Haitian wood had been tainted with an invasive bug at that time and we were warned to be careful. I then put it outside the back door to dry. I was living in Sheepshead Bay, Brooklyn at that time in a two-family row house with parking in the rear.

The next morning I went to retrieve my painting and discovered it was gone. I went to work feeling the loss of something special. A week later when I picked up the slides of all the pictures I had taken, the photo of the artist was nowhere to be found, but instead one slide had only black and gray shaded lines all across. I began to fear that Voodoo was at work here.

Four weeks after the disappearance of the Haitian painting from outside my back door, I was leaving for work when I spotted a stray dog trotting down my street with something large hanging from his mouth. He dropped it in front of me and stood there for a moment panting with his tongue hanging out to one side. I stooped down to pet him. He licked my hand and turned to go back down the street. I picked up the partially chewed object he had dropped. It was a picture frame. I turned it around and stared dumbfounded. It was my Haitian painting that disappeared weeks before.

I have no explanation. I now believe in Voodoo. I believe in magic. I still have that painting, but I had it reframed because I was concerned that the wood may have carried Haitian bugs or something more sinister.

DOMINICAN REPUBLIC SHARING HISPANIOLA WITH HAITI

Haiti is an independent country, once owned by France but not an island unto itself. It shares the island of Hispaniola with the Dominican Republic, a country once owned by Spain. The people of Haiti speak French and a French Patois, while Spanish is the language of the Dominican Republic. These two, very different, nations are separated by a huge mountain chain and have had little to do with each other.

Over the years I visited the DR, as the Dominican Republic is frequently called, many times on both press trips and then as a representative of the destination when I worked in public relations. Santo Domingo is a bustling city, one of the largest in the Caribbean and driving around Santo Domingo is a life threatening and often life changing experience. It reminded me of Italy where impatient drivers would skirt the traffic by driving on the sidewalk. There may be traffic lanes, but more often drivers just make their own lanes as they weave through the chaotic and crowded streets at blinding speeds.

I did have the pleasure of helping the DR in the early 1990s when I got invited down to meet with Ellis Perez, former US director of tourism for the country, who had become a personal friend. He was back in the DR and no longer working for the government, but had started working with the private sector to help restart the tourism industry that had all but disappeared from view because of lack of government funding to promote the destination.

He picked me up at the airport and on our way into Santo Domingo we were stopped in traffic along a crowded highway. Also, along this highway were an assortment of hawkers selling newspapers, fruit, water and clothing. At more than one point while we were stopped, the sidewalk sales people recognized Ellis with excitement. *"Ellie Perez, mi dio, Ellie Perez."* I asked him how come he was so recognizable by these people. He explained that aside from his tourism involvement, he was a Dominican Republic television talk show host, often referred to as "the Johnny Carson of the DR."

At our meeting in Santo Domingo we gathered with hoteliers, shop owners, attractions, local tour operators and travel agents. Out of that meeting we organized the *Consul a Promocion de Turistica* or Tourism Promotion Council. It was well funded to begin with and my fledgling company, Kahn Travel Communications, was hired to promote the DR in North America.

We were very successful and generated a lot of interest for vacationing in the DR in those early days. The problem was the Dominican Republic government was not interested in spending any money on tourism despite that taxes were flowing in from tourist dollars spent in the destination. This was a similar problem on several other Caribbean islands. Within five years after launching the CPT, on-island interest was beginning to weaken because tourists were flocking to the destination and they no longer felt that we were needed. They stopped paying us and after the debt got too high, we stopped working for the destination.

PUERTO RICO, THE OTHER SPANISH NATION

Puerto Rico, in the 1980s, became the connection to many other Caribbean destinations thanks to American Airlines using the San Juan airport as a hub for its extensive network throughout the region. This network, which dominated the Caribbean for more than twenty years, has since disappeared as the airline suffered the pangs that most other legacy carriers experienced based on the faulty proposition that used route dominance as the basis for making money. It never worked. Now JetBlue dominates the Caribbean with point-to-point flights that either make money or get eliminated. Other airlines have followed the same pattern in the last decade.

Puerto Rico benefitted from all those people connecting because many of them stayed a night or two in the island before or after going off to other destinations. Others found the destination affordable simply because of all the flights. I could take or it leave it, but had to go there often because the Caribbean Hotel Association had its headquarters there and I was both involved as a volunteer and later with my company as their official public relations agency.

One note of importance; never get into a taxi that is not part of the official taxi line. This is a good practice at any airport in any country including the US. I made the mistake once in Puerto Rico and got over-charged for a short trip from the airport to the Condado area, a fifteen- to twenty-minute ride that normally cost ten dollars back in the 1990s. I was charged twenty-five dollars because I accepted the invitation from a non-registered taxi who welcomed me as I exited the airport doors. I paid the fare and promised myself not to get stung again.

MARTINIQUE AND GUADELOUPE, THE FRENCH CONNECTION

Moving over from the Spanish destinations we find two islands, Martinique and Guadeloupe providing a true French experience in the Caribbean. Martinique was home to Napoleon's Empress Josephine who was born there and grew up in a small house with her small bed that is now a small museum from the 1700s. Everything was smaller 300 years ago.

Both these islands are filled with lush, tropical gardens and forests that provide great sightseeing. But beware when shopping because you will find that the shopkeepers speak French and often nothing else as the island caters to the French-speaking market and the local islanders are French islanders.

On one trip to Martinique with my son Josh, we stopped to buy some souvenirs. Josh was taking French in elementary school and although he was only eight-years-old, he proudly told me that he would help me get by in Martinique because he spoke French. He got to help me, but also got us thrown out of a shop empty handed when attempting to buy souvenirs. I asked him to translate and ask the shopkeeper how much the merchandise cost in US dollars. Josh smiled at the women and said *"Un, deux, trois."* The women said something to him and he just repeated *"Un, deux, trois."* This went on three or four times before we were physically pushed out of the store.

On another trip to Martinique, I was attending a travel industry conference. When breaking for lunch in an open-air restaurant overlooking the swimming pool, we witnessed the crew from the Air France flight, that had come in the night before, relaxing before having to fly back to France that afternoon. And relax they did as they stripped down to nothing with both men and women relaxed side-by-side totally naked enjoying the warm sun. These pilots and flight attendants worked together and relaxed together. They were French, and lived in a different culture than most of the others in the restaurant.

We all stared, not just because they were naked and had beautiful bodies, but because we could not embrace the fact that they would shortly dress and get back on the plane and work together. *"Vive la France."*

SAINT MARTIN, SINT MAARTEN, FRENCH & DUTCH LIVING TOGETHER

Another culturally diverse destination is Saint Martin/Sint Maarten, a small island that is shared by the French government controlling one side and the Dutch Netherlands Antilles overseeing the other side. These two diverse cultures live side by side and work on both sides of a small island. While the Dutch side may have the international airport welcoming most visitors, the influence of the French in restaurants and hotels can be found on both sides of this tiny island.

Orient Beach, back the 1970s, was the site of a popular gay resort at one end of the bay and little else along more than a mile of soft sand on a horseshoe shaped beach. On one of my trips there around 1976, I was relaxing on the far end of the beach at Orient Bay—away from the resort. This was where local residents came to take a break, get some unfiltered sun and swimming in the gentle waves of the cove.

One of these local residents was a man named Marcel Gumbs. Marcel worked in the air traffic control tower at the airport and since I had worked for *Aviation Week* we had something in common to talk about. We became friends, dined together and met up whenever I was on island as well as when he came to visit friends and relatives in New York. Marcel got into politics, became a senator in St. Maarten and went on to become a local celebrity on the island. He eventually became prime minister.

On one trip in the 1990s, Linda and I met up with Marcel (before he became prime minister) to have lunch at a local restaurant on the beach. It was like dining with a Hollywood star as everyone (I mean everyone) that passed stopped to say hello to Marcel. He apologized for the interruption and asked the proprietor to move us upstairs away from the passing crowds.

Years later, our firm was hired to handle public relations for St. Maarten after the island had been devastated by a hurricane and they needed to regenerate tourism. I'm proud to say that we jump-started tourism again for the island and increased the number of visitors by nearly twelve percent in the first year.

From time to time I would still meet with Marcel, who was now retired from politics, but working as a consultant. This didn't last too long as the government kept going through changes every year or two and Marcel was eventually called in to lead a coalition government to get things back on track. Now my long-time friend was the prime minister of St. Maarten and an official Head of State. We continued to talk on the phone from time to time, but getting to see him during his tenure as Head of State was not easy, not because he would not want to see me, but his official schedule kept him busy trying to get things back on track.

Marcel was not the only Caribbean prime minister I had come to know and work with over the years. Others included Michael Manley from Jamaica, Allen Chastanet from St. Lucia, Maurice Bishop of Grenada, Lester Bird from Antigua, Dame Billie Miller deputy prime minister of Barbados, and one of my favorites, Eugenia Charles of Dominica who, in 1980, was one of the first women in the world to become Head of State of a nation. My relationship with Marcel, however, was different, he was a personal friend before he became prime minister.

Meanwhile, US presidents were not shy about visiting St. Maarten for their vacation. I was on island once, staying at the exclusive La Samanna Hotel on the French side of St. Martin when all the guests, including me, received a notice that we would be restricted to certain very limited areas and one restaurant at the resort because of two special guests that were coming to the resort at the same time. President Richard Nixon was staying on one side of the resort, while former First Lady Jacqueline Kennedy was staying on the other side of the resort. It made for a very restrictive stay for other guests as well as these opposing personalities.

St. Maarten also has become famous for the location of its airport on Maho Bay where visitors can position themselves on a fence at the end of the runway and hold on for life when the wide-bodied jets land and takeoff. If you let go of the fence or just lose your grip, you will be blown backwards onto the beach behind the runway. Beachgoers relaxing on the beach take cover when airplanes are landing or taking off as the aircraft comes overhead and loose things on the beach (including small people) can be blown about. Many people have been seriously hurt as they have been blown into the air from the thrust of the aircraft jets. There are warning signs at both ends of the walkway and beach, but that does little to deter thrill seekers. There are many examples of this unique St. Maarten experience on YouTube.

Having visited St. Maarten/St. Martin so many times since the 1970s, I have observed the growth of the destination and the unfortunate traffic jams that often result from a growing visitor population. At one time, I could rent a car and circle the island, passing the famous sign that the French and Dutch governments agreed upon as the line that separates the two countries, drive through Marigot, the French capital, and back to Philipsburg, the Dutch capital in a little more than one hour. Now it could take you an hour or more to go from Philipsburg to the airport which used to be a fifteen-minute drive. Progress is not always a positive thing.

FLYING INTO ANGUILLA WITH RIFLES POINTED AT THE PLANE

Prinair was a small airline based in Puerto Rico that was focused on connecting the islands for both vacationers and commerce. Around 1980, then Prinair president Cesar Toledo was expanding the airline's routes and reached an agreement, or so he thought, with the ruling government of the small island of Anguilla which sat just off the coast of the French side of St. Maarten/St. Martin.

The airline was well known because they did a fair amount of self-promotion. Nothing wrong with that when you are trying to create a reputation and build business. Cesar Toledo invited both travel press and consumer press to join him on the inaugural flight from Puerto Rico to Anguilla.

The short flight was uneventful until approaching the small runway on the island and the pilot was told by the control tower that he did not have approval to land. Not only that, but he was warned that the armed soldiers standing on the runway would shoot the plane down if he came any closer to landing.

With quick reflexes, the pilot aborted the landing making an abrupt maneuver that shook up everyone in the plane. When the aircraft leveled off, Cesar Toledo got up from his seat and went into the pilot's cabin to enquire what was happening. He then got on the radio controls and contacted the tower to tell them he has prior approval to start service and land the first flight that day. He also explained that he had an aircraft full of press and this would be a huge embarrassment.

The chief minister of Anguilla (equivalent of prime minister or president) who had just taken over the government was Ronald Webster. His emissary got on the tower radio and reminded Toledo that his deal was with Emile Gumbs, the former chief minister, and if he wanted to land today or any other day, he would have to pay the new government a lot more money than previously offered. It was ransom, but Toledo felt his only other choice was to return red-faced to Puerto Rico.

He landed that day, saved face, but did not resume service to Anguilla and never paid the ransom to the new government of Anguilla. Too bad, Anguilla is a beautiful tiny island, but without adequate air connections to build tourism. It would be more than a decade after Prinair's attempt to build traffic before the island's tourism would take off and become successful.

THREE VERY DIFFERENT US VIRGIN ISLANDS

Nearby Puerto Rico, a three-island territory under United States jurisdiction has experienced a mixed bag of success. St. Thomas, St. John and St. Croix comprise the US Virgin Islands. And, just like Puerto Rico, these islands under US control, afford vacationers the luxury to bring back a large number of duty-free purchases.

The reason I say mixed bag of success is because St. Croix, a beautiful and lush island and the largest of the three Virgins, has experienced a devastating drop in tourist interest since 1972 following the much-publicized Fountain Valley Golf Course mass shooting massacre. What happened on Sept. 6, 1972 was that eight people, including four prominent US vacationers were shot dead on the golf course. Eight others were shot, and wounded. Five local black residents were charged with the murders and during the highly publicized trial it was made out to be a racial issue which exacerbated racial tensions on the island.

Just a footnote for those historians reading this: Sept 5, 1972 was the day Israeli athletes were taken hostage during the Munich Olympics and Sept. 6, 1972 saw the massacre of eleven Israeli athletes and one German police officer. These two events would dominate the news for a while. However, St. Croix never fully recovered from the stigma of the racial overtones of the Fountain Valley Massacre.

In the early 1980s St. Croix made strides to regain its prominence. On one of my many trips to help the island I stayed at the King Christian Hotel in downtown Christiansted, one of the two main cities on St. Croix. The King Christian Hotel was owned by an expatriate from the US named Betty Sperber.

As mentioned earlier, I did not know until years later that Betty and I had met more than a decade before when she was living her previous life as a business manager in the music business and representing my friend Richie Havens.

I was now sitting in St. Croix with Betty Sperber reliving those days. I kept a loose connection with Richie Havens, saw him at a couple of local events in New York, but with his touring and my traveling for work we were often miles apart. He never changed. He was always a shy person, but loyal to his friends.

Meanwhile, on one trip to St. Croix, I brought my son Josh who was six years old at the time. I asked him to recount his thoughts about this trip so I could write the story through the eyes of a child and show the public that St. Croix was a wholesome destination and not the racist island portrayed by the attorneys during the Fountain Valley trials. Josh told me his favorite part of the trip was going to Betty's island, (not really hers, but a beach just across the harbor from the King Christian Hotel). This became the headline for the story in *The Travel Agent* magazine.

St. Thomas, meanwhile, is the most popular of the US Virgin Islands, especially for cruise ships that stop and facilitate duty-free shopping for their passengers. St. John is a small nature lovers island good for hiking and great snorkeling just off the shores that surround the island.

It was my connection to a hotelier on St. Thomas that resulted in my second career as a public relations executive working with governments, hotels, tour operators, travel agencies and cruise lines around the world for 30 years.

I had left *The Travel Agent* magazine in 1989 because a newly appointed group publisher, who we will call Mr. B, wanted to control the publication that was, at that time, the most successful (and profitable) travel industry news magazine in the world. He also wanted to control me and told me (not asked me) not to travel anywhere without his permission. As editor and publisher, at that time, I was the face and voice of the publication and often sought by organizations to speak, head up or participate on a panel, or MC an event. I should not have needed his permission to do these events which helped keep the magazine in the forefront of everyone's eyes, ears and minds and resulted in a lot of advertising which fed the bottom line and made the publication successful.

I ignored his edict and continued to attend speaking engagements that had already existed. This eventually resulted in Mr. B declaring that I was fired for insubordination. And while Ken Fisher, the president of Fairchild Publications, owners of *The Travel Agent* magazine at that time, immediately rescinded that firing and had me reinstated in my position, I told Mr. Fisher that I would stay on until the end of the year (which was also the end of the ad sales period), but could no longer work with Mr. B because he was taking the publication on a course of self destruction. That predication came true a mere two years after I left when the publication lost money for the first time in its sixty-plus years of existence.

I left the magazine in January 1989, after sixteen years working there, and began an assortment of simultaneous consulting jobs including helping *Recommend Magazine* set up offices in New York and Los Angeles, writing and editing special sections on travel for *The New York Times* and the *Newark Star Ledger* and assisting Diana Orban Associates in reorganizing her public relations firm.

It was at Diana Orban Associates that Dick Doumeng, owner of Bolongo Bay Beach Club in St. Thomas, came to me to get help promoting his hotel and two others he was purchasing on St. Thomas. I brought Bolongo into Diana's company as a client and was overseeing the work being done on the account. When my job as consultant was finished, I left Bolongo in the good hands of Diana's staff.

Dick Doumeng did not see it that way and came after me asking that I take him and his three hotels on as my clients. I explained that I was not set up to be a public relations firm and actually detested public relations people. As a writer and editor, I found too many public relations persons to be more of a deterrent to getting information than the helpful individuals they were supposed to be.

I remember once calling a prominent PR firm asking for a photo of the president of a company they represented. I had just finished an interview with that president and was running the story in *The Travel Agent*. They told me that "Susie Q" was the account executive for that client and she would not be back until the following week and there was no one else to help me. They only had 150 employees in that office, but Susie Q was account executive on that important account and no one else cared to help get me a photo. She never called back. I ran the article without the photo. That's only one typical example of the poor service that many (not all) public relations firms provided me as a reporter and editor.

There are a few, mostly small public relations firms that do a good job of helping reporters and writers; only just a few.

Meanwhile, Dick Doumeng convinced me that he would guarantee me an agreed-upon fee with up-front funds that would enable me to start my PR firm and represent his hotels. He helped change my life as I entered a new phase and new career in public relations and marketing.

Kahn Travel Communications grew quickly into a successful firm with ten full-time employees, many part-timers and freelancers and more than twenty clients at the height of our business. Bolongo remained a client for twenty years and we promoted both the resort and St. Thomas.

I like to think that KTCpr was one of the few PR firms that helped, rather than hindered the important work that travel writers do. We made it a practice to hire persons fresh out of college and teach them our way of doing things which focused first on the needs of the media and second on our clients. In that way, we always served the needs of our clients in the end.

Aruba, One Happy Island

Far away from Puerto Rico, St. Maarten and the US Virgin Islands is Aruba. I had traveled to Aruba on press trips and vacations. It was an easy destination to fall in love with. Great hotels, great service, easy to get around in a rental car, and there were a dozen casinos and countless restaurants.

I was working as a consultant to Edison "Eddie" Briesen who had just become the new minister of tourism. Eddie had no tourism background, but was eager to learn and a fast learner. It was not unusual in the Caribbean to have a person with no knowledge or background in travel, tourism or hospitality to be named minister of tourism. It was considered to be a cushy position often given as a perk to some friend of the prime minister. A new government had just come into power in Aruba and Eddie won his district in the election and was named tourism minister. Over the years, we became good business friends. I liked him more than most others I had met.

Aruba was then dealing with overbuilding of hotels and resorts and enjoying a situation that most nations would love—virtually no unemployment. There were 65,000 residents on the small island, and anybody that wanted a job could easily find one in the growing tourism and hospitality industry. With all the new hotels coming on, the government had to open the floodgates and allow perspective workers to immigrate into Aruba. Some were already coming from neighbor and fellow Netherland Antilles nation Curacao. But there were not enough trained personnel.

I recommended that the hotels and restaurants seek out Philippine people because tourism was down in the Philippines and there were thousands of Filipino nationals that would love to come to Aruba to work. Filipinos could fit into the Aruba lifestyle very easily because, like Arubans, most of them speak fluent English and Spanish. To this day, some of the best employees in Aruba are those from the Philippines.

In the early 1990s, Kahn Travel Communications also helped open the 400-room La Cabana, an all-suites timeshare resort on Eagle Beach, Aruba. We put together a team of marketing companies including Stephen Hicks, a tour wholesaler and Peter Warren for advertising. Together with our public relations we had one of the most successful timeshare launches ever because we promoted and sold the resort as a mixed-use property for both timeshare buyers and transient guests. Many of the transient guests who filled the rooms in the early days, bought timeshares while vacationing at the resort.

One of our promotions included Gloria Estefan. She was just about to finish her "Into the Light" recovery tour with a final stop in South America. It was a worldwide tour that had propelled her to the top of all music charts at that time. Aruba sits just off the coast of Venezuela and a short hop on a plane.

One of our colleagues convinced Emilio, her husband, to extend the tour one more stop and bring Gloria and the tour group to Aruba. We got La Cabana to offer them some well-deserved rest and relaxation for a free week at the resort. They would do two shows for the residents of the island and a press conference to promote the opening of the La Cabana Casino. We got American Airlines to participate in the promotion to provide transportation and we put everyone up.

I had the privilege of being the MC at the press conference with Gloria Estefan seated next to me. She could not have been kinder and more gracious. The casino became an instant hit on the island and the three firms who partnered on the launch of La Cabana and its casino won accolades and awards for the innovative marketing that led to the quick success. We worked with La Cabana for more than twenty years and visited Aruba more than 100 times.

CAYMAN ISLANDS, VACATION OR BUSINESS

The Cayman Islands consists of three islands, Grand Cayman, Cayman Brac and Little Cayman. The main tourist attraction is Grand Cayman where downtown George Town has more banks than Nashville has bars (a slight exaggeration). These banks are known to hold a lot of hidden accounts for wealthy people around the world that hide their money from government taxes.

The Caymans are also well known for its legendary Cayman Wall where scuba divers flock like fish to view deep underwater sites not seen elsewhere. There is also Stingray City where hundreds of stingrays gather and mingle with vacationers to get fed and petted. "Just shuffle your feet lest you accidentally step on one of them and get stung by their tail," warns the guide that has a boat full of eager tourists about to step off and walk among the stingrays.

These fish seem to love human touch and I can't help but love their soft, smooth underbelly. When offering food to them, they suck it into their mouths like a vacuum, often taking fingers with the food, but usually returning your fingers intact. They actually scour the ocean floor looking for food. They are docile fish. But do be aware—they are related to sharks and they will use their tails to sting in defense. Walk softly and carry food, they will rise off the ocean floor to feed out of your hands. It's a wonderful experience for both children and adults.

MR. BAHAMAS, GEORGE MYERS

George Myers is Mr. Bahamas. He has been referred to that way by prime ministers in the Bahamas as well as many of the local residents and others across the Caribbean. However, George Myers is Jamaican; born and raised in the island of Jamaica. I don't know when he came to the Bahamas, but there is no doubt that he has had an enormous positive impact on the growth of tourism to the Bahamas islands, and in particular, Nassau, Cable Beach and Paradise Island.

I met George early on in my career, but did not get to know him for years. He was always surrounded by "groupies" and it was difficult to get near him. While I was rising to a prominent role within both the Caribbean Tourism Organization, representing all the government tourist offices around the region, as well as on the board of directors of the Caribbean Hotel Association, representing hundreds of hotels across the Caribbean, George Myers and I rarely had two words between each other.

George was CEO of Resorts International on Paradise Island in the late 1970s until the early 1990s. This was the largest resort in the entire Caribbean at that time with more than 1,000 rooms in two separate hotel complexes which were connected by an enormous casino. Resorts International was Paradise Island. All other hotels just reaped the benefit of whatever promotions Resorts International did. After the founder died, the company came under control of majority stockholder Merv Griffin in

1988, until it was sold to Sun International in the mid-90s and eventually morphed into Atlantis—which it remains today.

While running Resorts in the 80s and early 90s, George Myers could often be found sitting at his perennially reserved table at the corner of the open bar that overlooked the casino. All who passed from one hotel to the next had to pass this bar and the watchful eyes and ears of George. Anyone within his inner circle could gather at this or one of the other nearby tables in that bar. Merv Griffin and other television and movie stars could sometimes be seen at George's table.

It was many years before I was invited to sit there. It began when I had seen George earlier in the day. It was after I had been MC of an entertaining event that got a lot of laughs, many of them generated by, and directed at me, but all in fun to help build funds for education of Caribbean youth. George passed me with his entourage and called out, "Kahn, see you later in the bar."

"See you later" could mean a lot of things. I chose to take it that I should meet him there before dinner for cocktails. I was there at six o'clock. The table was empty. I wasn't concerned because George himself invited me. I sat down, but quickly attracted one of the servers who politely explained that this table was reserved. I smiled back, "I know, Mr. Myers invited me to join him here." The server smiled and asked me what I wished to drink. I had a glass of chardonnay.

I sat there alone for an hour, watching people pass as I had passed so many times. I even saw some of my colleagues and said hello to anyone I knew. At a little past seven o'clock, I got up, asked the server at the bar what I owed for the drink, was told there was no charge, and I went to dinner. Later that night I passed the bar again. There was a large group of George's buddies, but no George. I nodded at those I knew and walked past.

A couple of days later, I did get to sit with George Myers at his table at the bar. He told me that I should use this area any time I needed to meet or entertain, adding, "After all, you are part of our Caribbean family." Those words resonated within me and swelled my ego. I had officially made it. I was accepted by the elite of the elite. If you were acknowledged by George Myers, you were somebody.

Several years later, George Myers had left his post at Paradise Island and was heading up the revitalization and refurbishment of the Radisson

Cable Beach Hotel across the bay in Nassau. He called me and asked me to join him for breakfast in New York. He then asked me to take over the public relations and marketing for the Radisson Cable Beach, a 700-room hotel. I was flattered, but I told him that I could "not become one of his entourage and could not afford to provide the dedicated time that I had noticed he demanded from his employees. I had other clients that also needed my attention."

He smiled and said that I would not have to do any of that. He just wanted me and my firm to do what we had done for so many other resorts such as Spice Island Beach Resort in Grenada, Bolongo Bay Beach Club in St. Thomas, Mango Bay in Barbados etc. He accepted my terms and I worked for George for several successful years. By the way, when in his presence at travel industry events, I gave in and also became one of his "groupies."

Antigua & Barbuda, a Dichotomy of Islands

Antigua and Barbuda are a two-island nation that has never become as successful as they should. Barbuda is a sanctuary for wildlife and despite several attempts at building small luxury resorts there, the lack of connections (either a bumpy ferry ride or an expensive helicopter flight are the only options) and the few facilities on the island make it only good for a day trip from Antigua. It might have become a good private escape for the rich and famous, but none of the resorts were ever sustained long enough to be successful.

Antigua, on the other hand has a number of very good hotels including one of my top ten favorites in the Caribbean—Curtain Bluff. The resort has a legendary wine cellar, considered by many to be the best in the Caribbean. But many of the developments in the 1980s and 1990s were thwarted by the government with "alleged" corruption that prevented any real growth of tourism. While this makes no sense since more tourists would have surely generated more taxes for the government, it was believed by many that the only way to make anything happen in Antigua in the 1980s and 90s was to pay handsome ransoms.

We worked with the Antigua government in the early 2000s and tried to help them get more air lift by working out an agreement with Delta Air

Lines. The airline wanted a guarantee of minimum funding to provide regular air service from New York to Antigua which the government agreed to. But the lack of enough promotional funding from the government tourist office to generate interest in the US marketplace undermined the efforts at that time. Antigua continues to limp along generating some interest mainly thanks to promotional efforts from hotels.

BONAIRE, BAREFOOT CASINOS AND SNORKELING

Bonaire is a tiny island that is forever linked to Aruba and Curacao as the B in the ABC islands. It sits in the south end of the Caribbean just off the coast of Venezuela. Bonaire rivals the Cayman Islands for scuba diving and boasts the best shore diving in the Caribbean. This also means that snorkelers can enjoy the easily reached diving sights just off the beaches.

I once stayed at Captain Don's Habitat, a small beachfront resort with great diving within a short swim off the beach. There really is a Captain Don Stewart, an environmentalist who opened the resort in 1976. He was more colorful than the coral that lined the sea beds beneath the waves that lapped the shores of his resort. He looked like Hemingway's old man from the sea with his long white hair and longer white beard which framed the dark leather look of his perennially tanned face. He walked around the resort shirtless in a pair of weathered shorts and sandals, looking more like the gardener than the owner. He told stories about Bonaire and the Caribbean Sea that entertained visitors and anyone who would stop to listen. He was a very special person who was often featured on television shows promoting Bonaire in the US.

I was a good swimmer, competitor on the Erasmus Hall swim team, but never learned to scuba dive because of ear issues when diving too far down. In Bonaire I could swim out, do a relatively deep dive without gear and see some of the colorful sights just off the shore from the hotel. I also got to enjoy the colorful stories told by Captain Don in the open-air lounge facing the beach.

The nearby Divi Flamingo resort boasts the only "barefoot" casino in the Caribbean thanks to an island-wide relaxed dress code. I found this casino definitely more relaxing than most others I visited around the world and proceeded to lose money there like anywhere else I played. Bonaire, with its beachfront resorts, relaxed atmosphere and colorful figures is the quintessential Caribbean.

St. Kitts and Nevis Sing Praises of Hamilton

St. Kitts and Nevis are another two-island nation. St. Kitts is a large mountainous island and Nevis is a small, former plantation island that just happens to be the birthplace of Alexander Hamilton. Nevis has a number of small luxury resorts that were built out of the charming plantation homes from the 1700s. It also has an overrated Four Seasons resort that unfortunately did not live up to the reputation of the chain the three or four times I stayed there. St. Kitts, however, has a large Marriott resort that draws vacationers and business conferences and does live up to the Marriott brand name.

The best thing about these two islands is the small, boutique resorts that were once plantation homes. Most of them provide both excellent service and accommodations in what were massive plantation estates.

St. Lucia and its Walk-in Volcano

The island of St. Lucia is large enough to have two international airports. The problem is that one of the airports is on the other side of the mountain from the tourist resorts requiring a two-hour bus ride from the airport. Once there, vacationers will be treated with a great destination including the only walk-in volcano in the world where tourists can actually stroll along the upper ridge of the crater and view what was once a violent spot on the earth. There are also sulphur springs and black sand beaches.

While Linda and I were honeymooning in St. Lucia at a Sandals resort, we golfed among the cows until we were outnumbered and returned to the resort to rest.

Our PR firm also opened and promoted Jalousie Plantation Resort back in the 1990s when approached by Pascal Mahvi, a former Prince of the Persian Empire who escaped Iran during the fall of the Shah of Iran. Mahvi built Jalousie on a hillside that sits in between the Pitons, two mountains that can be seen from distant islands. Originally there were about ninety private villas, each with a personal plunge pool. These villas dotted the hills above the beachfront bungalows and a main house with typical hotel rooms.

The sights from the hillside villas were magnificent. A golf cart or mini-tram would pick up vacationers to take them down from these luxury villas to the main house for meals and the adjacent beach. A few years after we opened the resort, Mahvi brought in Hilton to manage and promote the property. Later it joined the Viceroy Resort brand as Sugar Beach Resort.

HIDING AWAY IN ST. VINCENT AND THE GRENADINES

St. Vincent and the Grenadines may sound like the name of a 60s rock band, but it is a group of islands that line the southern Caribbean and have been known for great sailing waters, good scuba diving and small, luxury resorts on several of the tiny islands. Some of these islands boast only one resort and little else. They offer an off-the-beaten Caribbean retreat that provides very special experiences and is often used as a hideaway by the rich and famous.

TRINIDAD AND TOBAGO, WHERE THE BEAT GOES ON

Another two-island nation consists of Trinidad, a bustling metropolis and commercial center and Tobago, the relaxed beach destination where the Trinis go when they want to get away. Trinidad is large and filled with a wide assortment of people who originated from other destinations including India, Guyana, Venezuela, China and the United Kingdom. There are more than a million people that live in Trinidad. This melting pot makes for a frequently unsettled nation. It is also a commercial connection between the Caribbean and South America.

Trinidad is well known for its annual Carnival celebration. It rivals Rio de Janeiro in Brazil and Mardi Gras in New Orleans. What makes Trinidad's Carnival stand out is the steel drum festival and competition. One January night I had the unique privilege of being among the few outsiders taken through the backstreets of Trinidad just prior to Carnival.

We had to wait until dinner was done and the dishes were cleaned. The sun was setting and slowly the steel drums began to appear. We traveled to the inner city where the streets are narrow and the locals live. Once there, I witnessed the steel drum bands preparing and practicing for the competition. With one band after another, I heard music that any classical group, rock band or folk group would have been proud to perform. I never knew these oil drum instruments could, with the right person, produce such great sounds. These drummers were truly musicians and the music they played was great.

Sailing Through the British Virgin Islands

If I were a sailor, I would fly to Tortola, get on a sail boat and wind through the fifty islands that make up the British Virgin Islands. Richard Branson (founder of Virgin Records, Virgin Atlantic airline and other companies) may have done that before buying Necker Island with its single resort that has accommodated both rich and famous as well as everyday vacationers for years.

Some of the more famous islands in this tightly knit chain include: Anegada, Frenchman's Cay, Jost Van Dyke, Norman Island, Peter Island (with its famous resort of the same name), Scrub Island, and Virgin Gorda. Some of the more interesting island names include: Cockroach Island, Dead Chest and Fallen Jerusalem.

The Irish Landed on Montserrat

Montserrat is a very Irish island with a heritage that dates back to the 1700s when the tiny island was settled by Irish escaping to the new world. The names of local residents are reminiscent of Irish names and street names are clearly reminiscent of Ireland.

This tiny mountainous island is a nice alternative to the many Spanish, French, Dutch and English islands, but a series of volcanic eruptions in 1995 from the mouth of the Soufriere Hills Volcano disrupted life on the island and for a while made it difficult for vacationers to enjoy this out-of-the-way destination.   The island provides a different vacation experience and it is once again safe to go and see what a volcanic island is all about. The people are wonderful and welcome visitors like few other islands in the Caribbean. And treks up to the volcano provide an experience that you can't find on the other destinations.

HOITY-TOITY ST. BARTHS

St. Barthelemy (better known as St. Barths) is a little bit of the South of France transported to the Caribbean. It is very French and enjoys the reputation of being one of the more exclusive, allusive and expensive islands. The rich and famous including movie stars, rock stars and others often flock to St. Barths in the winter to enjoy the sun, sand and surf. The hotels are small and provide a very attentive French-Caribbean experience. And the dining is French gourmet in many of the restaurants and resorts.

NEARBY TURKS AND CAICOS ISLANDS

The Turks & Caicos Islands are a string of mostly small islands and cays that sit just southeast of Florida, below the Bahamas, and on the beginning edge of the Caribbean Sea. Two of the islands dominate the tourist industry—Grand Turk and Providenciales (better known as Provo). Being so close to the US should have made Provo and Grand Turk more popular, but the development of the infrastructure left the Turks and Caicos lagging for many years. In the past decade it has become one of the growing popular destinations especially Provo with some very nice luxury resorts.

THE ELUSIVE LURE OF CUBA

Cuba, once the leading destination for vacationers from the US back in the 1950s, has continued to flourish over the past five decades with more than a million European tourists visiting each year. So, despite the fact that the US government banned travel to Cuba, the island grew its tourism infrastructure into a successful affordable vacation model.

Cuba flirted with membership in, and partnership with, the other nations of the Caribbean Tourism Organization. The Cuban hotel sector had been members of the Caribbean Hotel Association. However, not being able to promote in the US was a deterrent to continuing these relationships. Notwithstanding these difficulties, thanks to my role on the board of directors of both the Caribbean associations, I got to travel to Cuba on several occasions to have meetings with tourism officials and hoteliers. The idea was to help the island's tourism interests benefit from our collective expertise.

I found Cuba to be a throwback to a time in the past with mostly older hotels, restaurants and attractions. However, the Cuban people we met along the way were in many ways more accommodating than some others we had worked with in the other aforementioned islands. It is still an unspoiled destination that provides an enjoyable experience.

GETTING INVOLVED IN THE CARIBBEAN

You may have noted that I previously singled out the islands of Grenada and Jamaica. My experiences in those two islands warranted being singled out. To this day they remain my two favorite Caribbean destinations.

I had the great pleasure of spending a lot of time in the Caribbean since my first trip in the mid-1970s. Many of my trips were for business reasons because of my volunteer involvement with the associations as well as opening, marketing, and promoting more than a dozen hotels across the region.

Those special sections I wrote for the newspapers helped define me as an expert on the Caribbean and also helped me establish my fledgling public relations firm in the market. It all began with, and grew solely because of my volunteer work with the two regional associations. I can't stress enough that my volunteering and involvement with the travel industry associations and work on the board of directors were the building blocks that enabled me to gain prominence, first as a reporter and editor and subsequently as a public relations executive. The volunteer work was time well spent.

My only regret was that both the Caribbean Tourism Organization and the Caribbean Hotel Association (now the Caribbean Hotel and Tourism Association) often moved backward rather than forward and lost many opportunities to effectively promote the Caribbean as a region. And all too often the Caribbean Tourism Organization, made up of ministers of tourism, did not get along with the Caribbean Hotel Association consisting primarily of hoteliers in the region. Too many individuals who rose to prominence as ministers of tourism had self interest blind their path and obscure their role which was supposed to lead the Caribbean region forward. The graft and corruption on some of the islands were legendary. There are many stories that would be great fodder for movies.

And while tourism is the number one economic earner for the Caribbean, most governments failed to put any significant funds back into developing and promoting what clearly drove their economies. It never made sense and still doesn't.

It wasn't much different in the private sector. There were too many people who ran the Caribbean Hotel and Tourism Association solely to raise their egos above the interests of the organization, particularly the volunteer officers. I too volunteered with self-interest in mind as I knew that working side-by-side to help these hoteliers would benefit me, and my magazine would gain prominence and sell more advertising.

Unfortunately, what was, at one time in the 1980s and 90s, one of the strongest hotel associations in the world, failed to serve the changing needs of their rank-and-file small hotels that lined the beaches of more than thirty island nations. Great training and marketing programs and ideas fell apart because they were never adequately promoted to the membership and eventually the organization lost relevance with the member hotels and died. Interestingly, no one ever told the officials that their association died and it just kept dragging along helping only a few with anything of significance.

I really love the Caribbean and spent more time there than anywhere else in the world. It is the leading warm weather destination in the world for Americans. I do hope that both the Caribbean Tourism Organization and the Caribbean Hotel and Tourism Association will eventually find the same path to travel along. It will mean a lot to the residents of the islands. They need the support.

CHAPTER TWENTY-EIGHT

KOREA: THE
SOUL OF ASIA

Nobody wants to get drunk and get loud
And all my rowdy friends have settled down
••••••

"All My Rowdy Friends" by Hank Williams, Jr.

I often traveled to distant countries to attend tourism and hospitality industry conferences—sometimes as a speaker, always as a reporter. It was no different in 1983 when I planned on attending the American Society of Travel Agents (ASTA) World Travel Conference with 10,000 other delegates from around the world. This would be my tenth annual ASTA conference. Over the years I eventually attended nineteen ASTA conferences, more than a dozen Pacific Asia conferences, about twenty hotel industry conventions and over sixty Caribbean conferences.

Most of us delegates were scheduled to leave for Seoul, Korea on Thursday, Sept. 22, 1983. We were flying direct to Seoul from New York via Anchorage, Alaska on Korean Airlines Flight 007. Only the Russian government created some advance excitement, when on Sept. 1, 1983 a Soviet interceptor airplane shot down Korean Airlines Flight 007 with 269 passengers on board.

This unprovoked and unprecedented event shocked the world and almost brought the Cold War between the Soviet Union and the United States to a heated confrontation level. For several weeks after the Russians shot down this South Korean passenger plane, there was speculation of further altercations between various countries, allies and others to reciprocate and possibly get revenge for this mass killing of innocent people. There were questions about North Korea's involvement in this episode. There was also concern about whether or not China would step in and, if so, on which side?

For a while Korean Airlines had ceased flights on that route. But with the ASTA World Travel Conference coming up they reinstated service on Sept. 22. I can't say that I did not feel some trepidation getting on Flight 007 that day. But then I thought "the Russians would not be so bold to shoot down a second Korean flight which would surely result in a widespread war." But then I also thought "the Russians were pretty stupid to shoot down the first Korean airplane on Sept. 1 and so far, get away with it, so they might do it again."

Nothing happened. The flight was great. The service was great. We left New York in the early evening, stopped in Anchorage in the middle of the night and arrived the next day in Seoul.

I got to my hotel and while checking in, noticed there was a tent card on the front desk in the lobby promoting a relaxing massage to get the kinks out after a long flight. Well, I just had a long and somewhat stressful flight so I took the number down and when I got to my room I called for a massage. I have had an assortment of massages in various countries around the world, but this would end up being the best I ever had for a unique reason.

It started with a knock on my hotel room door. A man's voice proclaimed that the masseuse I ordered is here. I opened the door and there stood the same bellman who originally took me up to my room along with a young Korean woman dressed in an all-white uniform. I thanked him and welcomed her into the room. As she walked in, I began to feel that there was something strange about her. My intuition was confirmed when she reached out for the table in the room to put down her oils and towels. She was blind.

The bellman left and this young lady, in broken English, asked me to undress and lie on the bed. She then proceeded to massage me with a touch that I had never enjoyed before. It was like she was at one with my muscles and bones feeling and manipulating my back, my neck, my shoulders in such a way as to relieve all tensions that may have been built up over the thirty-nine years of my life. This was truly heaven. I never felt as good after a massage as I did that evening. I asked her what her name was so I could get her again if I had the time. It was Hyun-joo. I wrote it down.

The next day was uneventful with setting up booths at the convention hall. I returned to my hotel to change for a scheduled dinner with colleagues and decided to see if I could get another one of Hyun-joo's amazing massages. I called down to the lobby and asked if I could have Hyun-joo, the same girl I had the night before. I was told she was not available, but they could send up a very suitable replacement. I was disappointed, but had psyched myself up for a massage, so I agreed to have whoever they sent up.

A short while later, my favorite bellman knocked on my door again and this time presented a young Korean man in the same all-white suit that the young lady had worn the night before. He entered the room and felt his way around until he found the table to place his oils and towels. The bellman left and I followed the same procedure as the night before. And this, equally blind and equally talented man gave me an equally perfect massage as I had had the night before. I didn't bother to get his name as it was now evident that all the massage staff were blind.

On my way out of the hotel for my dinner with colleagues I stopped at the front desk and inquired: "I've had two massages over the past two days, both performed by young blind persons. Why is that?" The explanation was simple: "The Korean government provides for those with disabilities and trains blind people for various occupations that they can do without sight. Some have chosen to learn massage because they use their hands as their eyes and feel their way around the body better than those with sight so they are better at massaging."

I agree. I've never had a better massage than the two I had from those young blind masseuses in Korea.

The next day I took a pre-conference tour up to the DMZ, the demilitarized zone which is the border between North and South Korea. It is an army outpost where both Korean armies stand guard over their borders to prevent anyone from either side coming or going. I asked one of my South Korean colleagues how they felt about the possibility of North and South Korea reuniting. He told me that there was only one reason to reunite with the North and that was to reunite the families that were separated by the Korean War in the 1950s. He further explained that South Korea would end up supporting North Korea because the manufacturing and production in the South was far superior to the socialistic operations in the North.

The tensions at the DMZ were real. The guards on both sides of the border took their jobs very seriously and were prepared at all times for what might become a deadly altercation. Our tour group behaved and no one dared step in the wrong direction.

The conference began without incident and one afternoon I deviated and went shopping. I had heard that one could purchase hand-made western style cowboy boots made to order. I was directed to and stopped in a very unlikely dark and dingy shoe store and the sales person told me that they could have eel skin leather boots make to fit like no other shoes I have ever owned. After having the massage of my lifetime, I believed this salesman and got fitted for a pair of cowboy boots made of soft eel skin leather. The next day I had to stop by to see if the mold that was made of my feet fit right. It did. And later that day I had a pair of boots delivered to my hotel for the cost of $45. A pair like these would have cost $245 back in the US and would not have been made to fit every crevice of my feet. Again, I was in heaven.

The final thrill of this trip came as a result of my colleagues. Somehow several of them, including a couple of writers and public relations people, had discovered that I was celebrating my thirty-ninth birthday while at this conference in Korea. They decided to take me out for a night of celebration.

First, I must preface this with a note about Korean's use of garlic and Kimchi. Some say Kimchi is the national dish of Korea. Kimchi is a vegetable dish spiced with a variety of seasonings like chili and garlic and wrapped in cabbage. It is then sometimes stored underground in the garden where it ferments until ready to serve. In addition, the Korean's love their garlic. When getting on the elevator in the morning one can smell the pungent aroma of garlic emanating from the pores of everyone around you.

So, when my colleagues took me out for the evening of partying, we began by having a traditional Korean dinner with some Kimchi as well. This was a good thing because we would then smell more like a Korean and that made us more comfortable when we would later enter a Korean bar and dance club. At one such bar, as soon as we opened the door the strong smell of garlic hit us with a wave that could only be enjoyed and tolerated by other Koreans. We didn't go into that bar.

Ending up in an American-style bar we were enjoying beers and other drinks when my colleagues presented me with a hand-embroidered jacket for my birthday. On the back was a huge dragon, a symbol often used in Asia to depict a magical creature of power and vitality. On the front was an embroidered inscription "Happy Birthday Richard, Seoul, Korea, 1983." I still have that jacket.

CHAPTER TWENTY-NINE

TAHITI: WHERE EVERYONE WORKS FOR SOMETHING

I know it's late, I know you're weary
I know your plans don't include me
Still here we are, both of us lonely
Both of us lonely
We've got tonight, who needs tomorrow?
Let's make it last, let's find a way
. . . .
"We've Got Tonight" by Bob Seger &The Silver Bullet Band

"Everything in its Own Time, if Not on Time" — Mareva, Tahitian Woman

In the late 1980s, an American cruise line (which no longer operates) with small ships carrying less than 100 passengers, was launching cruises out of Pape'ete, the capital of French Polynesia in the South Pacific. I was invited to join the press trip for the inaugural sailing and decided to go to Tahiti a few days early to explore a couple of islands and hotels on my own.

I arrived after a long flight from San Francisco on Air Tahiti Nui and was met by a young lady named Mareva who happened to be the daughter of an official with the Tahiti tourist office and, who had just returned from studying abroad at the Sorbonne in Paris. Mareva could have been a poster girl for a Polynesian promotion. She was simply beautiful with dark mocha colored skin, jet black hair and bright green eyes. And she was very smart.

As this was French Polynesia, everyone spoke at least two languages, one being French and the other being Polynesian. A good deal of the population also spoke English so I had no problems getting around and communicating my needs. Mareva spoke five languages. I barely spoke English.

Mareva took me to my hotel to freshen up and then on a tour of Pape'ete. It was a bustling South Pacific city, busier than I thought, but still very relaxed as you might expect in the South Pacific. We had dinner together that night and she picked me up the next morning and dropped me off at the first of several hotel appointments scheduled for that day. I was planning on interviewing some general managers of the hotels to include them in my stories that I would take back from this trip.

My first appointment was with the general manager of one of the luxury hotels on the island. It was set for ten o'clock. I was there at ten. Introduced myself to the receptionist and was asked to take a seat. About twenty minutes later I got up and asked the receptionist if the general manager knew I was there for my ten o'clock meeting. She told me that he was aware that I was here waiting. I smiled and sat back down. Another fifteen minutes passed and I stood up again and asked the receptionist if the wait was going to be much longer as it was nearing eleven o'clock and my next meeting was scheduled for noon. I didn't want to be late for that meeting.

She explained that she could not predict how much longer it would be because the general manager had not arrived at the hotel yet. But she knew he was on the way and she assured me that he knew I was waiting.

I began to get concerned and asked to make a phone call to Mareva so she could adjust my schedule or tell me what to do. When I got Mareva on the phone I explained to her what was happening and she said:

"Please understand that Polynesian culture is different from your Western culture. We are very proud to be able to focus our attention on that which is most important at the moment and that sometimes means ignoring prior schedules and plans. Please don't mention the original scheduled meeting when the general manager arrives. That would be an insult to him because whatever he is doing now, at this particular moment in time, is perceived to be more important and we need to put aside our moment and respect his decision, as he would do the same for us. Everything will get done in its own time, if not on time."

Everything in its own time, if not on time. I liked that philosophy and vowed to try and incorporate that in my hectic life back home at the magazine. While I sat there for another ten minutes waiting for the general manager to arrive, I had time to reflect on this cultural philosophy and while it was currently an inconvenience to me, I relaxed and read a magazine.

When the general manager arrived, we went to the restaurant patio to talk. He had drinks and snacks brought over and we had a delightful time together exploring the differences in running a hotel in Tahiti as compared to other places in the world. He had worked for Hilton Hotels with resorts around the world and recognized that Tahiti had its challenges with its cultural differences. I thought that he had assimilated well since he ignored our scheduled meeting, but I followed Mareva's suggestion and did not refer to the delay or my other scheduled appointments. I just went with the moment and the moment felt good.

He told me that it is very difficult to get and keep hotel staff because most people in Tahiti do not need to work. The fruit and vegetables are so plentiful, growing all over the islands and accessible to everyone for free and the fish are equally available in the sea that surrounds the islands. "No one has to work for food in Tahiti."

He told me: "Right now we have more staff than we need and I am taking advantage of that situation by re-training everyone in various job rolls so that when we are short-staffed, I will be able to shift staff from one job to another."

"Why are you flush with staff right now," I asked.

"Everyone wants to buy the new Sony Walkman (it was the 1980s) that just came on the market and they need to have a job to get cash to pay for that. As soon as they make enough money to get what they want, they will quit. They will return to work when they want something else that needs cash money to acquire. It's a cycle that we live with."

I arrived more than an hour late for lunch that day, but the hotel manager that was waiting for me never mentioned it and I did not offer an apology. It felt strange, but good to just move forward. He and I also had a very good exchange of ideas and the interview went very well.

The next day I was scheduled to fly over to Mo'orea, one of the neighboring islands that attracts many vacationers in an assortment of beach-front resorts. Mareva picked me up and took me to the airport where we boarded a small four-passenger airplane for our short flight over to Mo'orea. She then commandeered an open-aired Jeep that was provided by the tourist office and drove me around the island before taking me to the Tahiti Ora Hotel where I would be staying for two nights before joining the cruise.

After checking me in and escorting me over to the thatched-roof hut that would be my accommodations for the next two days she bid me fare-well. I had grown very fond of her over the past few days. She was very intelligent, capable of talking about any topic that arose and had strong opinions about what was happening around the world; opinions that I shared. On several occasions we flirted with one another and joked fre-quently about her getting burdened as my guide and me getting stuck with her. Wow was I stuck.

I stood there in this idyllic setting. The round thatched-roof cottage sat directly on the beach about fifty feet from the water that gently rolled up on the shore. It was one large round room with a bed at one end, and a dresser near the bed. There also were some hooks for hanging things up. A tiny bathroom was enclosed by a curtain but as I remembered, it was little more than a glorified port-a-potty that needed to be emptied after several uses. The shower was outside and enclosed by a flimsy curtain. There were only a few of these huts on the beach. Most of the guests were accommodated in the more luxurious rooms that sat on stilts over the water. A series of thin wooden walkways led from the main house out over the sea to these rooms. I was very happy to be on the beach.

But I was not happy that Mareva was leaving me alone here and I told her, "The only thing that could make this more perfect would be your company." She smiled and answered with, "Does this mean you want me to stay?" I realized that this was just a fantasy and that all she had with her was the sarong and sandals she was wearing. But I was fast assimilating into the French Polynesian culture and this was a moment worth cherishing so I sheepishly grinned, "Yes."

She then took my hand and walked me outside. "Let's catch some fish for dinner and we'll see," she offered as she kicked off her sandals and walked towards the water. I did the same and stood in shallow water watching as she raised her sarong and stood knee deep in the water. She bent down, hands hanging loosely, but very still in the water and waited. It didn't take long before she scooped up a small fish in her bare hands and turned to smile at me: "Here, hold this, I will get one for you now." I took the fish from her but quickly lost it as it squirmed in my hands and slipped from my grip. "Never mind, I will get more," she laughed. And she did.

She then showed me how to clean and cook the fish on the beach. She grew up in Tahiti and told me that everyone learns how to survive and actually flourish in this natural environment. I was further impressed with her. Not only was she intelligent and beautiful, but she was capable of just about anything. I asked her "Now that you have returned to Tahiti, what will you be doing. "Teaching and maybe starting some business," she told me. "I don't know yet. I'm not finished learning myself."

Once again, I fell in love. But this time, I knew immediately that this moment—this Polynesian moment—would be just a moment in time. I was learning the culture and hoped that I would be able to return home without losing too much of what I had learned here. I realized that I too, was not finished learning.

Two days later I was walking slowly and aimlessly along the beach after a breakfast of local fruit and juices. I felt great. I was about to join the cruise when it made its first stop in Mo'orea after leaving Pape'ete the night before. Mareva came down the beach to find me and escort me to the pier to join the cruise. Once there, I said a teary-eyed goodbye to Mareva and held her in a long embrace noticing that she too appeared to regret having to say farewell. We both knew that it would be unlikely that we would see one another again. I was not sure how that fit into the Polynesian culture.

We traveled to several islands over the next week including some that were just atolls that would disappear depending on the height of the sea. Eventually we stopped in Bora Bora, often erroneously linked with the musical "South Pacific" because, like the island in the show, Bora Bora was a US military base in World War II. I had expected to find a tourist destination spoiled by too many vacationers. However, this was French Polynesia and nothing seems to spoil their land, their culture or the people who live there. I envied them and vowed to return some day just as the sailors in the musical proclaimed when they sang about Bali Hai (which some people think is an island in the South Pacific, but really doesn't exist).

I have not gone back—yet.

CHAPTER THIRTY

BROOKLYN: A CITY WITHIN THE CITY

If you're on your own in this life
The days and nights are long
When you think you've had too much
Of this life to hang on
Well, everybody hurts sometimes
Everybody cries
Everybody hurts, sometimes
• • • • • • •
"Everybody Hurts" sung by R.E.M

On my flight home from French Polynesia, I searched the sky above the clouds and marveled at the red strands that spread across the horizon signaling another magnificent sunset. I also reflected on all my recent experiences that showed me a simpler life. My life was anything but simple. I then began to reflect on how I got to this moment in time.

Growing up in Brooklyn, New York, we lived in a three-room apartment where my younger brother and sister and I slept in the same bedroom. I slept in a small single bed on one side of the room. My parents slept on the living room couch that opened into a full-size bed.

I was a bed-wetter. I hated being a bed-wetter. Besides the embarrassment of waking up in the morning wet and smelly from urine, it was uncomfortable. We never found out why I was a bed-wetter. My parents took me to an assortment of doctors, but no one was able to ascertain why I wet the bed almost every night. My parents were also embarrassed about this and they were angry at me as well. My mother would yell at me in the morning when the bed was wet and smelly. If I woke up early enough, I would strip the bed and deposit my pajamas and sheets in the laundry bin. Neither my brother or sister wet the bed.

I continued to wet the bed way beyond the normal bed-wetting stage that many children go through; not every night, but two or three times a week. This further angered my parents, who were now convinced that I was doing it on purpose. We fought about this regularly. Why would I wet the bed and lie in my own urine on purpose? My parents did not understand. I did not understand. My bed-wetting came to a complete end when I was around twelve-years-old. I don't know why. I haven't wet the bed since, but my wife is very glad about that.

I was also a shy kid. My closest friends Michael, who lived in the apartment directly below ours, and Robert, who lived across the hall from us, played with me from the time we were babies in the cribs together until they went off to school. They were a year and a half older and Robert soon moved out of Brooklyn and Michael found friends his own age in school. We continued to remain friends and Michael would always look out for me and sometimes include me in things his friends were doing. But they were all older, better athletes than me and I never did fit in with them. Michael and I are still in touch today. And even today he still looks after me and protects me. He is my accountant.

Robert had moved to Hewlett, Long Island and while we kept in touch, we didn't see enough of each other until he was dying from kidney disease at age 20. I did my best to reach out to him and stay connected at that time even though I was more than a thousand miles away at school in Kentucky. He never allowed anyone to pity him; he just went on with his life as best as he could.

One summer before he died, Michael, Robert and I took a weekend trip up to Lake George in the Adirondacks in New York State. We watched Robert go through his morning routine taking a large assortment of pills and supplements that were keeping him alive. He had once been a star quarterback at Lynbrook High School. He was now a frail shadow of himself and tired by mid-afternoon. But he would not let us do anything for him. And we did have a great weekend together. He died the following fall. I was devastated. This was my first, personal loss of a friend. It never got easy to lose a friend.

I came into my own at eleven years old in the sixth grade at PS 134 in Brooklyn. It happened overnight when I heard that Jack, one of the tough guys in the schoolyard, wanted to get a condom to have sex. I decided to steal one of my father's condoms (he had left the box on the top of his dresser in our bedroom). I gave it to Jack during recess in the schoolyard. The next day another kid asked me to get him a condom. I told him that it would cost him a quarter. That was the start of my short-lived career of selling condoms to kids in the schoolyard. Short-lived because my father eventually ran out of condoms or figured out that I was stealing them. I wondered if he realized he was not having that much sex that he had to replenish the condoms so often. For awhile, I was prince of the schoolyard. I was no longer just another stick standing in line at school. I was finally recognized—the kid who had condoms.

I can also recall being eleven-years-old walking down the road at Lake Paradise, just outside of Woodbourne, NY, and some man in a big car asked me and my cousins for directions to the Fink house. The Finks were mysterious rich people who had a real house in the back of the bungalow colony. The rest of us just had tiny bungalows, small cottages that served as summer homes by the lake. We didn't even own our bungalow, but rented it each year for the months of July and August.

Bungalow colonies, as they were called, dotted the Catskill Mountains and were filled with New York City dwellers who escaped to the country every summer for a breath of fresh air for a rental cost of about $1,000 for the summer. The area was popular during the 1940s, 1950s and early 1960s and included several major hotels such as Grossinger's and The Concord. A generation of kids from New York City grew up on the lakes, rivers, creeks and in mountain forests that made up the Catskills. And then they went off to college, came back to the asphalt city and went to work; often forgetting the pleasures of those summer months splashing in the lake, cooking on the homemade firepit, and riding with the breeze of the country roads.

We fished (I never caught anything) in the fishing lake and swam in the small swimming lake. We played softball against other bungalow colonies on weekends when the fathers were up from the city. During the week we did little else other than gather at the pavilion that sat just behind the beach at the swimming lake. We spent eight summers at Lake Paradise from the time I was five until I was thirteen. I walked around all summer in just a pair of swim trunks, no shirt and no shoes. My hair, which was blond until I was ten, had begun to darken. My skin was tan from July to September. And there was handholding with Susan. It was a wonderful time of my life.

I was fourteen when I came out of my shy shell and started to hang out with the kids that lived along the two long blocks on 18th Avenue between Ocean Parkway and Coney Island Avenue. It was Brooklyn in the 1950s and that's what kids did. My parents were thrilled that I had started hanging out with others because previously I would keep to myself, listen to music and pretend to be singing along with every record as if they were my own creations. Sometimes I would stand in front of the mirror in the bedroom and perform. I was supposed to be doing homework, but more often shirked that responsibility and just mimicked the rock and roll singers that I saw on TV.

I knew every popular song of the day—*There Goes My Baby* by The Drifters and *Oh Boy* by Buddy Holly, The Elegants with *There You Are Little Star*, anything from Dion and the Belmonts and others from that early rock and roll era. I found my thrill on *Blueberry Hill* with Fats Domino and was in *My Blue Heaven* when I saw "the Fat Man" in person at the Little Theater on 44th Street in Manhattan while attending Dick Clark's Saturday Night Beechnut Show.

That same night I got turned on to Jackie Wilson performing *Night* and I began to imitate the great crooner with his majestic voice. Only I did it with silent lip synching while the music roared from the record player or radio. The Dick Clark Show on Saturday nights became a regular stop for me and a couple of friends. Bob and Morgan were the two regulars, the twins Alan and Sherman were two others. Earlier in the day we often went to a Saturday matinee in the same theater district. Most often we would purchase "standing room only" tickets at a fraction of the regular price and usually midway through the first act, we would find empty seats in the orchestra. It was a perfectly acceptable procedure and the ushers would even help us find seats once the play was on the way.

At one particular musical, *The Bells Are Ringing*, starring Judy Holiday and Hal Linden, Bob and I became regulars at the Saturday matinee. The ushers knew us so well they helped us find seats even before the show started. We would also stop by the stage door before and after the show and talk with Judy Holiday and Hal Linden and have (long-since faded) photos taken with them from week to week.

One Saturday afternoon in 1958, when Judy Holiday arrived, she called me and Bob over to her limousine and said: "How would you boys like to do me a favor?" Without waiting for an answer, she explained: "My nanny who watches Jonathan is sick and I did not have time to find a replacement baby sitter. He's six and loves the Zoo. My driver will take you there and pay for everything, pretzels, soda and everything. I will see you back here at five and take you all to dinner at the Carnegie Deli. Okay?" She then took a breath and waited for an answer which was, of course, "Yes." And we were off on a great experience which cemented our relationship with a Broadway star. After that, the management allowed us entrance to "standing room" without paying.

Many years later, in 1982, I was a guest of Gerry Cohen at *Night of a Thousand Stars*, a charity production at Radio City Music Hall produced and directed by his parents Alexander Cohen and Hildy Parks, famous writers and producers who, for many years, orchestrated the Tony Awards on Broadway. Gerry was married to Jane Lasky, at that time, and she worked with me as an editor and reporter at *The Travel Agent* magazine. The show had vignettes and walk-ons from hundreds of Broadway and Hollywood stars.

There was a typical red-carpet welcome outside the theater and when I arrived by limo, dressed in the customary tuxedo, I too was greeted by the paparazzi with cameras flashing and even had a couple of young ladies behind the red velvet ropes asking for my autograph. I, of course, obliged and scribbled something illegible so they could make up whoever they thought I was when showing the autograph to their friends.

At the end of the taping of the show, all the stars were to walk out the front of Radio City Music Hall and up 6th Avenue on another red carpet that was laid out from Radio City to the Hilton Hotel where there was a big dinner planned in the massive ballroom. The only problem was that the taping of the show ran two hours late and it was nearly eleven o'clock when everyone was exiting for what was supposed to be a street lined with adoring fans. As I walked alongside Hal Linden, who pretended to remember me as that star-struck kid from 24 years earlier, I heard Tyne Daly complain about the empty streets and lack of fans: "Why did we do this if not for the fans. Where are all the fans. Alex Cohen promised us the fans." "This was for a charity," Hal Linden reminded her as he smiled knowingly at me.

That experience provided me with a glimpse into the ego of some of the stars and also reminded me of my own ego needs and how I felt after making a speech and having a throng of guests come up to ask me questions. When there were no followers, I was left with an empty feeling. I could now understand Tyne Daly's disappointment.

As star-struck kids in the 50s we also used to go to the taping of the Gary Moore Show every Friday evening at the Ed Sullivan Theater on 7th Avenue. For this weekly excursion I was joined by Alan and Sherman, Mary, Bev, Marilyn, Nardina, Geri, Bob, Morgan, Dave and Phil and Sammy (another set of twins). Our large group of kids, ranging from fourteen to sixteen years of age, would stand on line in front of the theater each week, sometimes for an hour or two, hoping to get in to see the weekly taping of the show. Almost without failure, we made the cut and enjoyed the variety show which featured a young comedian named Carol Burnett. There too, we hung out and met the cast and were readily welcomed by all the stars. We were just kids who were adoring fans and provided the stars with young, friendly faces each week. Years later I learned it meant nothing to them.

One night after the taping, in which there were only a few of us present, we were invited to join the cast for dinner at the Chinese restaurant adjacent to the theater. Gary Moore picked up the tab, but Derwood Kirby paid the bill. He was Moore's sidekick on the show and possibly in real life as well.

On another occasion, what started as a joke turned into a real-life Fan Club. I joked with Bob about how much I loved Hermione Gingold, an older British actress who often performed as a comedic caricature of herself. Bob got tickets to the Tonight Show starring Jack Parr when Hermione was scheduled to appear and he and I went to the show. Prior to the taping, the audience was often handed cards in which they could write questions for Jack Parr in hopes that he would answer them right after he did his monologue. I addressed my question to Hermione Gingold and asked if she had a fan club in the US.

After his monologue Jack Parr picked up a few of the question cards and read two of them which resulted in answers that produced laughter.

Then he got serious and said: "This next question is actually not for me, but for my next guest, so let's bring her out here to answer this herself. Ladies and gentlemen, join me in welcoming one of my favorite guests, Hermione Gingold."

Hermione came on stage, smiled, waved in her exaggerated way and sat down to talk with Jack Parr. They spoke for a moment and he then offered up the question saying, "Hermione, we have a question from a young man in our audience that wants to know if you have a fan club here in the America."

"Where is this wonderful man," Hermione immediately answered. And the next thing I knew, I was standing in the audience with a microphone thrust in front of me and appearing on national television talking with Hermione Gingold about starting a fan club for her in America. "What a darling you are," she said. She told me to meet with her back stage after the show and she would introduce me to her manager that would help me start a Hermione Gingold Fan Club.

This resulted in the start of a real Hermione Gingold Fan Club which very quickly had hundreds of members communicating by mail. I was in college at that time and I created a newsletter and sent out photos of Hermione to anyone who wanted one. The Hermione Gingold Fan Club lasted only about two years because I found that there was not enough going on in her career to keep up regular communications. Also, this was happening in the 1960s before computers and everything was by mail and too costly for me to absorb. There were no dues to pay so no money to cover the costs. The Hermione Gingold Fan Club just faded away.

Meanwhile, we were a large group of kids that hung out together in the schoolyard at PS217 and at Red's Candy Store and it was only natural that we gravitated to dating one another. Mary and I were the relationship brokers of sort. Everyone came to either Mary or myself or both of us for advice on how to handle one or another relationship in the group. We were an early form of matchmakers and she and I talked often about all the friendship issues and disputes that arose from within our larger than normal group of friends.

Relationships evolved between Alan with Bev, Sherman with Mary, Morgan with Marilyn and me with Nardina for a short while and then Geri for nearly three years. Sherm and Mary were the only couple that stayed together over a long period of time. They got married after high school and they are still married today with a family full of kids and grandkids.

After hanging out in the early evenings, the boys would end up on one of the street corners, usually Ocean Parkway and 18th Avenue to sing. Yes. teenagers did stand on the street corners in Brooklyn singing in the 1950s and early 60s. We harmonized well. Even then I had a deep voice and was relegated to doing the base parts of the songs which sounded like "boom, da-boom, da-boom, da-boom" or "boom-ditty-boom-ditty-boom." I could not use my long-practiced expertise in lip-synching all those songs because once the actual sounds came out of my mouth, they never matched the tune of the song. I may have known the words, but could not carry the tune.

As we grew older, the group expanded. Soon we even had a member of the group that had a car. Good old Sheldon. He might not have even become part of the group if he didn't have that old car, but once he was let in, he became well liked by everyone. The car gave the guys wings to fly. And the big experience of the evening was driving from Brooklyn to Idlewild Airport in Queens which was subsequently renamed as John F. Kennedy International Airport.

In those days, we would park alongside the end of the runway and lay on the hood or roof of the car and watch the airplanes come in for a landing. It was dangerous and fun for a bunch of teenagers looking for a harmless thrill. The only real problem was that we often did this after going to the movies or bowling and sometimes didn't come home until four or five o'clock in the morning. Needless to say, most, not all, of the parents were franticly worried. I was punished over and over again, but persisted in doing this because it was my social life and that was important for a kid, who prior to age fourteen, had limited social interaction.

At fourteen, I found my second real love with a cute Italian girl a couple of blocks away. Her name was Nardina and her mother worked in the same place as my mother so that gave the connection a blessing from the parents.

By age sixteen, I had fallen in love with another one of our group— Geri. She was a bit younger at only fourteen, with sparkling eyes and a wide smile that never ceased. We began a relationship that lasted nearly three years and only ended when I went away to college in Kentucky. I'm convinced today that we would have been married had I not gone away to college.

Meanwhile, at sixteen, I was still learning about girls and relationships and had the better part of a year in high school in which I was tutored by a young bus driver who drove the school bus we took to Erasmus Hall High School. It started very innocently one day when I wanted to avoid a test and asked the driver, if I could stay on the bus when everyone exited at the school. He had a couple of other runs, but had no problem with my company.

Following his next run, he was talking with two girls at Midwood High School and convinced them to stay on the bus for some fun. After that run he headed to Prospect Park where he parked the bus in a remote parking lot. He turned on some music and immediately took one of the two girls to the back of the bus to "make out."

I didn't know what to do and felt uncomfortable, but the girl that was sitting in the front with me was less shy and more experienced. She waited a short while for me to make a move and when all she got was some small talk, she moved over on my seat and put her arms around me and began to kiss me on the neck. Thus, I began to learn my way around fast women. This, however, did not help when confronted with normal women in regular potential relationships.

That winter, I cut classes—a lot. I actually skipped school every day for nearly five months from November to early March. I intercepted the mail at home to make sure that my parents did not get the many notes that the school sent asking where their son was and why I hadn't been in school for months. My new friend, the bus driver helped with this making sure that we stopped by my apartment building every day to get the mail.

He was a bus driver by day, but a musician by night and this also provided me with my first connection to the music industry. He would appear as a drummer on stage backing up some famous musicians appearing in New York's Greenwich Village in the 1950s and early 1960s. He provided me with access to some of the clubs that I wouldn't otherwise be allowed to enter at age sixteen. That's when I first started hanging out at Cafe Wha and became a regular there.

When I eventually got caught by a truant officer, I was place under the jurisdiction of Dean Shamus at Erasmus and had to check in every morning at the Dean's office before being escorted to my first class. After each class I had to return to the Dean's office to get my next escort to my next class.

Sometimes the escort was waiting for me outside my class and saved me the time of going back and forth. I was a prisoner in Erasmus Hall High School.

One afternoon my cousins Steven and Bobby came looking for me. The three of us were very close in age and besides being cousins were very close friends. We did a lot together, including getting into trouble together. Steven attended Brooklyn Tech high school on the other side of Brooklyn and Bobby lived on Long Island. They were heading out west to escape the tyranny of parents and came to Erasmus to break me out of jail. They went to the administration office and told them there was a family issue and they were sent to bring me the message. Could they see me for just a moment to give me this personal message?

Of course, the people in the administration office knew who I was. I was now famous for cutting more classes than anyone in the history of Erasmus. They also knew that I was in the dean's office between all classes so they sent a note to dean Shamus who suspected foul play and immediately called the police. The dean then escorted me to the administration office to meet with my cousins, but upon hearing the police sirens, Steven and Bobby disappeared on their own and when I got to the office my cousins were long gone. They didn't get too far having stopped in Philadelphia at one of my aunt's friends for the night; where he convinced them to return to New York the next day.

Growing up in Brooklyn in the 1950s was both a pleasure and a challenge. The stories about gangs like the Amboy Dukes were legendary—and true. As a young kid and a loner, I had dreamed about being a member of a gang protected by my fellow gang members. Selling condoms to the tough guys in elementary school was the closest I came to that realization.

However, there was a small, local gang in our neighborhood led by a huge guy we will call Mr. Big. And they thought that I was the leader of our gang—our large group of guys and girls that would play softball, basketball and tag in the schoolyard and hang out at Reds candy store. There wasn't a fighter among us, but we did something to offend them and they were out for revenge.

Marilyn was having a party at her apartment one Saturday night. It may have been a birthday party. There was a knock on the door and several guys from this local gang wanted to come in. Marilyn did not want them in her apartment, nor did anyone else. They were not our friends and their reputation was not good. I saw that they were about to push their way in and interceded and told them they were not invited and shut the door in their faces. No, I was not being brave. I was tall and weighed over 225 pounds. I was big. That's all.

Several weeks later, when some of our group were hanging out watching the trains go by from a bridge over the Newkirk station this same group of guys spotted us and came after us. That night we outran them and got away. We were not as lucky a few weeks later as Sherm, Alan and I were walking home on Newkirk Avenue after taking our respective girlfriends' home and we were suddenly surrounded by a dozen of this gang—including the boss himself, Mr. Big. Despite that fact that I was big and played on the Erasmus Hall high school football team, Mr. Big was larger than me and could have been the entire front line of the team. He was built like an oversized brick. His head sat directly on his shoulders. His chest was a barrel and his arms were like baseball bats.

"We're sorry about your friends and the party, but it was a private party," I squeaked out. He growled back at me: "You and your 18th Avenue gang dissed my friends here. You gotta pay now with your faces." We were surrounded. It was ten o'clock at night with no one else on the street. Mr. Big nodded to his gang and suddenly they were upon us throwing punches and kicking. I managed to find a hole to run through like we practiced on the football field and leaped over the front of a parked car and up the street towards Coney Island Avenue where I hoped that car traffic would deter further pursuit.

"Get him, he's the leader of the gang," shouted Mr. Big. And all twelve guys came after me. They were mean and there were a lot of them, but they were not in shape to run long distance. I outsprinted them to Coney Island Avenue where I got across a well-lighted and heavily trafficked four-lane street which then protected me. Meanwhile, Alan and Sherm ran the other way when the gang left to chase me. They were bruised, but not beaten. We all had some black and blue scars from this adventure and the admiration (pity) of the girls.

That was only the beginning of an episode in my life filled with fear that any day I would fall victim and be beaten and possibly killed. Rumors spread that they were coming after me. I began to fear going to Reds Candy Store in the evening because they knew where we hung out and had been seen there looking for me. I feared walking Geri home at night because she lived down the block from Mr. Big. I didn't sleep well at night and was nervous during the day. I was a mess overcome with fear.

I saw him or his cronies on several occasions and ran in opposite directions to avoid them. One Sunday afternoon I was on a bus coming home from Manhattan Beach on the far end of Sheepshead Bay in Brooklyn when I noticed three guys on the bus staring at me. Mr. Big was sitting behind them. I figured they might have recognized me so I jumped off the bus at the next stop just as the doors were closing even though it was nowhere near my stop. It was a long walk home that day, but I was safe once again.

After two very long years of fearing the inevitable, it finally came to a head one Saturday afternoon at the local bowling alley. Bob, Sherm, Alan and I were bowling and enjoying ourselves. In comes Mr. Big and a bunch of his gang. He walks up to the alley where we are bowling and loudly declares, "I've got you now Kahn." I knew he knew my face, but hoped he didn't know my name. I was wrong. He then further declared, "Do you want me to mash you face here on the alley or do you want to step outside?"

From two alleys down came: "What's going on here?" It was Steve Colletti, the 250-pound star fullback from the Erasmus Hall football team. Colletti was my teammate and lived in the neighborhood. We practiced together and played softball together at times, but he was not part of our close-knit group of friends. He was not part of anything other than the high school football team where he was a star.

"Mind your own business Colletti," shouted Mr. Big.

"This IS my business, Mr. Big, this is my friend. These are all my friends and your threats against them end here and now, ya hear me?" Most of the kids had heard about these threats in the neighborhood and my fears were warranted.

Mr. Big looked back at Colletti and again told him to mind his own business. "I have no beef with you Colletti, but I am going to beat the crap out of him so stay out of it." I was shaking with fear but resigned to just get beat up and lie down and be done with this fear. It had consumed me for two years and I wanted relief.

Colletti came forward and stepped in between Mr. Big and me. Mr. Big did not take his eyes off of me. Colletti interceded on my behalf and let's just say that was the end of any threats from Mr. Big and two years of fear had suddenly dissipated.

"You okay?" Colletti said to me. "Thanks to you we all are. Thanks Steve." I never saw either of them again.

CHAPTER THIRTY-ONE

I LOVE NEW YORK

There isn't another like it. No matter where you go.
And nobody can compare it. It's win and place and show.
New York is special, New York is diff'rent'
cause there's no place else on earth quite like New York and that's why –
I love New York
• • • • • • •

a New York State jingle by Steve Karmen

The music builds to a crescendo as the chorus repeats "Iiiiiiii. . . love New York" over and over again. It's really an exhilarating song. I got to hear this performed every day and night for more than two weeks by an ensemble of Broadway stars that carried the message across South America as part of a New York tourism promotion back in the 1980s. More about that later. Meanwhile, listen to the song on *YouTube* and you may get caught up in the emotion that so many people feel about New York. I felt it then, I feel it now, but I didn't always feel that way about New York.

I couldn't wait to get out of New York in 1962. Growing up in Brooklyn was full of turmoil. Getting down to Murray, Kentucky was the best thing that I did as a child. I grew up and matured there (although some say I never matured). Despite the great growth and learning experiences I had in Murray, I needed to get to work on my career and returned to New York in September 1968. Only I was not welcomed back with the open arms that I had expected. My parents had moved and there was no longer room for me in their apartment. The job market was cruel. Doors would not open, even for an accomplished journalist that had newspaper and radio news experience. I was a small-town reporter. New York was the big town, the Big Apple. Day after day I walked the streets of New York just trying to get an interview with very little luck.

Walking in midtown Manhattan, New York City, is like being in the middle of the pack in a marathon race surrounded by thousands of other people. You never can win the race, but you may have small gains and losses as you maneuver through a tight web of bodies. And, depending upon the time of the year, the strong stench of body odor may prevent you from making any headway through the masses. It's a never-ending race.

There are all sorts of people walking the streets of New York City representing the entire world's population, including every nation, race, religion and ethnicity. There are tall people who stand out in front of you, short people who may cause you to stumble as you almost trip over them, skinny people that you can easily slip past and fat people, a lot of really fat people, too many fat people, forcing you to slow down until a passing opportunity enables you to quickly glide by—only to find another mass of person or persons in your way.

Most of the people are going in the same direction as you are going making this race ever more competitive. But you can never forget that there is also a steam of individuals and sometimes groups coming at you from the opposite direction. Where they are going is anybody's guess, but they also can be a force and obstacle in your path to get where you are going.

These opposing figures are in their own race, often to nowhere in particular and of no concern to you. But you can't get in their way. As much as they may impede your speed and direction you have to allow them the freedom to go wherever they might be going.

Often this pack comes at you on the left side of the sidewalk closest to the tall buildings that climb as endless grey monoliths into the sky. You are walking on the right side of the sidewalk closest to the street where, depending on foot traffic, you are often too close to speeding taxis and buses that dominate the streets of Manhattan.

If you look out into the street you will see little else other than a yellow sea of taxi cars with an occasional large white bus coughing its way from one corner to the next, unloading and loading people who do not want to race anywhere. These bus riders pay for the privilege of not being in the

RICHARD S. KAHN

race. They are complacent to be late for just about anything they are going to attend. They are comfortable hanging on and being jostled, shaken, not stirred, and deposited a few blocks latter to find that they exited one block too soon and now have to join the race they paid to avoid.

Few regular people drive in Manhattan because they don't want to compete with the taxis that dominate the blacktop. These taxis know every oily ounce of the streets, every turn that is allowed and every nuance of the red and green lights that are supposed to control the flow. However, traffic lights often create wars between intersecting avenues of cars that want to claim a section of the street as their own before moving up or down the next street. When the war gets really involved, and many more cars and taxis get engaged, you have New York City Grid Lock, a form of impasse that can last from minutes to an hour, especially if too many of the drivers are sporting the ego driven heads of pigs.

Meanwhile, back on the sidewalks you are fighting for your space, searching for lanes to keep moving forward. You will also occasionally see a lone pedestrian coming directly at you, straight out of the middle of the opposing pack. You may wonder what this idiot is doing cutting against the grain in the opposite direction of your pack. He forces you to use your honed avoidance system as you twist away and somehow keep moving forward. Then you recall you have done this yourself in the past as you were forced into oncoming bodies to make your way. You duck your head and forgive him as you brush shoulders, knocking each other off pace, neither of you providing an apology for the infraction.

Back in the race, you will find that over years of practice, you can actually move rather quickly through the pack and make decent progress along the streets and avenues of New York City. There are tricks that you may need to learn, but nothing difficult. First you must be both limber and quick in your decision making. These are two good attributes that can be used to navigate the streets of New York as well as in various life situations that will benefit you in both business and your personal life.

Limber and quick decision making come into play as you move with the pack and suddenly find nearly everyone in front of you stopping, often for no reason other than the pack has gotten backed up and there is nowhere to move forward. This phenomenon also happens on the highways where cars will be moving along at 60 miles per hour and suddenly come to a halt behind a seemingly endless string of cars ahead. Then, as suddenly as you stopped, the cars will begin to move and in moments you are back up to 60 miles per hour with no sign of what caused the traffic in the first place. It happens for no reason at all. It just happens.

It is the same on the streets of New York City. Once moving quickly, you suddenly find the pack has slowed and sometimes stopped. However, you are not in a car on a highway. If you are limber and quick, you can bob and weave and dart and glide as you keep moving either past or through the pack. You must be careful not to walk into the middle of this pack as you will surely get hit, jostled and sometimes even punched as you interfere with others going in the opposite direction. Other times you may go right and skirt the border along the street, always keeping a careful eye on the taxis and buses that could clip you, essentially ending your day in the hospital fixing broken bones or worse.

And, I almost forgot to warn you about the bicycles that speed by, often faster than the taxis and often in the opposite direction, making it impossible to see them in advance. These bikers, mostly messengers and delivery people, hate pedestrians more than they hate taxis. It is the pedestrians that step off the curb and block the bikers from speeding past red lights and onto their destination. It is these bikers that sometimes purposely hit pedestrians as they pass at the speed of light, knocking down their victims and claiming another victory for bicycles in the inner city. It took me a long time to recover from the ankle injury I got from a passing messenger on a bike going the wrong way on Fifth Avenue in Manhattan as he passed a red light clipping me with his purposely outstretched foot. I went down, he went on to wherever he was heading, chalking up an imaginary score with his raised hand that waved victory as he disappeared up the avenue.

Passing through the pack of walkers with agility is an art form. Doing it with the same speed you are walking is what makes you a champion. If there were an Olympic sport for walking through crowds in New York City, there would be thousands that could compete. I was proud to be among them. Years of walking these streets rather than taking subways, buses or the take-your-life-in-your-hands taxis, has prepared me well for the Olympics. I have trained nearly daily for more than thirty years and have learned how to find the holes that enable me to squeeze through crowds of people to get in front of a group, only to find another similar group in my face.

I know when to stop at the red light and squeeze my way to the front of the crowd so that I am off and walking as soon as the light turns green. I know when to cross the avenue to the other side of the street in preparation for turning a corner and moving up the street to another avenue. It takes timing. It takes stamina. It takes practice. I've put in my time on the streets and can confidently say that I have earned "street smarts" when it comes to walking.

But I am not the only one. And sometimes I find there is a competitor beside me that is keeping pace with me. I glance over at him and he sometimes looks back. We know that we are in the race. We know what is at stake. There may not be an Olympic medal at the end of this race, but there is the knowledge, the pride that we have won and that we remain the undisputed Champion of New York City Street Walking.

But we don't always win. Sometimes, simply because we get behind the wrong person or our competitor finds the right hole, we are left a few steps behind and we can't catch up before we reach the next street and cross the finish line with the glowing green lights above us. Other times we manage to sprint walk the last 100 yards just managing to pass our challenger as the crowd roars with pleasure and the light changes from green to yellow to red and he is left behind—standing still as a crane on one leg—the ultimate shame for a street walker. It is a scenario played out hundreds of times over many years. Good exercise for the body and for the mind as well.

On a warm day in September 1968, I finished one of my Olympic-style walks from the subway to the McGraw Hill building, at that time on Eighth Avenue and 42nd Street in the heart of Manhattan. Thanks to McGraw Hill human resources department, I landed a job as a copy desk editor—aka proofreader.

I was thinking about that lucky day I was hired by McGraw Hill and eventually ended up as a reporter for *Aviation Week & Space Technology*. I was in the right place at the right time that day. I was also in the right place at the right time when I, as the office gofer, was sent over to the United Nations to get the papers on the Comsat satellite communications and interviewed the Indian Ambassador that led to my first big story and a reporter's job on *Aviation Week*. And it was another right place, right time meeting Eric Friedheim, owner of *The Travel Agent* magazine that led me to the major travel industry news magazine and sixteen years of travel around the world and fame as the editor and eventually publisher of the magazine.

But I was not in the right place on a very hot August 14, 2003, when I was once again walking across town in New York City for a meeting with a potential client. I bought a bottle of water at Penn Station, took the train uptown and across town and arrived on Lexington Avenue and 51st Street for my meeting with hotel executives at a newly refurbished and renamed hotel that I was pitching for their public relations account. The meeting went well and I left with a good feeling that I would get the account.

I poised at the elevator bank and decided that I was only on the third floor and I would take the stairs instead. I didn't like elevators under normal circumstances and getting into a hot, and potentially crowded, elevator did not appeal to me. It actually frightened me. There are few things more frightening than having your elevator stop between floors and have the doors open to expose only a solid brick wall. You stand there powerless in a state of disbelief and start pressing buttons, any and all buttons, to hopefully make the elevator move again.

There was the time when as a child going down the elevator in my building (when I still took the elevator) and it skipped the lobby and went straight down to the basement. There in the dark and musty building basement filled with legends of superintendents from the past, I ventured out, running past the laundry room, flying past the boiler room with its large Buddha-like structure always rumbling like an angry god waiting to strike. Finally, I reached the door that led into the alley and back out to daylight on the street. I was safe from those dark secrets held in New York City basements.

Living and working in Manhattan with all the skyscrapers reaching thirty or forty stories into the sky, I had to take elevators—reluctantly. But when given the choice to take the stairs, I always would choose stairs, especially on a hot summer day. So, on that particular hot August day in 2003, I turned from the elevators and entered the stairs under the sign "Exit to Lobby" and walked down three flights of stairs and into the lobby. I did notice a little commotion at the elevator bank and heard someone say "What's wrong with the elevator?" but paid no attention to it as I left the hotel and walked towards the subway which was three blocks north of the hotel on Lexington Avenue.

I hadn't walked far when I heard people referring to the possibility of another terrorist attack because power was out across all of Manhattan. It was less than two years after September 11, 2001, and talk of another potential terrorist attack was like a strong odor that permeated the air, especially on this stifling hot and humid August afternoon. I called my office on Long Island using my cell phone and was told that there was a power outage that seemed to be impacting random spots in the New York tri-state area. They had power in my office and as far as they knew Long Island was okay. No one really knew what was happening.

I turned and walked in the opposite direction from which I was headed. I didn't know if the subways were affected, but I surely wasn't going down into a hot sticky underground putting myself in jeopardy of getting stalled in between stations with hundreds of other sweaty and anxious people. As I passed back in front of the hotel, there was a stream of people coming out complaining about having to walk down the stairs to get out of the stuffy hotel. The air-conditioning had shut down with the power outage and so had the elevators, some with people stuck inside. I suddenly felt sick. I could have been one of those stuck inside the elevator when the power shut down.

I began to get nervous and walked faster. I wanted to get to the Long Island Railroad and get a train out of Manhattan and back to my family. Some of the people along the way were talking about the blackout and how it was spreading across the entire Northeast. Others seemed oblivious to the fact that anything out of the normal was happening. Still others were annoyed that something was disrupting their routines—those were the real New Yorkers.

The walk to Penn Station was long. It was twenty-two blocks south and four avenue blocks west. The avenue blocks are the equivalent of two to three regular blocks. It was about two miles from the hotel where I was to Penn Station at three o'clock in the afternoon, the hottest time of the day. When I arrived at Penn Station it was nearly four o'clock and the crowds outside of the two entrances on 7th Avenue were enormous. At first, I thought to myself that I would just stop into one of the coffee shops across the street to get out of the heat and wait until the crowds dissipate, but then I listened to a police officer telling some women that the Long Island Railroad was not running because of the power failure and they were evacuating Penn Station.

I quickly turned and went straight for the Hotel Pennsylvania which sits directly across from Penn Station. The lobby was darker than normal, but there were emergency lights strategically placed as well as some light coming in from the doors on both 7th Avenue and 32nd Street. I went to the lobby restroom to relieve myself, bought another bottle of water, some chocolate bars and took a comfortable seat on a couch in an alcove off the lobby to wait out the blackout.

There was only one other person in the alcove when I first sat down. I called home to get an update on what was happening. Information was still sketchy, but the blackout appeared to be spreading way beyond New York City. Rumors were that it started in Canada and it may have been a terrorist act. No one seemed to know and the fact that there was no electricity there was no radio or television to give us the news.

My thoughts turned to what I imagined was appearing on all the television news stations. They would probably be trying to inform a public that has suddenly been thrust into the dark about the blackout. Did they realize that only those not impacted by the blackout could see and hear the news reports? The rest of us were sitting in the dark—really in the dark. We couldn't see or hear their warnings or heed their advice as to what to do. Their coverage was worthless to anyone in the blackout. Cell phones were the only communication link. I turned mine off to preserve the battery.

By five o'clock the lobby was beginning to fill up as people realized that the crowds in front of Penn Station were not going away and it was too hot to stand there in the street. My alcove was now filled with people sitting on the couches and the floor leaning against the walls and the posts. I looked across the lobby and there were people standing everywhere. The front desk had a long line of people waiting to talk with anyone available about a room. I heard someone say that there were plenty of rooms but no way to get to them because the elevators were not working and the hotel did not want people walking up ten to twenty flights of stairs without supervision.

By six o'clock the lobby was packed. I gave up my seat to a pregnant lady with a young child. She was trying to reach her husband, but by now cell phone service was spotty at best as millions of people were trying to use their cell phones to connect to someone to find out what was happening. And it wasn't just New York City, it was the entire Northeast from Virginia to Montreal. It also seemed like the entire population of the Northeast were all crowding into the Hotel Pennsylvania. To make matters worse, many of the guests staying in the hotel were streaming down the stairs to get out of their dark and stuffy rooms. The manager at the hotel made the hard decision to lock the doors to prevent an even more overcrowded lobby.

At seven o'clock there was no longer room to walk without stepping over someone. You need to picture this: the lobby at the Hotel Pennsylvania was huge. It began at the 7th Avenue entrance and went a quarter of a block down with a side entrance on 32nd Street. There were now more than a thousand people standing, sitting and laying across the floor of this enormous lobby. Getting around was beginning to become a chore. But I had to go to the restroom and I wanted to see if I could get something to eat so I asked my alcove mates to save my spot, which they did, most likely because I had given up my comfortable couch seat for a floor spot so the pregnant lady could be comfortable with her little girl.

I ventured across the lobby, first to the restroom, which now had a long line and then to the snack bar which now had very little left. I got some chips and some more water. I still had my candy bars. I was saving them for my dinner. I returned to the alcove ate my candy and chips and drank a little water. Then I made myself comfortable as it started to get dark. Linda and the kids were at home on Long Island and while they had no power, they were fine. All the neighbors were out talking to each other and I felt comfortable that they would be okay. I was told that my nephew Jessie was heading to the Hotel Pennsylvania, but there was no way I could find him as it was only dimly lit by a few emergency lights and there were too many people laying all over the lobby floor.

By eight o'clock it was almost dark outside, but the emergency lights in the lobby provided a calming mood for all of those strangers huddled together. Conversations were growing friendly. People found once again that it is truly a small world as they talked about others that they mutually knew and restaurants that they loved and past blackouts they had endured and, of course, about the attack on September 11, 2001. People were getting comfortable together. I was getting worried and I was not comfortable being there. But I had carved out my space on the floor next to a post so that I could lean against it and be protected from someone just walking by and stepping on my head.

Suddenly there was a commotion at the front door that a lot of people seemed interested in hearing. After loudly explaining and pleading with the security team at the front door, one of the guards radioed the general manager who agreed to let this frantic man inside to search for his wife. One of the security guards escorted him as he weaved his way across the lobby looking in all the alcoves which is where his pregnant wife had told him she was stationed. When finding her in our cozy alcove, he cried out, and then cried. She and her daughter embraced him as if he had just come back from the war. Everyone in our alcove joined in and cried. It was a very moving sight. The security escort reported back to the general manager and everyone was happy. The reunited family sat down on the couch; the father sat in front of her on the floor. I sat back against my poll and smiled. I was getting more comfortable.

I must have dozed off to sleep because the next time I looked at my watch it was 10:30 p.m. and there was another commotion across the other side of the lobby near the front desk. I could not make out what was going on, but I could see several security guards rushing over with flashlights. Whatever was happening quieted down quickly. Our corner was very quiet. Most of the people were sleeping or talking quietly. There were additional people there that were not there when I dozed off around 8:30 p.m. It was very crowded. Space had become non-existent. Nearly everyone was touching someone else.

I tried falling back to sleep, but around 11:30 p.m. I had to go to the bathroom again. I told everyone in my close proximity where I was off to and asked if anyone wanted anything from the snack bar—if it were still open and if there was anything left. No one wanted anything, which was just as well as the store was closed having run out of supplies sometime earlier.

I reached the dark stairs leading up to the restrooms and almost tripped up the stairs. Someone mercifully turned a flashlight on the stairs and I could see that the line to both the men's room and the women's room were long. I queued up on the men's room line and noticed that there were at least two women on the line ahead of me. The men's room line was shorter than the women's room line and it was moving somewhat faster.

When I got into the completely dark men's room, I was lucky that several people had flashlights. I found an empty urinal and relieved myself. The women that were waiting alongside of me were waiting to get into the adjacent stalls. No one paid attention to this detail. No one cared that there were several women standing there as we used the urinals. No one cared that they could see us exposed as some men used flashlights to see what they were doing. We were all in this together and the facilities were being pushed to their limits. At least one of the urinals was overflowing and could not be used. The floor of the men's room was completely wet. The odor of urine permeated the air and torched my nostrils. But everyone waited patiently for their turn at relief and returned to the dim light of the lobby below.

I found my way back to my corner and had to now squeeze into my ever-smaller space that I had long ago carved out for myself. I tried not pushing, but was forced to use my body and to excuse myself several times as I reestablished my space where others had now encroached. No one complained. Everyone accepted whatever space they had. I vowed not to leave this space again for fear that it would not exist when I returned. I tried to get comfortable again, but had trouble falling asleep. I nuzzled up against a young couple who were intertwined and lay next to me.

Despite the fact that I was determined to sleep through the night and not move from my cozy spot on the hard marble floor of the Pennsylvania Hotel lobby, I awoke somewhere around 3:30 am. The lobby population had somehow grown to nearly 2,000 people, most of whom were sleeping on the floor. It was now very quiet. You could hear people snoring from several spots around the immense lobby. No one was talking. Everyone was sleeping or trying to sleep. I seemed to have gained some space during the night as I was almost stretched out in my corner. I still had the tangled couple to one side and two heavy women to the other side. There was a small man by my feet and the poll by my head, a small comfort in the darkness that now completely surrounded us.

I looked around the lobby. The emergency lights had given out or were turned off and the temporary emergency flashlights that were distributed by the hotel staff earlier, had mostly dissipated leaving a very dark lobby. There were bodies everywhere. I got up once more to venture to the bathroom, thinking that this was a good time to go. I had to step over bodies every single step I took. There was no walking room, just spots where you could step over and in between bodies. Several times on this particular trip to the bathroom I stepped on people. I was careful to step lightly and they moved as my foot touched their bodies. I apologized and then realized I was disturbing others with the sound of my voice. So, I just moved through this sea of bodies in silence, trying not to hurt anyone and trying not to fall on anyone.

I reached the dark stairs to the restrooms and carefully made my way up stairs. There were no beacons of light to share now. Only darkness stared back at me. At the top of the stairs I found there was only one line, much smaller than the previous lines and it went toward the men's room. Just to be sure, I whispered "Is this the line to the men's room?" The answer came from two people who said "The women's room is flooded and closed." And despite the fact that this one line was shorter than previously, it moved much slower because most of the people on the line were women waiting to get into a stall in the men's room. When I got closer, to the opening, the stench of urine was overbearing. I almost turned back, but my weak bladder asked me to forebear so I held my nose and moved forward.

Returning to my space was more difficult than I had expected. The darkness compounded by the carpet of bodies lying across the lobby floor made it tough for me to find my corner. I stepped on more bodies than I had on my way to the restroom, but eventually found my way back into my tight spot. Once again, I had to reestablish my space, but found it easier to move people who were fast asleep this time. I lied back down, but never really fell asleep. It was hot in the lobby and there was no way I could get comfortable. I tossed and turned for the next few hours until a glimpse of light started to come through the lobby windows and doors. I did not want to look at my watch, but I figured it must be around six a.m. I felt some relief. We made it through the night.

I then heard a commotion and talk about buses being available to take people to Queens to connect to the Long Island Railroad in Jamaica where diesel-fueled trains were being used. I saw a number of people leaving and walking across the lobby which was now more tolerable. I waited to hear verification of this transportation news because I did not want to leave the relative comfort of the hotel and my personal space which I was getting very fond of, especially the poll that I used to lean against.

One young girl confirmed that there were buses lining up on 32nd Street. I walked outside the hotel, turned around and took a fond look at what had been my comfort zone for the night and squinted as I walking into the morning sunlight. It didn't take long to verify that there were buses out there and I figured it was time to leave. I then found out that the buses were there since three a.m. taking people out to Queens. However, I was told this by someone standing on line since 3 a.m. when the buses came because they filled one bus at a time and there were thousands of people waiting on line.

I then began to walk with others along the line that stretched down 32nd Street to 7th Avenue and was told to follow the line which wrapped down 7th Avenue to 31st Street and back up towards 6th Avenue. I got out of the line to check on what was really happening and as I walked past hundreds of others standing on line, I noticed a number of buses pulling up and wondered how they would do this. I went to the back of the line knowing that I had just walked past more than a hundred patient people who were also waiting. I just stood there and waited. I did not call home because I did not want to wake anyone.

I waited about twenty minutes with nothing happening and then the line started moving slowly, but steadily. I was actually surprised how fast the line suddenly began to move. A step here, a step there and then another step. We would then pause for about a minute and then move a few more steps. I was beginning to feel optimistic.

Then something great happened. A dispatcher was separating people going to Brooklyn and two different sections of Queens. I chose the one going to Jamaica Queens where I could get on the Long Island Rail Road and eventually home. I boarded the bus and felt great. I sat in the third row by the window. The bus filled up pretty quickly, but ended up taking off with a couple of empty seats which I thought was strange. Once underway, the driver announced that he was taking us to several stops in Queens ending in Jamaica at the Long Island Rail Road. He noted that the trip would be about an hour because there were no traffic lights and he had to follow a course that was controlled by traffic cops and volunteers who were directing traffic.

We arrived at the Jamaica train station within about forty minutes. And that's when I found out that no trains were running at all. The talk about the Long Island Rail Road using diesels had been nothing more than rumor. The entire rail system was shut down. I was now apparently stranded in Jamaica, an area that was known for high crime statistics. I was concerned as I started to get off the bus. However, there were dozens of people that began refusing to get off the bus, several of which were anxiously questioning the bus driver about this new development and asking where was his next stop?

The bus driver was sympathetic to our plight. After all, most of the Northeast was blacked out and he and his family were in the same predicament. He slept in the bus barn the previous night so he could drive today. After more passengers refused to get off the bus, he called his dispatcher and was told that he was now going on the Merrick Road run. I asked where that went and almost cried with joy when he told me that it went through Valley Stream, Lynbrook, Rockville Centre, Oceanside, Baldwin. . . and I did not hear anything else.

At that time, I lived one block from Merrick Road in Baldwin. Suddenly, by the grace of God, I was on my way home by bus. It took a long time, about an hour and a half from Jamaica. There were only about a dozen people remaining on the bus when we stopped in Baldwin. I got off and breathed the fresh breeze that often wafted over from nearby Atlantic Ocean. I relaxed and walked the half block to my home. As far as I was now concerned, the blackout was over for me.

Despite some trying times in the big city, I really did love New York. So much so, that when I got a call in the mid-1980s inviting me to be the only scribe on a promotional tour for the "I Love New York" campaign, I took a two-week leave of work to go along. The plan was to take Broadway stars to key cities in South America to highlight the best that New York has to offer tourists. Tourism officials would speak, show films of all the vacation areas across New York State, and provide brochures and contact information for local travel agents and tour operators.

Presentations were followed by the real draw, a medley of songs from current Broadway shows. Performers from shows like *Aint Misbehavin* and *The Best Little Whorehouse in Texas* were among the highlights. I got to know the stars of all the shows. Even the most famous among them were humble in this traveling environment. They were like kids at a circus. Many of them had not traveled extensively outside of the US. They treated me as their travel guru because I was at home with the traveling. I was awestruck by their talents. They performed so effortlessly. They were a group of stars and backup performers that worked both individually and together as a cohesive group. And the guests that attended the performances were starstruck and eager for autographs and photos. I stood on the side watching this day-after-day, night-after-night and appreciated it all. I was getting great material for my stories that I would write upon our return.

On a stop in Caracas, Venezuela, I took a morning walk in a local park. I stopped to sit on a large boulder overlooking the city and the sea below. I also noticed a young lady sitting on an adjacent boulder writing in a notebook. I awkwardly waved at her to get her attention and she smiled back at me before turning back to her writing. She was small, light cocoa colored with short black hair and large round brown eyes. She was very, very pretty.

When I got down from my rock and walked past, I offered a very feeble "*Hola*" with a wave of my hand. She smiled and said in perfect English "Good morning *senior.*" I stopped and asked a stupid question: "You speak English?" She laughed and said, "Yes, I studied in your country." She then came down from her rock and we walked over to a nearby cafe and had coffee and talked about her studies at Mississippi State and her life in Venezuela. Her name was Gabriela and she and I had a lot in common. She came from an inner city, studied in a small town in the South and returned to her home city to work as a journalist.

We talked for nearly two hours and she never asked for anything. She did however express excitement about the "I Love New York" show that was in town, saying: "Everyone is talking about the Broadway stars that have come to Caracas. It must be wonderful to travel with them and listen to them each night."

I, of course, offered to get her passes to attend the show at the theater that night. She explained that she was staying with her mother and sister and asked if it would be possible to get three tickets. Tickets were hard to come by. Wherever we went, Caracas, Sao Paulo, Buenos Aires, etc. the theaters were always too small to hold all the people that wanted to see these Broadway stars. They may have not been the biggest stars in the world, but in South America, they may have been the biggest stars they have ever seen live.

I promised I would get her three tickets and told her where to meet me. at the theater. Now I had to convince the producers, my friends at the tourist office, that I needed three passes for the evening performance. Not easy to do when there are no seats available. Fortunately, they were able to give me VIP passes to get them in and told me to try and find empty seats in the balcony.

I met Gabriela and her mother and younger sister at the front of the theater. When I first arrived, they were about to be escorted away by a police security officer. I interceded and explained that they were my guests. He smiled and let them through. We hugged and walked into the theater and up to the balcony where we chose seats that I was told might be empty.

Gabriela took my hand and smiled at me. We then held hands like teenage children. She and her mom and sister were so excited to see the show. After the show, I surprised them by taking them back stage to meet some of the performers. Gabriela kept squeezing my hand and kissing my cheek. She could not contain her glee. Neither could her mom or sister. I had made a hit with all of them just by bringing them back stage to meet the stars.

Afterwards, I walked them outside where her mom and sister said goodbye and waited on the side while Gabriela and I said our farewells. Neither of us wanted this brief encounter to end, but I was leaving very early in the morning and she had work the next day, so we kissed, embraced and parted with telephone numbers and addresses for the future. As usual, my future was just another stop on a tour of the world and work—more work.

We were from different worlds. We never talked or met again. But it was another glorious moment in my life and one that plays like a movie in my mind.

CHAPTER THIRTY-TWO

AROUND THE US, IT'S ALL HOME TO ME

Let us be lovers, we'll marry our fortunes together
I've got some real estate here in my bag
So we bought a pack of cigarettes and Mrs. Wagner's pies
And we walked off to look for America
Kathy, I said as we boarded a Greyhound in Pittsburgh
Michigan seems like a dream to me now
It took me four days to hitchhike from Saginaw
I've gone to look for America
• • • • • • •
"America" by Simon & Garfunkel

I am ashamed to say that with all my travels (to more than 120 countries) I have not been to all fifty states in my own country. I have been to forty-four states and have enjoyed every moment of my travels for both business and pleasure including some special memorable times across our own country. Here are just a few of them:

CALIFORNIA DREAMING

California is so much more than Los Angeles. I say this because Los Angeles, Hollywood and Anaheim (with Disneyland) are the main attractions for vacationers. I worked in Los Angeles for a short time on two separate occasions in my life and found the area to be less than exciting. The legendary fog in the morning may burn off with the afternoon sunshine, but the warm weather cannot overcome the distances and traffic that surrounds the area and the people themselves.

San Diego, on the other hand, may be the most perfect place on earth to live if weather is important to you. The climate is not cold at all, but also not too hot. You can go snow skiing in the morning in the nearby mountains and water skiing in the afternoon in the bays or Pacific Ocean. I don't know anywhere else that has that diversity. Neil, a good friend of mine, who also happened to be my haircutter, moved his family to north San Diego around 1990 and never looked back.

He and I were making changes in our lives around the same time and we both needed to move from our Brooklyn nests. He moved to San Diego and I moved to New York City. My problem was that he had been cutting my hair since 1968 when I first moved back from Kentucky to Brooklyn. When I lived in Kentucky, I rarely cut my hair. It was a time when hippies ruled the college campus and I fit right in with shoulder length hair and a full beard. When I returned to Brooklyn, got an apartment in Sheepshead Bay and found Faces Haircutting Salon right around the corner I met Neil, one of the owners, and got my haircut. I also ended up getting a great friend and confidant.

Neil was like a therapist. All his clients would sit in the chair and tell him their darkest secrets as he cut their hair. Like any good therapist, he would offer solutions to all their problems. For women this could be an hour of hair styling and therapy. For men, it was fifteen minutes of quick repair of mind and hair. For me, it was the beginning of a friendship that came at an important part of my life and lasted twenty-two years until he moved to San Diego and distance slowly destroyed the relationship.

It was Neil who talked me into running so that I could lose some of the 252 pounds that I had built up doing nothing but traveling and eating good food. Travel and dining are strongly linked together. And when one travels as a journalist, the food is heaped upon the plates from first class flights to luxury hotels and gourmet restaurants. As I have said before, I was blessed.

The first time Neil got me out to run, I could not make it around one city block. I was so out of shape that my lungs could not keep up with air escaping everywhere. Slowly, through walking and running, walking and running and then running and walking, I build up strength and stamina and was able to run a quarter of a mile, then a half a mile and finally a full mile in ten minutes time.

I kept up the running as I watched the pounds drift off my body until one full year after this excruciating experiment began, I found myself weighing only 198 pounds and running five miles a day at eight minutes a mile. At age thirty six, I had lost fifty-four pounds. When Neil moved to San Diego ten years later, I felt I lost even more.

Meanwhile, with my new found running passion (and yes, I experienced the runner's high, especially after about forty-five minutes of jogging), I got the magazine to sponsor a travel industry 10K charity race in Flushing Meadow Park in Queens, New York. The race was organized by Carefree David Travel and was open to anybody in the travel industry to compete.

I arrived at Flushing Meadow Park and met with the other organizers and posed for pictures with some of the travel industry dignitaries from the airlines, cruise lines and travel agencies. Then I heard someone announcing via a bullhorn "Will all the five-minute-milers step forward. Everyone else step back. The race is about to begin." I was standing in the front because our magazine was a sponsor and I felt that I should be there. Then the gun went off and everyone began to run—including me.

The first thing I noticed was that I was third from the front and there were more than 1,000 runners behind me. I can win this race I thought and pushed hard to get even with the two leaders. I kept this pace up for maybe five minutes and then my lungs began to burn and my legs began to buckle like rubber. I had run the first mile in about five minutes and I was done. I had never run a race before and did not know how to pace myself. I had run myself out. I tried several times to restart the legs, but ended up walking most of the rest of the five miles left in the race as I watched old men and women pass me.

Future races would find me in the middle of the pack at the start. When the gun would go off, I would close my eyes and just get into my rhythm so I could run my own pace of eight minutes a mile. I was comfortable with that and ran half-marathons without burning my lungs or turning my legs into rubber sticks.

On one press trip to the wine country in Northern California, in the mid-eighties, a group of journalists I was traveling with went from one winery to another over several days enjoying the wide variety of wines produced in the state. I don't remember much of that trip because we were drunk most of the time.

However, I do remember taking a side trip one afternoon down to San Jose to attend (actually crash) a wedding that was taking place. One of our hosts (an airline public relations person) had a friend who worked for the Sacramento Bee and was getting married to someone that worked in California government. The California Secretary of State was performing the wedding ceremony and the bride walked down the aisle in the back yard of this magnificent home to the tune of "Looking for Love in All the Wrong Places." The food for the wedding turned out to be a variety of chili dishes as part of a chili bake off contest. I like California weddings. They are unique and fun. I would have liked to have crashed some others.

St. Louis, Archway to the Midwest

Living in Kentucky, far away from my family in New York, I had very few choices of where to spend Thanksgiving, a family holiday, always spent with family as I was growing up. I remember the Thanksgiving at my Aunt Vivian's house in Brooklyn with vivid visions of my Grandmother having a heart attack. The entire family of 26 was there, five aunts and uncles, more than a dozen cousins and my own family of five. It was always chaotic, but I loved the contact with my cousins and my grandmother survived that one to live many more years.

That was my mom's family, all of which lived in New York. My father's family was spread out from Pittsburgh (Donora and Duquesne) Pennsylvania, to New York, Florida and St. Louis. My favorite, Uncle Jack and Aunt Fannie with cousins Marcia and Harriet resided in Creve Coeur, a suburb of St. Louis. Harriett and I were about the same age and I really liked her. When I was in college in Kentucky I got an invitation to spend Thanksgiving with their family, I jumped at it. St. Louis was a little more than three hours from Murray. For the next few years, Thanksgiving in St. Louis became my family ritual.

Harriet was attending Emporia State University in Kansas and so was my cousin Bobby who was from my mother's side of the family and lived on Long Island. I introduced Harriett and Bobby and while they were from two different sides of my family and not related, they treated each other as cousins. Harriet invited Bobby to come to Thanksgiving in St. Louis one year and promised to set him and I up with a couple of her girlfriends for a night out.

Bobby had a car so he drove Harriet home that Thanksgiving. Dinner was great. Aunt Fannie knew how much I loved pumpkin pie so she made me my own pumpkin pie for dessert. Marcia, Harriet's older sister, and her husband Sidney and their two kids Tony and Amy were there and the kids did not understand why I got my own pumpkin pie. I ended up sharing it with them.

After dinner, Bobby and I met Harriet's girlfriends and we went out for a night on the town. Bobby was a budding alcoholic at that time and drank too much. I ended up driving the girls home as he threw up in the back of his own car. When we got stopped by the police, I explained that my cousin got food poisoning and I was rushing him home. He helped to show them how sick he was by throwing up again, this time outside the car at the feet of the police. They told me to get him back in the car and get him home. I'm glad they didn't ask to see my driver's license as I didn't have one yet.

I didn't get my driver's license until I was twenty-years-old. As a matter of fact, when I took my diving test in Murray, Kentucky, the state trooper who gave me the test asked why I was so old and didn't have a license. Most kids in Kentucky had their licenses by age sixteen. I explained that I didn't need the license because I couldn't afford a car, but that now that I had a job, I needed a car and therefore a license. Despite that fact that I did several things wrong (like when he said park the car and I was a half mile from the curb, or when he told me to pull into the driveway so that I could turn around and go back up the street and I did a U-turn in the driveway to avoid backing out onto a busy street) he passed me because he thought I was "a mature boy." Not even close.

Thanksgiving in St. Louis became a staple for me and much more of a rich family tradition than Thanksgiving in New York. And I got to enjoy a wonderful Midwest city with a very welcoming culture and a rich history with a feel of visiting someplace special and unique. It was as if St. Louis and its residents stood a little bit above the average city, but not with a snob-bishness that is often found in New England towns. I also liked listening to stories about St. Louis from Marcia and Sidney. They had some great experiences to share about living in St. Louis, especially Sidney, who had a great sense of humor.

Washington, DC Wears a Regal Atmosphere

The first time I visited Washington, D.C. was for a March on Washington in 1968 to try and get Congress to end the Viet Nam war. I was part of a conservative group that believed that we should not be spending our time and losing the lives of thousands of our soldiers thousands of miles away in a jungle just because it was a so-called strategic position. We marched in unison with the Liberals, but our vision was more focused on those soldiers wasting their lives than the political battle at home. It was a weekend protest march that got a lot of media attention, but achieved nothing.

On another trip a few years later, I was hosted for a private lunch with J. Willard "Bill" Marriott Sr. just prior to the grand opening of the first JW Marriott Hotel. As a journalist I was very used to martini lunches and never shirked my responsibility to have a vodka martini (very dry), glass of wine or beer at lunch. Bill Marriott Sr. was the founder of the Marriott Corporation (now the biggest hotel company in the world). I was warned that he was a Mormon and did not drink. I sat to the right of Bill Marriott at the end of a very long conference room table. He sat at the end. We both had great views of Washington D.C. out the window across the room. When asked by the waiter what I wanted to drink, I said a glass of milk. Marriott smiled. That's what he was drinking for lunch. We had a great interview after that and I had an exclusive story about the future of the hotel chain.

Many trips to D.C. over the years allowed me to see what made our capitol special. Eventually I was able to take Linda to D.C. for a three-day escape. We had hoped to do this during cherry blossom season, but year-after-year we missed the early spring bloom. We eventually made the trip in late spring and did get to spend a day on the Mall viewing the Viet Nam Memorial, the even more impressive Korean War Memorial, and other sites along this vast park. The next two days were spent visiting more than a dozen museums and there were dozens of others we never reached, some of which, like the Newseum, are now closed because of lack of funding.

We also visited one of the most impressive churches I have ever seen. The Basilica of the National Shrine of the Immaculate Conception. The plans for the church were conceived in 1846, and donations were raised over the next few decades to build this magnificent structure to rival the ancient churches of Europe. It was completed and opened in 1920, and has more than eighty chapels, many named for foreign people such as those from Austria, China, Cuba, Philippines, France, Germany, Hungary, India, Ireland, Italy, Korea, Poland, Slovenia, and Viet Nam to name just a few.

The Basilica is off the beaten path and we had to take a taxi there and the driver offered to wait as we probably would not find a taxi to return to downtown D.C. The Basilica does not hold regular masses and has only had a couple of funeral masses and weddings over its long history. We spent the better part of an hour and could have spent more time walking around this massive structure and sitting in these revered pews.

EATING OUR WAY ACROSS NEW ORLEANS

It was a special birthday for Linda and we decided to spend a long weekend in New Orleans. We both loved jazz and enjoyed good food. New Orleans was well known for both. We were not disappointed. At least we were not disappointed in the food. The music, on the other hand, had morphed from primarily jazz to rock. It wasn't hard to understand this as we passed one packed club after another and the clientele were primarily under thirty years old. We did find a few jazz clubs and got to enjoy walking around the French Quarter people watching, which is always fun.

The first day we walked around exploring and had Po'boys (New Orleans style subs) for lunch. The first night there we took a taxi to the Garden District and dined at Commander's Palace, one of the established tourist spots, but one that provides great Creole cuisine. The next day we had the famous "breakfast at Brennan's" complete with champagne mimosas, omelets and pancakes and their Bananas Foster desert. I was in heaven, but I must caution you that it may be the most expensive breakfast on this planet (over $100 before tip).

We spent most of our time in the French Quarter, a great walking venue. Lunch was at Café du Monde where we had local Creole sandwiches. Dinner was at Galatorie's for gourmet French food. Our next lunch was at Pat O'Brien's Pub (we were hitting all the tourist stops), then dinner at Café Dauphine for Cajun local cuisine. Lunch the next day was at another tourist spot, Court of Two Sisters where we sat outside in the courtyard and enjoyed their jazz brunch buffet. Dinner was at Broussard's Restaurant, another fancy French/seafood spot.

By the last night at Antoine's Restaurant, Linda had enjoyed too much rich French food and opted for plain roast chicken. I continued to enjoy the rich sauces and spices from the combined French, Creole and Cajun cuisines for which New Orleans is famous. We really ate our way across New Orleans with breakfast, lunch and dinners at wonderful restaurants and had to loosen our belts a notch or two. And while we did not get to enjoy as much live jazz as we would have wanted, we did get a taste of traditional New Orleans at Preservation Hall.

Twenty years later, Linda and I returned to New Orleans, along with Tom and Karen, Pete and Peg, and Hutch and Sheila—three couples we love to travel with. In the interim, New Orleans was devastated by Hurricane Katrina. While the city fully recovered, it was never fully restored or revived. I had been back several times over the years and watched the recovery take place. It was slow and steady, but something changed. It was no longer the jazz city it once was. And while there are more restaurants than ever, the food and atmosphere were never the same.

We spent another long weekend there with these friends and took them around. We stayed in a boutique hotel in the heart of the French Quarter where renovations were still underway. We walked the streets both day and night and found too many homeless people asking for help. And the jazz and zydeco music were all but gone. Bourbon Street was one rock and roll club after another. And while we enjoyed some really good rock music in several clubs, we wanted more diversity.

We did find it on Frenchmen Street, a fifteen-minute walk from the heart of the French Quarter and Bourbon Street. And while our friends enjoyed their experience exploring New Orleans, we remembered the past and did not duplicate the wonderful experiences from our trip twenty years prior, once again proving you can't go home again.

Two Hot Towns, Tucson, AZ and Las Vegas, NV, But it's Dry Heat

I love Las Vegas. It is truly a 24-hour town where entertainment venues never fully close. You can gamble, see shows, dine and do other unmentionable things at any time during the day or night. The casino hotels offer a Disney World atmosphere for adults. These are not just casino hotels, they are themed hotels that provide a 24-hour lifestyle with shops, entertainment, dining and, of course, gambling.

The Paris Hotel gives you a little bit of a romantic city within its walls. The Eiffel Tower stretches above Las Vegas and the restaurant at the top is costly, but superb. The Venetian Hotel comes complete with Italian canals and a gondolier that takes guests for a ride through the inner parts of the hotel. New York Hotel gives guests a piece of Central Park and shops and restaurants that mimic the Big Apple city. And those are just a few of the many, many themed hotels that make Las Vegas one big gigantic theme park in itself. You don't have to stay in any one of these hotels to enjoy all that they have to offer. Just walk along the Strip and stop in any hotel to take advantage of what they have to offer.

However, walking along the Strip in summer can be dangerous as the heat can be truly unbearable. My cousin Steve, who moved there to help with his arthritis would tell me "It's dry heat, so you don't feel as hot as you would on the East Coast." Well, dry or wet, arid or humid, when the temperature rises above 100 degrees Fahrenheit it becomes hot and dangerous.

One July afternoon, while attending a conference in Las Vegas, I decided to take a leisurely walk along the strip. When I left the hotel, the temperature on my smart phone read 105 degrees. I stopped at a convenience store and bought a bottle of water. As I walked along the Strip, which was primarily empty of other strollers, I sipped on the water and enjoyed the sights. I felt hot, but not extraordinarily uncomfortable. Within less than fifteen minutes of walking I took my last sip of water and tossed the empty bottle in a trash can. Shortly after that I began to feel the heat. Very quickly I began to feel a slight dizziness. I quickly ducked into one of the casinos and sat down on a couch.

I had been out for only fifteen minutes, had only walked a few blocks and was on the verge of heat stroke despite the fact that I was drinking cold water. I sat for a while and then went out the casino lobby to get a taxi to take me back to my hotel. The taxi driver said, "Your hotel is only three blocks up the strip. You can walk it. It's too short a trip for me." I gave him a blank stare and said, "Please take me back to the hotel, I'm not feeling well." He did and didn't charge me anything.

Years later I got another taste of walking within an oven when attending our son Ryan's graduation from the University of Arizona in Tucson. It was a beautiful sunny day in May in Tucson with the temperature reaching a ridiculous 109 degrees. We only had to walk across the campus to get from the stadium to our parked car. We ended up touring most of the campus buildings as we ducked in and out of one building after another including a stop in the U of A store where we bought some T-shirts, hats and even sweaters (not to wear, but to take back East).

No one can convince me that temperatures at that level are not hot. There is no relief from that sort of heat. No breeze can cool you off when the temperatures are 109 degrees. It's like blowing hot air across hot skin while cooking the body in an outdoor oven. Nothing can compare.

But Tucson, like Las Vegas, has a lot of character and is a great city about eight months out of the year where the University gives the town a young atmosphere that's also great for dining. Add the foothills to this picture and you have a scenic wonderland to enjoy and photograph.

Nashville, Music City
Not Just for Country Folks

Having been to Nashville so many times when I lived in nearby Kentucky, I couldn't wait to take Linda there to have her enjoy the center of country music that we both loved so much. Finding the right time was always the issue. The right time came 50 years after graduating from Murray State University. The excuse was that Murray State was having a reunion for my class. It was October 2018 and I convinced Linda to come with me to Murray and we would then spend three days and nights in Nashville.

We had to fly into Nashville anyway, so we rented a car, drove the two hours north to Murray, spent three days enjoying the hospitality of the Alumni Association, seeing a few, very few old friends that I was not really close with while at Murray and then drove back down to Nashville to spend the next three days enjoying country music. Our friends, Karen and Tom Olivadotti flew up from Florida to join us for the Nashville end of our trip and we proceeded to explore the bars along Broadway, take a "Comedy" bus tour, and visit Andrew Jackson's Hermitage which was a true educational morning.

We stayed at the Gaylord Opryland Hotel which is a very unique place. The lobby and walkways between buildings are all enclosed, but present as an outdoor space complete with gardens and fountains and a river that runs through it. And yes, you can take a boat ride on that river and explore the sights. We sat on our balcony and watched people walking alongside the river. We walked around and explored the many shops and restaurants. And, at night, we took the shuttle the short distance to the Grand Ole Opry for a show.

For decades the Grand Ole Opry was hosted in the Ryman Auditorium downtown Nashville. Ryman is a small old theater that seats under 2,400 people. The new Opryland theater seats over 4,000 and sits in the Opryland Theme Park which draws visitors from all over the world.

We were there for the music. We purchased tickets for one evening and sat right up front where we could not only hear, but see everything including the radio announcer. Now let me explain. As we are watching one performance after another, the announcer, who has been introducing these wonderful acts, suddenly pauses and begins to read a commercial. His deep, melodic voice resonates across the auditorium and the airwaves of country radio.

Linda leans over to me and says, "That's cute the way he is doing that as if this was a radio or TV show." I then explain that while it is cute, it is also live. "This is the Grand Ole Opry which still is a twice weekly live radio show broadcast 'very live' from either Opryland or the Ryman Auditorium for more years than I can remember. They do commercial breaks on the radio and everything you see on stage can be heard over the airwaves." The whole staging then becomes even more fascinating to Linda, Karen and Tom.

Nashville was great fun and walking around Broadway from early morning until late at night (or early the next morning) you can find music. Broadway has more bars with live music than anywhere else in the world. There is literally one bar after another on both sides of the street and many more on the side streets. And they all have live music for free. People just walk in, stand about listening to music and if they want a drink, they get one. If not, they just stand there enjoying the music. Nashville is a music lovers heaven. While country music dominates Nashville, there are more than enough bars that have bluegrass, Americana, folk music and an assortment of rock and roll. Nashville is, after all, Music City.

BOSTON, A COOL CITY BY THE SEA

Boston is a small city that has so much surrounding downtown that it gives a big impression. I visited Boston many times for work and did get to see quite a bit of this very Irish town. But it was a pleasure trip that Linda and I took with Hutch and Sheila that really allowed me to appreciate the warmth and coolness of this great city.

We stayed on the Cambridge side of the Charles River and walked to Harvard University to observe the students and absorb the atmosphere. It felt invigorating.

Faneuil Hall Marketplace and Boston Market are entertaining afternoon stops that also offer shops and dining for breakfast, lunch or dinner. Mark and Donnie Wahlberg, Boston natives, were introducing their own hamburger venture—Wahlbergers—while we were there and this drew crowds hoping to meet any one of the many Wahlberg brothers, all of which were somehow involved.

Paul Revere's House is really there and so is Cheers, the famous bar "where everyone knows your name" and was the basis for the long-running television comedy series of the same name.

In the evenings we found music and entertainment everywhere. Boston, for all its sophistication and strong economic base is still just an overgrown college town with several great schools besides Harvard and the students permeate every aspect of this old town by the sea. It's that youthful grasp on Boston that makes this city very special.

One night we explored Harbor Walk along the Boston Waterfront and the many Wharfs that line the harbor with shops and restaurants to please every taste. We ate at the Long Wharf and walked around a crowded waterfront filled with people of all ages. We had a great time at Howl At The Moon, a very lively place to eat and listen to dueling bands coming at you from separate stages. We were probably the oldest guests in this venue. But we were fine with it and enjoyed the jumping atmosphere. A long weekend in Boston is great any time of the year.

New York City, Center of the World

People either love or hate New York City. It is both a large city encompassing the five boroughs including Brooklyn (which was, at one time, really a city on its own), Queens, Staten Island, Manhattan and The Bronx. Nine million people live in New York City, four million in Brooklyn alone. But it is Manhattan that most people think of when they conjure images of New York City. And even those living in the outer boroughs often say "I am going to the City" when referring to Manhattan.

New York City has more restaurants than you can imagine. Every type of cuisine can be found on one of the side streets of the City. And some of these restaurants provide foods that can be found nowhere else like Himalayan cuisine (whatever that is). Shopping is diverse with luxury stores lining Fifth Avenue and bargain shopping on Orchard Street.

For those interested in viewing art or learning about history or just learning about different things, there are more than 100 museums of every sort in New York City. And, Manhattan may be the entertainment center of the world with nightclubs, dance clubs, jazz clubs, and, of course, Broadway.

New York may not be the 24-hour town that Las Vegas is, but it comes closer than anywhere else in the world. And when you pack in all that you can do, you have what is still my favorite city for visiting. I still choose to live nearby just so I can take advantage of all that New York City has to offer.

Charlestown and Savannah, Two Southern Belles with Charm

Our friends, Lou and Marlene, kept telling us that we should visit Savannah, Georgia and Charlestown, South Carolina. They said that both are very quaint, charming Southern cities with a lot of historic sites as well as great bars and restaurants for drinking and dining.

We had just leased a new car while wintering in Florida and were planning on driving back to New York for the summer. Linda was not enthusiastic about this planned road trip, but when we decided to make it a week-long adventure with stops in Savannah, Charlestown, and Washington, D.C., it changed the purpose and made it more palatable.

Driving from Florida north in May we experienced the splattering of the sticky "lovebugs" across our windshield, creating a very treacherous driving condition on the highway. These bugs that travel in pairs can actually cover a windshield creating a real hazard. Early in our trip out of Florida we paused at a highway rest stop and I tried to wash and scrap these bugs off of my windshield. Using all my strength and full force I was only able to clear a portion of the windshield so I could see to drive. Fortunately, it began to rain and anyone who has traveled to or lived in Florida knows that rain often comes in sheets of water with such force that it cuts through everything—even the lovebugs on my windshield that I was unable to clear.

Horse and buggy rides, walking the cobblestone streets, visiting the local churches and museums and dining at waterfront restaurants made both Savannah and Charlestown educational and fun cities in which to stay. Savannah provides a surprisingly Irish flair having been settled by the Irish is the 1800s. I'm told that the St. Patrick's Day parade and festivities rival those in Boston and New York.

Charleston has a similar look with its cobblestone streets downtown, but has nearby beaches that draw crowds in summer and a young and vibrant art scene.

These are true Southern cities from the Antebellum period and worth the visit. Thanks, Marlene and Lou for the suggestion.

DALLAS, A LOT OF BULL AND BRAVADO

Dallas is a sprawling city made famous by the TV show of the same name and the assassination of President John F. Kennedy. Both the location of the filming of Dallas on TV at Southfork Ranch and the route that Kennedy traveled on that fateful day in November 1963, are must see stops while visiting Dallas. Nearby Fort Worth has the Stockyards with regular rodeos for live entertainment.

On one of my many trips to Dallas, I visited Gilley's Bar, the famous bar in the movie Urban Cowboy where riding the mechanical bull challenged some of the most famous stars, politicians and plain old patrons. I felt no obligation to get on the bull. The original Gilley's burnt down and was replaced by a new Gilley's which is a sprawling entertainment center.

I was also in Dallas for the opening of the Loews Anatole Hotel, a Trammell Crow developed hotel that was, at that time in the 1980s, state of the art for any hotel in the world and centerpiece of the Dallas Market Center downtown. My room at the Loews Anatole had more push-button conveniences than I could ever use. Everything was activated by remote control and some even voice activated. You never had to get out of bed. I almost didn't one morning thanks to the room darkening curtains that had me convinced it was still the middle of the night.

SOME OTHER FAVORITES

Omaha, Nebraska is a cross between a farm town and a western village. The Old Market is a great historic walking site. **Des Moines, Iowa** is the quintessential Midwest farm city. Its downtown Farmers Market is a daily gathering place. **Alexandria, Virginia** is a great quirky city just outside Washington, D.C. The main street and harbor are lined with great restaurants. And you will find that there are more association headquarters in Alexandria than anywhere else in the world which means that a lot of the lobbying efforts emanate from Alexandria. **Saratoga Springs, NY** is one small upstate town with a big reputation. One main street and a few side streets with great restaurants and mineral springs define this city that also has one of the oldest racetracks in the country. **Key West, FL** is the southern-most point in the US, has the Hemingway house and President Truman's summer home, but only the brave should venture there during the Fall Fantasy Fest where naked body painting features bodies of all ages and shapes.

CHAPTER THIRTY-THREE

CRUISING, A TRUE ESCAPE FROM REALITY

When I get to heaven, I'm gonna shake God's hand
Thank him for more blessings than one man can stand
Then I'm gonna get a guitar and start a rock-n-roll band
Check into a swell hotel, ain't the afterlife grand?

·······

"When I Get to Heaven" by John Prine

The year was 1973, my first year at *The Travel Agent* magazine, and Home Lines was doing a press trip from New York to Bermuda. I got to go and thus began my love affair with cruising. Home Lines was a small Italian cruise company with decent ships carrying 400 to 600 passengers. It opened my eyes to the benefit of being at sea.

In the 1970s and 1980s there were no cell phones and making telephone calls at sea was accomplished with very costly satellite communications. You only used the telephone while at sea if there was an emergency. My recollection was that calls at sea cost $12 a minute and there were connection charges as well. This was a good thing. It protected me from unnecessary distractions while at sea. Being at sea gave me respite from the fast pace workplace. It was the ultimate vacation in which I vacated mind and body for a short while and truly relaxed and ate great food. No one would contact me and I didn't worry about anything that might be happening back at the office. I couldn't do anything anyway—so why worry.

Cruising also allowed me to indulge in my eating and drinking pleasures. Great breakfast buffets (my favorite meal) where I could stock up on extra portions of smoked salmon, omelets, waffles and Danish to finish off a morning feast. This was often followed by a nap (eating took energy), then a walk around the ship before lunch for another lavish buffet. Afternoons were spent with interesting people and taking another nap. Sometimes I would read or write some poetry.

Evenings began with cocktails followed by a gourmet sit-down dinner. The all-you-can-eat stories are very true. The servers were more than happy to provide extra portions, two or more appetizers or entrees and desserts to please their guests. Their tips could depend on how well they served up dinner.

On one particular cruise, our good friend Steve Czarnecki set a record, and received a standing ovation, by ordering ten lobster tails at one sitting. It started out innocently. He first ordered escargot for an appetizer. Then came a pair of lobster tails with all the trimmings for the main course. When finished, he asked for a second helping. A new plate of lobster tails soon arrived, again with all the trimmings. When he finished that he asked if he could have two more tails, but without the rest of the sides. When that came, we noticed that they had another pair of lobster tails in the waiting. He smiled and said, "Bring em on." They did just that until he had consumed ten lobster tails and waived them off with "I'm done, thanks so much." He still had room for dessert. He was a big man; in more ways than size.

After dinner we would have after dinner drinks in one of the bars or pubs or nightclubs. Then there was the big show and some of the performers were really great. There is a lot of talent out there that are honing their craft on cruise ships. Singers, comedians, magicians and dancers. After the show we might stop and lose some money at the onboard casino, but more often we would find a lounge for dancing followed by drinks and singalongs in the piano bar. The evening would end at the disco which usually didn't open until midnight and last until everyone left, whenever that was.

By the way, the Midnight Buffets, which, on most ships no longer exist, were so lavish that one could indulge their dining fantasies with everything from breakfast, through lunch and dinner and lavish desserts—all in one midnight meal. I only consumed another dessert of two with coffee so that I could stay awake for disco dancing. The next day it would start all over again. These were the lazy days and fun-filled nights while at sea. This was a vacation that truly defined the definition of vacation—to get away from it all and relax and enjoy life.

I loved the days at sea best of all because it gave me that perfect vacation from work. However, the port stops were good too, especially for those that had not traveled much. In the Caribbean there were many islands to see, in the Baltic Sea there were northern European capitals to visit, in South America, a variety of countries, and in Southeast Asia, new cultures. River cruises on small intimate ships provided a closer look at the inner cities of the US, Europe and Asia.

Cruising quickly became my vacation of choice. Thanks to work-related press trips and connections I was making with the cruiseline executives, I was taking three or four cruises each year. One year in the early 1980s I actually took seven cruises in one year, all but one was for business. As of this writing, over the past forty-seven years I have taken well over 100 cruises. I lost count along the way.

Not all cruise lines are the same. Home Lines, my first experience was a basic cruise line. I soon upgraded to Holland America, one of the premier lines, but still not the top of the crop. Lines such as Silversea and Crystal Cruises are at the luxury end of the spectrum. Norwegian Cruise Line is at the bottom of the experiences and Carnival and Royal Caribbean provide first time cruises with the best experience to lead vacationers into a life at sea.

Our personal favorite cruise line is Celebrity Cruises. We sailed Celebrity and Holland America more than any other lines. Celebrity offers an upscale experience without the high cost of the more intimate ships. It costs slightly more than its sister line at Royal Caribbean, but you get more. You get what you pay for.

Speaking of "you get what you pay for" the cruises are NOT all-inclusive. You do get all meals and entertainment on board, but that's it. You pay for all drinks and all excursions while in port. And you are expected, but not required to tip the cabin stewards and restaurant servers.

When looking at river cruising, Uniworld on European destinations and Victoria Cruises for sailing the Yangtze River are two examples of small ships carrying 100-300 passengers that stop for day trips along the rivers to allow in-depth sightseeing. These river cruises cost more because all the sightseeing is included as well as all meals and usually drinks on board. But, on these ships the amenities and nightlife are limited because river cruises are geared toward seeing the sights.

One of the things we love about cruising is that you can go with a group of people and everyone can find their own pace and things to do. The one thing we would tell everyone is that, "This is your cruise too, and you pick and choose what you want to do. We don't have to be tied at the hip." (Although my friend Tom Olivadotti did once bring a leash to tie himself to my hip so he wouldn't get lost while we were traveling in Europe.) Our normal routine on a cruise included meeting for cocktails and dinner and exchanging stories about our experiences during the day. It works well on a cruise.

We started taking an annual winter cruise when Charlie and Sheila, our next door neighbors on Cossayuna Lake suggested after spending so much time together during the summer, we should get together for a week in mid-winter. We ended up with a group of friends from both Cossayuna Lake and long-time friends Tom and Kathy Minlionica from Long Island.

On one particular cruise in the Caribbean with some friends from Cossayuna Lake we even met up with another couple from the lake who were coincidently on the same winter cruise. This couple, Mike and Sue Roach, were ardent sailors and great fun to be with. Mike was never far from his cooler filled with beer and Irish whiskey, even on shore excursions. He understood the full meaning of escaping and enjoying the moment. Years later I noticed that same cooler on the back of his golf cart whenever we played a round of golf. It was reassuring to have it there and he was always quick to offer everyone and anyone a beer.

The one thing that has upset me over the past few years is the relaxed atmosphere that has permeated most cruise lines and the fact that jackets for men have disappeared from the dinner tables at night and it is rare to see a tuxedo on men and cocktail dress on women on the formal nights any more. This is a tradition that made cruise travel very special going back to the 1920s (I don't go back that far). I'm sorry that this has been lost, but then dress codes have changed for everything and if that makes people more relaxed, I guess that's a good thing since vacations are supposed to be for relaxation.

The two objections I often hear from people that do not want to try a cruise is that they fear eating too much and think they will be bored. Yes, I eat too much and often gain a notch on my belt by the end of a seven-day sailing. But I am never bored. Take a vacation. Get away on a cruise.

CHAPTER THIRTY-FOUR

IRELAND: JOHN WAYNE, RONALD REAGAN AND ALL AMERICANS

I learned the path to heaven Is full of sinners and believers
Learned that happiness on Earth Ain't just for high achievers
•••••••

"Red Dirt Road" by Brooks & Dunn

I've saved Ireland for last—primarily because it has become first in my heart. Ireland has recently replaced Australia as my favorite destination in the world. This was no easy feat, but the Irish people are up to the task. And they have moved the destination trophy on my mantle from the Aussies just by being themselves and opening up the widest welcome we have ever received anywhere in the world.

The Irish people love Americans. It began with John Wayne, when in 1952, he filmed "The Quiet Man" with Maureen O'Hara, a transplanted Irish movie star. John Wayne and Maureen O'Hara filmed five movies together and their posters can be seen all over Ireland. Wayne could have run for Mayor of Dublin and won a unanimous victory.

I had been to Ireland for business on several occasions, but mostly to Dublin for meetings. I ventured into the countryside a couple of times, but again, mostly for VIP sightseeing. Then, a couple of years ago, Linda and I, along with Hutch and Sheila, two close friends with whom we have traveled extensively, planned a seventeen-day road trip around Ireland. At first that might sound like a lot of time for one destination. I can tell you that we spent most of that seventeen days driving around, stopping only for short breathers in some quaint Irish towns and only touched a small portion of Ireland. We need to go back. There is so much we didn't see, so many people we have yet to meet and even some local beers we have yet to drink.

We flew over from New York to Shannon on Aer Lingus. A very suitable airline with very tight seating in coach. I was in the aisle seat in hopes that I could extend my long legs into the aisle. Linda was on the window seat. When a tall young man came along to claim the center seat, Linda made the generous mistake of offering to switch so he could have the window and she could sit next to me.

Don't get this wrong. Linda and I are very close. We have a good marriage and do most things together. But sitting on an airplane for seven hours is not where we need to cling together. I sleep. She doesn't. She reads. She would have been better at the window, but instead found herself in the center of two tall men who slept fitfully through the night and at times used her for a pillow. It was awkward and uncomfortable for all of us. I could not stretch out and vowed never to sit in coach on Aer Lingus or any other airline ever again. Yes, I was spoiled by all those upgrades I received as a travel writer. But now, with my older bones, I will gladly pay just to get the room my body needs. (And that is exactly what we did when we upgraded to business class on our return flight three weeks later.)

We landed in Shannon at 6 a.m. and I walked stiffly off the plane. We picked up our rental car and was luckily given a Range Rover Discovery which provided us enough room for luggage for four people traveling for more than two weeks. Hutch and I agreed to share the driving and vowed that while one of us was driving the other would be the navigator. This was mandatory since the steering wheel is on the right side and cars drive on the opposite side of the road from the US. My biggest job, aside from watching the map and trying to find street signs so we could make the correct turns, was making sure that we didn't clip the trees, bushes and stone walls that lined the left side of the road. It was tight at times and sometimes I just closed my eyes and yelled our code word for getting too close to the wall which was "Wall."

We drove from Shannon north past Galway to County Mayo where we checked into Ashford Castle in Cong. Built in 1228, it was the first of two ancient castles that we would be staying in rather than traditional hotels. We chose two castles because we wanted to experience how it might have felt to be living in Ireland hundreds of years ago when Medieval knights fought to protect the interests of their kings and their fair damsels.

Ashford Castle is a five-star hotel that provides the look and feel you might expect in a castle with long narrow hallways, winding stairways, large ornate bedrooms, four-poster beds and converted bathrooms with modern toilets. It was all there. We walked around the grounds, explored the expansive gardens and huge tree-lined paths. We were exhausted, but happy, when we returned to our rooms to rest before dinner. We dined like kings and queens and retired to bed early that first night as we were tired from our sleepless flight over, the drive from the airport, the close calls with the lovely Irish stone walls that line the roads, and the walk around Ashford Castle.

The next morning, we somehow found our way into Galway and explored the sights in this old cobblestone city with a knowledgeable guide. We loved the old churches dating back to a time we have only read about and seen in the movies. It all came to life in front of us. And then the sky opened and the rain came pouring down with a furry. We ducked into a pub just in time and looked at our watches. It was lunch time anyway so we had a few beers and ate local pub food.

The beer of choice in Ireland is *Guinness*. I've heard that when you drink *Guinness* draft in Ireland it is like no other *Guinness*. I was never a big beer *aficionado,* but when I had my first *Guinness* draft in Ireland, I became a convert. It is now my beer of choice whenever available. The smokey, chocolate taste that reaches your palate when you have a correct draft of *Guinness* is amazing. The bartender must know what he or she is doing and slowly pour the beer from the draft, allowing some of it to settle before continuing to fill the ice-cold mug. Then, when completely filled, the beer still must settle, allowing the head to firm up and dark brew to overtake the glass before drinking. It is an art form and worth the wait to take a sip of a very special beer—which somehow happens to have less calories than most other beers including some light beers.

Pub food in Ireland is pretty standard and very decent fare. No matter where we went there were fish and chips, hamburgers, chicken sandwiches and corned beef sandwiches. Sometimes the pub had Shepherd's pie with beef and lamb, carrots and peas and potatoes, lots of potatoes. We recalled that Ireland was famous for its unfortunate potato famine which resulted in a lot of Irish leaving their country for the US and elsewhere. Many of the dishes were cooked in *Guinness* gravy for added flavor. But corned beef and cabbage was not always available as one might have expected. The food was always good, the beer always cold, and the conversation with locals always vibrant and friendly.

After lunch we decided to explore the countryside on our own. We got lost. But we did see some beautiful rolling hills covered with lush green carpeting that mother nature provided. Ireland was as green as a leprechaun's coat. There was green everywhere and every road was covered with a canopy of green trees. We got very lost.

As we drove down one desolate road, we saw a farm as we came over a hill. We stopped at this farm house and pulled into the driveway to ask directions. The farmer came right out of his house to see who was coming into his driveway. He probably didn't have too many unannounced visitors. He gave us a strange look, most probably because we were strangers. I got out and told him that we were lost and wanted to find the right road back to Cong. He smiled when he heard my American accent and said: "Ah, Americans. Are you from New York? I have cousins that live in New York. Do you know Jack O'Malley?"

I told him sadly no and introduced Linda, Hutch and Sheila and repeated that we were sorry for coming up his driveway and disturbing him, but we were lost. We just need to find the right road back to Cong. He said, "Wait a minute, I'll be right back." We waited and watched him walk into the house and back out again. He then got into his car and drove over to where we were parked in his driveway. He got out, walked over to us and said: "Just follow me. It's a little confusing so I will get you to the main road back to Cong." With that he went back to his car, as did we, and he drove past us waving us on to follow him. We did. We followed him for nearly twenty minutes and dozens of turns until he waved us past him as we got to the main road where we were facing a sign that read "Cong 10 miles." He had driven a great distance just to get us back on track. This was hospitality at its best. This was Ireland.

On our last morning at Ashford Castle we visited the Cong Abbey and cemetery. The Abbey dates back to the 12th Century and is an example of gothic architecture. A walk through the small cemetery across the road from the Abbey took us across the centuries. There are many grave stones that have lost part or all of their marks over the centuries and others that can be linked from the 1400s through the 20th century.

Our next stop was the Dromoland Castle, one of the more celebrated (and expensive) five-star castle hotels in Ireland. The castle sits just outside of Shannon. The grounds are very well kept and the interior is more of a cross between a luxury hotel and an old castle. Every room we walked through was large and ornate. Dinner was excellent with a menu more extensive than our pub food of the past few days. After dinner we retired to one of the lounges where the King or Earl or Duke may have stopped to have an after-dinner drink and conversation.

While relaxing in the lounge we were entertained by a family of Irish farmers that were on vacation from the north, but not Northern Ireland which is part of the United Kingdom. The farmer (who it turned out was a very wealthy cattle farmer) along with his wife, teenage daughter and son, were traveling around their country enjoying the sights as we were. They, as all Irish people we met along the way, wanted to engage us Americans in conversation. We soon discovered they love the US and everything about our country, especially the movies and our presidents. Everyone talked about John Wayne and Maureen O'Hara with a reverence that most Catholics reserve for the Pope. And then there was President Ronald Reagan, and even President Bill Clinton that did so much for the Republic of Ireland. They all wanted to know if we knew presidents Reagan and Clinton and what they were really like. We admitted that we did not know either of them.

The farmer was a very generous person and was suddenly buying all of us rounds of Jameson Irish whiskey. We were all having a great time. But soon, our farmer friend was complaining about the Fawkin sheep. At first, I thought he was referring to sheep from the Falkland Islands. But he kept correcting me and got louder as he did; "No, no, I'm tawkin about all the Fawkin sheep. Din ya see all the Fawkin sheep long the road. Too much Fawkin sheep."

The next day, as we drove along the roads to the Cliffs of Moher, we began to notice that there were a lot of sheep. Everywhere we looked there were sheep. Even in the front yards of some of the small homes in the small towns and villages, there were sheep. Everyone had some sheep. These were the "Fawkin sheep" he was talking about. Too many "Fawkin sheep." And this became the phase that carried us across Ireland as we saw the "Fawkin sheep" everywhere we looked.

The Cliffs of Moher are a massive and impressive sight high above the Atlantic Ocean that sits far, very far below. It is one of the most viewed tourist sites in Ireland and there are many viewing positions along a walkway that goes on for about ten miles. It is a must-see site in Ireland, even more so than the Blarney Stone which sits atop the Blarney Castle just outside of Cork (more about that shortly). We walked along the Cliffs with hundreds of other sightseers from around the world and took pictures that do not portray the immense strength of these natural walls along the ocean.

We moved on from Shannon to Killarney to a small hotel right downtown, took a horse and carriage ride around the city, and had a great dinner in a local restaurant. From this central location in the south of Ireland we visited two of the more famous sites, the Ring of Kerry and the Dingle Peninsula. Both of these day trips take the better part of a full day and require the dexterity of a race car driver. Not that the driving is fast, but the course for both the Ring of Kerry and the Dingle Peninsula takes you on what amounts to a single car highway up and around the mountainside for a thrilling ride of a lifetime. Few rollercoaster rides including those in Disney World can match the adventure of riding up and around the mountainsides of the Ring of Kerry and the Dingle Peninsula.

The following is not an exaggeration: We were strongly advised by my friend David Callaghan, a native Irishman, now living in Miami, to hire a car and driver to take us around the Ring of Kerry and the Dingle Peninsula so that we would arrive home safe. The road is narrow as it winds its way up and around the mountainside with breathtaking views of the ocean below.

There are many spots where there are absolutely no way two cars can pass one another without one car careening off the mountain to the rocks and sea way down below. When going up the mountain and coming across a car, or even worse, a bus, coming down the mountainside, one vehicle must give way to the other. And when there is no room to pull over, one must either back up or back down. There is no choice. And the reality of this is that I could do neither back up or back down. So, I took Dave's advice and we hired a car and driver for the two days of excursions to the Ring of Kerry and Dingle Peninsula. And they were exactly as advertised. And we did, at several times, find ourselves in precarious positions of having to maneuver to allow another vehicle to get by. We all took a collective deep breath and held it until we got past a car or bus coming down the mountain and facing us.

Following those two days of exciting excursions we took the long road south, east and then north with our eventual destination Dublin. We stopped several times along with way to see the sights along the countryside. One of those sights was the Blarney Castle. To get to the Blarney Stone you need to walk up a narrow stairway to the top of the castle. Once there you are held by your feet as you bend over backwards in between a narrow wall where you will find this limestone that has been kissed by hundreds of thousands of people. Supposedly you gain the gift of gab after kissing the Blarney Stone. I think it's a lot of blarney. But the view of the countryside from the top of the castle was expansive.

Once we arrived in Dublin, we relinquished the car that had protected us along the treacherous west coast of Ireland and had taken us on the modern fast-moving highway into Dublin where we would spend the next four days. Dublin is a great city for walking and we no longer needed the car.

Dublin did not disappoint. Some people had told us not to spend too much time in Dublin. We could have spent a week or more meeting people each day and night as we cruised through the sites and restaurants and bars of this vibrant city. One evening after dinner we set out to explore The Stags Head, one of the more popular bars where we were ushered past the very crowded front bar, further past the equally crowded second lounge and bar into the back room where there was yet another bar and a slew of high tops filled with drinkers. One of the staff took us to a private booth in the back where we could sit and drink. But we wanted to mix and meet with the locals so we declined to drink there and ordered drinks to be brought to us while we stood on the side of this large lounge.

After a short while, we noticed that several of those gathered around one of the high tops were leaving and just two people remained standing there. Linda and I walked over and asked if we could join them. Upon hearing our American accents, they welcomed us and our friends Hutch and Sheila to join them and immediately bought us a new round of drinks even though we hadn't finished our current ones. We spent the next three hours standing there getting pleasantly drunk with these two Irishmen who both invited us to their homes while admitting they would be in trouble with their wives for getting home late for dinner. It was near 10 p.m. and long past anyone's dinner.

This scene as described above was basically repeated in every bar and pub and restaurant we entered during our stay in Dublin. We were so welcomed as visitors, but even more welcomed as American visitors because of the connection to their kinfolk. Everyone in Ireland had a relative living in America, most of them in New York. "Do you know my cousin Colleen? She lives in Queens," is an example of a common question.

We also took the train up to Belfast for a day trip to see another side of Irish life in Northern Ireland. At this time, the hostilities and terrorist activities between Northern Ireland and the Republic of Ireland had subsided. But two days before we were scheduled to train up to Belfast, the capital city of Northern Ireland, Gerry Adams, the leader of the Irish Republican Army (IRA) was placed under house arrest for past crimes, portending a possible resurgence of hostilities.

We were a little concerned and so was our hired London Cab driver-guide who was escorting us around Belfast. When we came across a group of protesters painting and drawing murals on the walls that line many of the streets in Belfast, he urgently told us not to get out of the car. But wanting to get some good photos of the action, we did not heed his advice and took a number of pictures before being dragged back into our car and driven away. We also discovered that the gates between the Catholic and Protestant sections of Belfast were still being closed at night to prevent any possible hostile exchanges in the dark. Nothing happened and we returned to Dublin safe and sound.

After seventeen days, dozens of cold mugs of *Guinness*, numerous close calls along narrow roads and mountain paths, and hundreds of encounters with warm, welcoming Irish people, we left Ireland realizing that this was one of the best vacations we ever experienced. And we had only seen a small portion of Ireland and Northern Ireland. It's no wonder that people return to Ireland many times.

CHAPTER THIRTY-FIVE

TIME CATCHES UP

So wake me up when it's all over
When I'm wiser and I'm older
All this time I was finding myself
And I didn't know I was lost

....

"Wake Me Up" by Avicii

I started this journey in Brooklyn many years ago, passed through my beloved Murray, Kentucky, back to Brooklyn, a short stint living in Manhattan and on to Long Island. From there it was a four-hour-plus drive to Cossayuna Lake, New York for summers and a short flight to Sarasota, Florida for a winter break in nearby Venice.

Along the way I was privileged and blessed to be able to see the world as I traveled, for both business and pleasure, to 129 countries.

The memories are vivid. The pictures in my mind are worth more than money can buy. The experiences I have had, both scary and exhilarating, are part of my personal history. These experiences are me and I am them. I have dined on gourmet food and had the pleasure of a $300 bottle of wine (that I didn't have to pay for thanks to a cruise line president). I have also enjoyed and savored the simpler, yet equally delicious street food in New Orleans, Trinidad and many other places. I learned that good food comes from the people who prepare it and you can't put a price on that.

The most significant thing I have learned is that the people I have met along the way have made my life more interesting, more fun and more memorable. I make no mistake about their friendship or lack thereof, but accept their moments in my life as important connections and recognize their significance, even if I was nothing more than a passing spec to them.

As noted earlier, I did not plan on getting into the travel business. I was a journalist, a wannabe news reporter that fell into a job at an aviation travel magazine and was lucky enough to find a home at a second travel publication which propelled me into a key role in the travel industry as a reporter, editor, speaker, radio host and eventually public relations executive.

My growth along the way was propelled, in part, by my volunteer work with the associations such as the Hospitality Sales & Marketing Association International (HSMAI) and the two previously mentioned Caribbean associations as well as the Society of American Travel Writers, the New York Travel Writers Association, the American Society of Travel Agents, the Pacific Asia Travel Association and SKAL, a charitable organization of travel industry personnel.

How I found time to give to these associations and do my job as well as live my life is beyond my own comprehension. I somehow found the time and it paid off in riches of relationships that were forged and business that was developed, first for the magazines and newspapers I wrote for and then for my own public relations firm and radio show.

Volunteering has become a lost art. I realize that times have changed, but I fear that the younger generations do not fully appreciate the learning, networking and friendships that are generated through volunteer work. It takes an effort to volunteer and it is more than just sitting on the board of directors as some opportunistic volunteers have always done.

I have often wondered why more people do not participate in these volunteer endeavors. Had I not done so, I would not have gained the prominence that I enjoyed in the travel industry. My volunteer efforts were very much a part of my success. And also, part of my rewards.

Once I thought the goal was for rewards and acknowledgement to satisfy my ego. But it turned out to be the actual journey that made this all worthwhile. I had often dreamed about getting awards, but when I finally received the Lifetime Achievement Award from my peers in the travel industry, I realized that the real rewards were gained as I traveled along the path that brought me to the podiums to accept the accolades and trophies.

I suddenly felt rich, but not in the monetary sense. The richness came from my family, my friends, the love that surrounded me all through the years and the travel experiences and people I met along the road.

I had two successful careers; twenty-two years as a fulltime employed travel writer and editor and thirty years running a public relations and marketing company. I was one of the lucky ones. I loved my job. I loved the work. Loving what one does for a living leads to a happy life. I was blessed, truly blessed.

I know that what I have done has not changed the world, but if along the way I have had even the smallest impact on some of those that I have interacted with on my travels, if I have set an example of why people should volunteer and help others, then I have been very successful. But even then, that feeling of success is not important.

Our true success is in the memories that line the corridors of our mind.

My memories are vivid colors of people and experiences that have blessed me with a very rich life.

Music has always been an important part of my life from those early days of lip syncing to rock and roll music in the 1950s, to my days running the Nowhere Coffee House in Kentucky, to today as I listen to a variety of genres including folk, country, classic rock, jazz and classical. Therefore, I close with a verse from a song which has an important meaning for me as did all the other song quotes that I offered throughout this book.

Many moons I have lived,
My body's weathered and worn
Ask yourself how would you be,
If you didn't know the day you were born
Try to love on your wife,
And stay close to your friends
Toast each sundown with wine
And Don't let the old man in
· · · · · · ·
"Don't Let The Old Man In" by Toby Keith

COUNTRIES VISITED

by Richard Kahn between 1968 and 2019

1.	Algeria	28.	Dominica
2.	Anguilla	29.	Dominican Republic
3.	Antigua and Barbuda	30.	Ecuador
4.	Argentina	31.	Egypt
5.	Aruba	32.	El Salvador
6.	Australia	33.	Estonia
7.	Austria	34.	Fiji
8.	Bahamas	35.	Finland
9.	Bahrain	36.	France
10.	Barbados	37.	French Polynesia
11.	Belgium	38.	Germany
12.	Belize	39.	Gibraltar
13.	Bermuda	40.	Greece
14.	Brazil	41.	Grenada
15.	British Virgin Islands	42.	Guadeloupe
16.	Canada	43.	Guatemala
17.	Cayman Islands	44.	Guyana
18.	Chile	45.	Haiti
19.	China	46.	Honduras
20.	Colombia	47.	Hong Kong
21.	Cook Islands	48.	Hungary
22.	Costa Rica	49.	Iceland
23.	Croatia	50.	India
24.	Cuba	51.	Indonesia
25.	Cyprus	52.	Ireland
26.	Czech Republic	53.	Israel
27.	Denmark	54.	Italy

55.	Jamaica	94.	Portugal
56.	Japan	95.	Puerto Rico
57.	Jordan	96.	Qatar
58.	Kenya	97.	Reunion Island
59.	Kiribati	98.	Romania
60.	Kuwait	99.	Russia
61.	Latvia	100.	St. Kitts and Nevis
62.	Lebanon	101.	St. Lucia
63.	Lithuania	102.	St. Vincent and the Grenadines
64.	Luxembourg	103.	Samoa
65.	Macau	104.	Serbia
66.	Malaysia	105.	Singapore
67.	Maldives	106.	Slovakia
68.	Malta	107.	Solomon Islands
69.	Martinique	108.	South Africa
70.	Mexico	109.	South Korea
71.	Micronesia	110.	Spain
72.	Monaco	111.	Sri Lanka
73.	Montenegro	112.	Suriname
74.	Montserrat	113.	Sweden
75.	Morocco	114.	Switzerland
76.	Nauru	115.	Taiwan
77.	Netherlands	116.	Tanzania
78.	Netherlands Antilles	117.	Thailand
79.	New Caledonia	118.	Tonga
80.	New Zealand	119.	Trinidad and Tobago
81.	Nicaragua	120.	Tunisia
82.	Nigeria	121.	Turkey
83.	Norway	122.	Turks & Caicos Islands
84.	Oman	123.	United Arab Emirates
85.	Pakistan	124.	United Kingdom
86.	Palau	125.	Uruguay
87.	Palestinian territories	126.	US Virgin Islands
88.	Panama	127.	Vanuatu
89.	Papua New Guinea	128.	Vatican City
90.	Peru	129.	Venezuela
91.	Philippines		
92.	Pitcairn Island		
93.	Poland		